Sixth Workshop on Syntax, Semantics and Structure in Statistical Translation 2012

(SSST-6)

Held at the 50th Annual Meeting of the Association for Computational Linguistics (ACL 2012)

Jeju, Republic of Korea
12 July 2012

Editors:

Marine Carpuat
Lucia Specia
Dekai Wu

ISBN: 978-1-62748-345-2

Printed from e-media with permission by:

Curran Associates, Inc.
57 Morehouse Lane
Red Hook, NY 12571

CURRAN ASSOCIATES INC. proceedings.com

Some format issues inherent in the e-media version may also appear in this print version.

Printed by Curran Associates, Inc. (2013)

For permission requests, please contact the Association for Computational Linguistics at the address below.

Association for Computational Linguistics
209 N. Eighth Street
Stroudsburg, Pennsylvania 18360

Phone: 1-570-476-8006
Fax: 1-570-476-0860

acl@aclweb.org

Additional copies of this publication are available from:

Curran Associates, Inc.
57 Morehouse Lane
Red Hook, NY 12571 USA
Phone: 845-758-0400
Fax: 845-758-2634
Email: curran@proceedings.com
Web: www.proceedings.com

Introduction

The Sixth Workshop on Syntax, Semantics and Structure in Statistical Translation (SSST-6) was held on 12 July 2012 following the ACL 2012 conference in Jeju, Korea. Like the first five SSST workshops in 2007, 2008, 2009, 2010, and 2011, it aimed to bring together researchers from different communities working in the rapidly growing field of structured statistical models of natural language translation.

We selected 13 papers for this year's workshop, many of which reflect statistical machine translation's movement toward not only tree-structured and syntactic models incorporating stochastic synchronous/transduction grammars, but also increasingly semantic models and the closely linked issues of deep syntax and shallow semantics. Semantic SMT research includes context-dependent WSD (word sense disambiguation) for SMT (Carpuat and Wu 2007, 2008; Chan, Ng and Chiang 2007; Giménez and Màrquez 2007); SRL (semantic role labeling) for SMT (Wu and Fung 2009); and SRL for MT evaluation (Lo and Wu 2010, 2011). In the second year since "Semantics" was explicitly added to the workshop name, the work exploring SMT's connections to semantics, predicate-argument structure, and deep syntax has continued to grow.

There is increased interest in modeling semantic and deep syntactic structure intranslation. Quernheim and Knight lay a foundation for modeling semantics in SMT by developing weighted acceptors and transducers for feature structures. Haugereid and Bond show how semantic transfer rules for rule-based MT can be extracted from corpora using SMT phrase aligners. Han, Sudoh, Wu, Duh, Tsukada and Nagata introduce source prereordering rules for Chinese-Japanese translation, based HPSG deep parses of Chinese sentences.

Semantic and syntactic models continue to provide rich models of source context. Apidianaki, Wisniewski, Sokolov, Max and Yvon use word sense disambiguation models as n-best reranking features and local language models to improve translation quality. Wang, Osenova and Simov integrate rich morphological and grammar-based information in a factored SMT framework. Source preprocessing is also used to model verbal constructs in English-Hindi translation (Arora and Sinha), zero prounoun resolution in Japanese-English translation (Taira, Sudoh and Nagata), and clause structure (Koeva, Leseva, Stoyanova, Dekova, Genov, Rizov, Dimitrova, Tarpomanova and Kukova). Wetzel and Bond build training examples designed to improve the translation of negated sentences.

Conversely, existing SMT systems and resources can be used to enrich existing semantic resources. Arcan, Federmann and Buitelaar show how SMT can be used in combination with other techniques to translate the vocabulary of a domain-specific ontology.

The challenges of correctly evaluating the semantics of MT output are also explored. Lo and Wu show how to automate the tuning of semantic role based MT evaluation metrics for English. Bojar and Wu investigate the porting of SRL based MT metrics to a very different language, Czech. Rosa, Dušek, Mareček and Popel show how to improve rule-based correction of SMT output by designing a parser specifically for that task.

Thanks once again this year are due to our authors and our Program Committee for making the SSST workshop another success.

Marine Carpuat, Lucia Specia, and Dekai Wu

Acknowledgements

This work was supported in part by the National Research Council Institute for Information Technology (Marine Carpuat); by the Department of Computer Science at the University of Sheffield (Lucia Specia); and the Defense Advanced Research Projects Agency (DARPA) under BOLT contract no. HR0011-12-C-0016 and GALE contract nos. HR0011-06-C-0022 and HR0011-06-C-0023, the European Union under the FP7 grant agreement no. 287658, and the Hong Kong Research Grants Council (RGC) research grant GRF621008 (Dekai Wu). Any opinions, findings and conclusions or recommendations expressed in this material are those of the authors and do not necessarily reflect the views of the RGC, EU, or DARPA.

Organizers:

Marine CARPUAT, National Research Council (NRC), Canada
Lucia SPECIA, University of Wolverhampton, UK
Dekai WU, Hong Kong University of Science and Technology (HKUST), Hong Kong

Program Committee:

Marianna APIDIANAKI, Alpage, INRIA and University Paris 7, France
Wilker AZIZ, University of Wolverhampton, UK
Srinivas BANGALORE, AT&T Research, USA
David CHIANG, USC ISI, USA
Colin CHERRY, National Research Council (NRC), Canada
Mona DIAB, Columbia University, USA
Alexander FRASER, University of Stuttgart, Germany
Daniel GILDEA, University of Rochester, USA
Nizar HABASH, Columbia University, USA
Yifan HE, Dublin City University, Ireland
Kevin KNIGHT, USC ISI, USA
Philipp KOEHN, University of Edinburgh, UK
Alon LAVIE, Carnegie Mellon University, USA
Yanjun MA, Baidu, China
Daniel MARCU, USC ISI and Language Weaver, USA
Lluìs MÀRQUEZ, Universitat Politècnica de Catalunya, Spain
Sudip Kumar NASKAR, Dublin City University, Ireland
Hwee Tou NG, National University of Singapore, Singapore
Daniel PIGHIN, Universitat Politècnica de Catalunya, Spain
Markus SAERS, Hong Kong University of Science and Technology (HKUST), Hong Kong
Libin SHEN, IBM, USA
Matthew SNOVER, City University of New York, USA
John TINSLEY, Dublin City University, Ireland
Stephan VOGEL, Qatar Computing Research Institute, Qatar
Taro WATANABE, NICT, Japan
Deyi XIONG, National University of Singapore, Singapore
François YVON, Université Paris Sud 11, France

Table of Contents

Conference Program

Wednesday, June 29, 2005

8:45–9:00 Opening remarks

Session 1: Source language modeling

9:00–9:30 *WSD for n-best reranking and local language modeling in SMT*
Marianna Apidianaki, Guillaume Wisniewski, Artem Sokolov, Aurélien Max and François Yvon

9:30–10:00 *Linguistically-Enriched Models for Bulgarian-to-English Machine Translation*
Rui Wang, Petya Osenova and Kiril Simov

10:00–10:30 *Enriching Parallel Corpora for Statistical Machine Translation with Semantic Negation Rephrasing*
Dominikus Wetzel and Francis Bond

10:30–11:00 Coffee break

Session 2: MT output evaluation and processing

11:00–11:30 *Towards a Predicate-Argument Evaluation for MT*
Ondrej Bojar and Dekai Wu

11:30–12:00 *Using Parallel Features in Parsing of Machine-Translated Sentences for Correction of Grammatical Errors*
Rudolf Rosa, Ondřej Dušek, David Mareček and Martin Popel

12:00–12:30 *Unsupervised vs. supervised weight estimation for semantic MT evaluation metrics*
Chi-kiu Lo and Dekai Wu

12:30–2:00 Lunch

Wednesday, June 29, 2005 (continued)

Session 3: Semantic dependencies

Session 4: Poster session at Coffee break

4:00–5:00 Panel

WSD for n-best reranking and local language modeling in SMT

Marianna Apidianaki, Guillaume Wisniewski†, Artem Sokolov, Aurélien Max†, François Yvon†

LIMSI-CNRS
† Univ. Paris Sud
BP 133, F-91403, Orsay Cedex, France
firstname.lastname@limsi.fr

Abstract

We integrate semantic information at two stages of the translation process of a state-of-the-art SMT system. A Word Sense Disambiguation (WSD) classifier produces a probability distribution over the translation candidates of source words which is exploited in two ways. First, the probabilities serve to rerank a list of n-best translations produced by the system. Second, the WSD predictions are used to build a supplementary language model for each sentence, aimed to favor translations that seem more adequate in this specific sentential context. Both approaches lead to significant improvements in translation performance, highlighting the usefulness of source side disambiguation for SMT.

1 Introduction

Word Sense Disambiguation (WSD) is the task of identifying the sense of words in texts by reference to some pre-existing sense inventory. The selection of the appropriate inventory and WSD method strongly depends on the goal WSD intends to serve: recent methods are increasingly oriented towards the disambiguation needs of specific end applications, and explicitly aim at improving the overall performance of complex Natural Language Processing systems (Ide and Wilks, 2007; Carpuat and Wu, 2007). This task-oriented conception of WSD is manifested in the area of multilingual semantic processing: supervised methods, which were previously shown to give the best results, are being abandoned in favor of unsupervised ones that do not rely on pre-annotated training data. Accordingly, pre-defined semantic inventories, that usually served to provide the lists of candidate word senses, are being replaced by senses relevant to the considered applications and directly identified from corpora by means of word sense induction methods.

In a multilingual setting, the sense inventories needed for disambiguation are generally built from all possible translations of words or phrases in a parallel corpus (Carpuat and Wu, 2007; Chan et al., 2007), or by using more complex representations of the semantics of translations (Apidianaki, 2009; Mihalcea et al., 2010; Lefever and Hoste, 2010). However, integrating this semantic knowledge into Statistical Machine Translation (SMT) raises several challenges: the way in which the predictions of the WSD classifier have to be taken into account; the type of context exploited for disambiguation; the target words to be disambiguated ("all-words" WSD vs. WSD restricted to target words satisfying specific criteria); the use of a single classifier versus building separate classifiers for each source word; the quantity and type of data used for training the classifier (e.g., use of raw data or of more abstract representations, such as lemmatization, allowing to deal with sparseness issues), and many others. Seemingly, the optimal way to take advantage of WSD predictions remains an open issue.

In this work, we carry out a set of experiments to investigate the impact of integrating the predictions of a cross-lingual WSD classifier into an SMT system, at two different stages of the translation process. The first approach exploits the probability distribution built by the WSD classifier over the set of translations of words found in the parallel corpus, for reranking the translations in the *n*-best list generated by the SMT system. Words in the list that match one of the proposed translations are boosted and are thus more likely to appear in the final translation. Our results on the English-French IWSLT'11 task show substantial improvements in translation quality. The second approach provides a tighter integration of the WSD classifier with the rest of the system: using the WSD predictions, an additional *sentence specific* language model is estimated and used during decoding. These additional local models can be used as an external knowledge source to reinforce translation hypotheses matching the prediction of the WSD system.

In the rest of the paper, we present related work on integrating semantic information into SMT (Section 2). The WSD classifier used in the current study is described in Section 3. We then present the two approaches adopted for integrating the WSD output into SMT (Section 4). Evaluation results are presented in Section 5, before concluding and discussing some avenues for future work.

2 Related work

Word sense disambiguation systems generally work at the word level: given an input word and its context, they predict its (most likely) meaning. At the same time, state-of-the-art translation systems all consider groups of words (phrases, tuples, etc.) rather than single words in the translation process. This discrepancy between the units used in MT and those used in WSD is one of the major difficulties in integrating word predictions into the decoder. This was, for instance, one of the reasons for the somewhat disappointing results obtained by Carpuat and Wu (2005) when the output of a WSD system was directly incorporated into a Chinese-English SMT system. Because of this difficulty, other cross-lingual semantics works have considered only simplified tasks, like blank-filling, without addressing the integration of the WSD models in full-scale MT systems (Vickrey et al., 2005; Specia, 2006).

Since the pioneering work of Carpuat and Wu (2005), several more successful ways to take WSD predictions into account have been proposed. For instance, Carpuat and Wu (2007) proposed to generalize the WSD system so that it performs a fully phrasal multiword disambiguation. However, given that the number of phrases is far larger than the number of words, this approach suffers from sparsity and computational problems, as it requires training a classifier for each entry of the phrase table.

Chan et al. (2007) introduced a way to modify the rule weights of a hierarchical translation system to reflect the predictions of their WSD system. While their approach and ours are built on the same intuition (an adaptation of a model to incorporate word predictions) their work is specific to hierarchical systems, while ours can be applied to any decoder that uses a language model. Haque et al. (2009) et Haque et al. (2010) introduce lexico-syntactic descriptions in the form of supertags as source language context-informed features in a phrase-based SMT and a state-of-the-art hierarchical model, respectively, and report significant gains in translation quality.

Closer to our work, Mauser et al. (2009) and Patry and Langlais (2011) train a global lexicon model that predicts the bag of output words from the bag of input words. As no explicit alignment between input and output words is used, words are chosen based on the (global) input context. For each input sentence, the decoder considers these word predictions as an additional feature that it uses to define a new model score which favors translation hypotheses containing words predicted by the global lexicon model. A difference between this approach and our work is that instead of using a global lexicon model, we disambiguate a subset of the words in the input sentence by employing a WSD classifier that creates a probability distribution over the translations of each word in its context.

The unsupervised cross-lingual WSD classifier used in this work is similar to the one proposed in Apidianaki (2009). The original classifier disambiguates new instances of words in context by selecting the most appropriate cluster of translations among a set of candidate clusters found in an automatically built bilingual sense inventory. The sense inventory exploited by the classifier is created by a cross-lingual word sense induction (WSI) method that reveals the senses of source words by grouping their translations into clusters according to their semantic proximity, revealed by a distributional similarity calculation. The resulting clusters represent the source words' candidate senses. This WSD method gave good results in a word prediction task but, similarly to the work of Vickrey et al. (2005) and of Specia (2006), the predictions are not integrated into a complete MT system.

3 The WSD classifier

Our WSD classifier is a variation of the one introduced in Apidianaki (2009). The main difference is that here the classifier serves to discriminate between unclustered translations of a word and to assign a probability to each translation for new instances of the word in context. Each translation is represented by a source language feature vector that the classifier uses for disambiguation. All experiments carried out in this study are for the English (EN) - French (FR) language pair.

3.1 Source Language Feature Vectors

Preprocessing The information needed by the classifier is gathered from the EN-FR training data provided for the IWSLT'11 evaluation task.[1] The dataset consists of 107,268 parallel sentences, word-aligned in both translation directions using GIZA++ (Och and Ney, 2003). We disambiguate EN words found in the parallel corpus that satisfy the set of criteria described below.

Two bilingual lexicons are built from the alignment results and filtered to eliminate spurious alignments. First, translation correspondences with a probability lower than a threshold are discarded;[2] then translations are filtered by part-of-speech (PoS), keeping for each word only translations pertaining to the same grammatical category;[3] finally, only intersecting alignments (i.e., correspondences found in the lexicons of both directions) are retained. Given that the lexicons contain word forms, the intersection is calculated based on lemmatization information in order to perform a generalization over the contents of the lexicons. For instance, if the EN adjective *regular* is translated by *habituelle* (feminine singular form of the adjective *habituel*) in the EN-FR lexicon, but is found to translate *habituel* (masculine singular form) in the other direction, the EN-FR correspondence *regular*/*habituelle* is retained (because the two variants of the adjective are reduced to the same lemma).

All lexicon entries satisfying the above criteria are retained and used for disambiguation. In these initial experiments, we disambiguate English words having less than 20 French translations in the lexicon. Each French translation of an English word that appears more than once in the training corpus[4] is characterized by a weighted English feature vector built from the training data.

Vector building The feature vectors corresponding to the translations are built by exploiting information from the source contexts (Apidianaki, 2008; Grefenstette, 1994). For each translation of an EN word w, we extract the content words that co-occur with w in the corresponding source sentences of the parallel corpus (i.e. the content words that occur in the same sentence as w whenever it is translated by this translation). The extracted source language words constitute the features of the vector built for the translation.

For each translation T_i of w, let N be the number of features retained from the corresponding source context. Each feature F_j ($1 \leq j \leq N$) receives a total weight $\mathrm{tw}(F_j, T_i)$ defined as the product of the feature's global weight, $\mathrm{gw}(F_j)$, and its local weight with that translation, $\mathrm{lw}(F_j, T_i)$:

$$\mathrm{tw}(F_j, T_i) = \mathrm{gw}(F_j) \cdot \mathrm{lw}(F_j, T_i) \tag{1}$$

The global weight of a feature F_j is a function of the number N_i of translations (T_i's) to which F_j is related, and of the probabilities (p_{ij}) that F_j co-occurs with instances of w translated by each of the T_i's:

$$\mathrm{gw}(F_j) = 1 - \frac{\sum_{T_i} p_{ij} \log(p_{ij})}{N_i} \tag{2}$$

Each of the p_{ij}'s is computed as the ratio between the co-occurrence frequency of F_j with w when translated as T_i, denoted as $\mathrm{cooc\_frequency}(F_j, T_i)$,

[1] `http://www.iwslt2011.org/`

[2] The translation probabilities between word tokens are found in the translation table produced by GIZA++; the threshold is set to 0.01.

[3] For this filtering, we employ a PoS and lemmatization lexicon built after tagging both parts of the training corpus with TreeTagger (Schmid, 1994).

[4] We do not consider hapax translations because they often correspond to alignment errors.

and the total number of features (N) seen with T_i:

$$p_{ij} = \frac{\text{cooc\_frequency}(F_j, T_i)}{N} \quad (3)$$

Finally, the local weight $\text{lw}(F_j, T_i)$ between F_j and T_i directly depends on their co-occurrence frequency:

$$\text{lw}(F_j, T_i) = \log(\text{cooc\_frequency}(F_j, T_i)) \quad (4)$$

3.2 Cross-Lingual WSD

The weighted feature vectors corresponding to the different translations of an English word are used for disambiguation.[5] As noted in Section 3.1, we disambiguate source words satisfying a set of criteria. Disambiguation is performed by comparing the vector associated with each translation to the new context of the words in the input sentences from the IWSLT'11 test set.

More precisely, the information contained in each vector is exploited by the WSD classifier to produce a probability distribution over the translations, for each new instance of a word in context. We disambiguate word forms (not lemmas) in order to directly use the selected translations in the translated texts. However, we should note that in some cases this reduces the role of WSD to distinguishing between different forms of one word and no different senses are involved. Using more abstract representations (corresponding to senses) is one of the perspectives of this work.

The classifier assigns a score to each translation by comparing information in the corresponding source vector to information found in the new context. Given that the vector features are lemmatized, the new context is lemmatized as well and the lemmas of the content words are gathered in a bag of words. The adequacy of each translation for a new instance of a word is estimated by comparing the translation's vector with the bag of words built from the new context. If common features are found between the new context and a translation vector, an association score is calculated corresponding to the mean of the weights of the common features relatively to the translation (i.e. found in its vector). In Equation (5), $(CF_j)_{j=1}^{|CF|}$ is the set of common features between the translation vector V_i and the new context C and tw is the weight of a CF with translation T_i (cf. formula (1)).

$$\text{assoc\_score}(V_i, C) = \frac{\sum_{j=1}^{|CF|} \text{tw}(CF_j, T_i)}{|CF|} \quad (5)$$

The scores assigned to the different translations of a source word are normalized to sum up to one.

In this way, a subset of the words that occur in the input sentences from the test set are annotated with their translations and the associated scores (contextual probabilities), as shown in the example in Figure 1.[6] The WSD classifier makes predictions only for the subset of the words found in the source part of the parallel test set that were retained from the initial EN-FR lexicon after filtering. Table 1 presents the total coverage of the WSD method as well as its coverage for words of different PoS, with a focus on content words. We report the number of disambiguated words for each content PoS (cf. third column) and the corresponding percentage, calculated on the basis of the total number of words pertaining to this PoS (cf. second column). We observe that the coverage of the method on nouns and adjectives is higher than the one on verbs. Given the rich verbal morphology of French, several verbs have a very high number of translations in the bilingual lexicon (over 20) and are not handled during disambiguation. The same applies to function words (articles, prepositions, conjunctions, etc.) included in the 'all PoS' category.

4 Integrating Semantics into SMT

In this section, we present two ways to integrate WSD predictions into an SMT decoder. The first one (Section 4.1) is a simple method based on n-best reranking. This method, already proposed in the literature (Specia et al., 2008), allows us to easily evaluate the impact of WSD predictions on automatic translation quality. The second one (Section 4.2) builds on the idea, introduced in (Crego et al., 2010), of using an additional language model to

[5] The vectors are not used for clustering the translations as in Apidianaki (2009) but all translations are considered as candidate senses.

[6] Some source words are tagged with only one translation (e.g. $stones\_\{pierres(1.000)\}$) because their other translations in the lexicon occurred only once in the training corpus and, consequently, were not considered.

PoS	# of words	# of WSD predictions	%
Nouns	5535	3472	62.72
Verbs	5336	1269	23.78
Adjs	1787	1249	69.89
Advs	2224	1098	49.37
all content PoS	14882	7088	47.62
all PoS	27596	8463	30.66

Table 1: Coverage of the WSD method

you know, one of the intense_{intenses(0.305), forte(0.306), intense(0.389)} pleasures of travel_{transport(0.334), voyage(0.332), voyager(0.334)} and one of the delights of ethnographic research_{recherche(0.225), research(0.167), études(0.218), recherches(0.222), étude(0.167)} is the opportunity_{possibilité(0.187), chance(0.185), opportunités(0.199), occasion(0.222), opportunité(0.207)} to live amongst those who have not forgotten_{oubli(0.401), oubliés(0.279), oubliée(0.321)} the old_{ancien(0.079), âge(0.089), anciennes(0.072), âgées(0.100), âgés(0.063), ancienne(0.072), vieille(0.093), ans(0.088), vieux(0.086), vieil(0.078), anciens(0.081), vieilles(0.099)} ways_{façons(0.162), manières(0.140), moyens(0.161), aspects(0.113), façon(0.139), moyen(0.124), manière(0.161)} , who still feel their past_{passée(0.269), autrefois(0.350), passé(0.381)} in the wind_{éolienne(0.305), vent(0.392), éoliennes(0.304)} , touch_{touchent(0.236), touchez(0.235), touche(0.235), toucher(0.293)} it in stones_{pierres(1.000)} polished by rain_{pluie(1.000)} , taste_{goût(0.500), goûter(0.500)} it in the bitter_{amer(0.360), amère(0.280), amertume(0.360)} leaves_{feuilles(0.500), feuillages(0.500)} of plants_{usines(0.239), centrales(0.207), plantes(0.347), végétaux(0.207)}.

Figure 1: Input sentence with WSD information

directly integrate the prediction of the WSD system into the decoder.

4.1 *N*-best List Reranking

A simple way to influence translation hypotheses selection with WSD information is to use the WSD probabilities of translation variants to produce an additional feature appended to the *n*-best list after its generation. The feature value should reflect the degree to which a particular hypothesis includes proposed WSD variants for the respective words. Rerunning the standard MERT optimization procedure on the augmented features gives a new set of model weights, that are used to rescore the *n*-best list.

We propose the following method of features construction. Given the phrase alignment information between a source sentence and a hypothesis, we verify if one or more of the proposed WSD variants for the source word occur in the corresponding phrase of the translation hypothesis. If this is the case, the corresponding probabilities are additively accumulated for the current hypothesis. At the end, two features are appended to each hypothesis in the *n*-best list: the total score accumulated for the hypothesis and the same score normalized by the number of words in the hypothesis.

Two MERT initialization schemes were considered: (1) all model weights are initialized to zero, and (2) all the weights of "standard" features are initialized to the values found by MERT and the new WSD features to zero.

4.2 Local Language Models

We propose to adapt the approach introduced in Crego et al. (2010) as an alternative way to integrate the WSD predictions within the decoder: for each sentence to be translated, an additional language model (LM) is estimated and taken into account during decoding. As this additional "local" model depends on the source sentence, it can be used as an external source of knowledge to reinforce translation hypotheses complying with criteria predicted from the whole source sentence. For instance, the unigram probabilities of the additional LM can be derived from the (word) predictions of a WSD system, bigram probabilities from the prediction of phrases and so on and so forth. Although this approach was suggested in (Crego et al., 2010), this is, to the best of our knowledge, the first time it is experimentally validated.

In practice, the predictions of the WSD system described in Section 3 can be integrated by defining, for each sentence, an additional unigram language model as follows:

- each translation predicted by the WSD classifier can be generated by the language model with the probability estimated by the WSD classifier; no information about the source word that has been disambiguated is considered;
- the probability of unknown words is set to a small arbitrary constant.

Even if most of the words composing the translation hypothesis are considered as unknown words, hypotheses that contain the words predicted by the WSD system still have a higher LM score and are therefore preferred. Note that even if we only use unigram language models in our experiments, as senses are predicted at the word level, our approach is able to handle disambiguation of phrases as well.

This approach has two main advantages over existing ways to integrate WSD predictions in an SMT system. First, no hard decisions are made: errors of the WSD can be "corrected" by the translation. Second, sense disambiguation at the word level is naturally and automatically propagated at the phrase level: the additional LM is influencing all phrase pairs using one of the predicted words.

Compared to the reranking approach introduced in the previous section, this method results in a tighter integration with the decoder. In particular, the WSD predictions are applied before search-space pruning and are therefore expected to have a more important role.

5 Evaluation

5.1 Experimental Setting

In all our experiments, we considered the TED-talk English to French data set provided by the IWSLT'11 evaluation campaign, a collection of public speeches on a variety of topics. We used the Moses decoder (Koehn et al., 2007).

The TED-talk corpus is a small data set made of a monolingual corpus (111,431 sentences) used to estimate a 4-gram language model with KN-smoothing, and a bilingual corpus (107,268 sentences) used to extract the phrase table. All data are tokenized, cleaned and converted to lowercase letters using the tools provided by the WMT organizers.[7] We then use a standard training pipeline to construct the translation model: the bitext is aligned using GIZA++, symmetrized using the grow-diag-final-and heuristic; the phrase table is extracted and scored using the tools distributed with Moses. Finally, systems are optimized using MERT on the 934 sentences of the `dev-2010` set. All evaluations are performed on the 1,664 sentences of the `test-2010` set.

5.2 Baseline

In addition to the models introduced in Section 4, we considered two other supplementary models as baselines. The first one uses the IBM 1 model estimated during the SMT system training as a simple WSD system: for each source sentence, a unigram additional language model is defined by taking, for each source, the 20 best translations according to the IBM 1 model and their probability. Model 1 has been shown to be one of the best performing features to be added to an SMT system in a reranking step (Och et al., 2004) and can be seen as a naive WSD classifier.

To test the validity of our approach, we replicate the "oracle" experiments of Crego et al. (2010) and estimate the best gain our method can achieve. These experiments consist in using the reference to train a local n-gram language model (with n in the range 1 to 3) which amounts, in the local language model method of Section 4.2, to assuming that the WSD system correctly predicted a single translation for each source word.

5.3 Results

Table 2 reports the results of our experiments. It appears that, for the considered task, sense disambiguation improves translation performance: n-best rescoring results in a 0.37 BLEU improvement and using an additional language model brings about an improvement of up to a 0.88 BLEU. In both cases, MERT assigns a large weight to the additional fea-

[7] `http://statmt.org/wmt08/scripts.tgz`

method		BLEU	METEOR
baseline	—	29.63	53.78
rescoring	WSD (zero init)	30.00	54.26
	WSD (reinit)	29.58	53.96
additional LM	oracle 3-gram	43.56	64.64
	oracle 2-gram	39.36	62.92
	oracle 1-gram	42.92	69.39
	IBM 1	30.18	54.36
	WSD	30.51	54.38

Table 2: Evaluation results on the TED-talk task of our two methods to integrate WSD predictions.

PoS	baseline	WSD
Nouns	67.57	69.06
Verbs	45.97	47.76
Adjectives	51.79	53.94
Adverbs	52.17	56.25

Table 3: Contrastive lexical evaluation: % of words correctly translated within each PoS class

tures during tuning. When rescoring n-best, an improvement is observed only when the weights are initialized to zero and not to the weights resulting from the previous optimization, maybe because of the difficulty to exit the local minimum MERT had found earlier.

As expected, integrating the WSD predictions with an additional language model results in a larger improvement than simple rescoring, which shows the importance of applying this new source of information early in the translation pipeline, before search space pruning. Also note that the system using the IBM 1 predictions is outperformed by the system using the WSD classifier introduced in Section 3, showing the quality of its predictions.

Oracle experiments stress the high potential of the method introduced in (Crego et al., 2010) as a way to integrate external sources of knowledge: all three conditions result in large improvements over the baseline and the proposed methods. It must, however, be noted that contrary to the WSD method introduced in Section 3, these oracle experiments rely on sense predictions for all source words and not only content words. Surprisingly enough, predicting phrases instead of words results only in a small improvement. Additional experiments are required to explain why 2-gram oracle achieved such a low performance.

5.4 Contrastive lexical evaluation

All the measures used for evaluating the impact of WSD information on translation show improvements, as discussed in the previous section. We complement these results with another measure of translation performance, proposed by Max et al. (2010), which allows for a more fine-grained contrastive evaluation of the translations produced by different systems. The method permits to compare the results produced by the systems on different word classes and to take into account the source words that were actually translated. We focus this evaluation on the classes of content words (nouns, adjectives, verbs and adverbs) on which WSD had an important coverage. Our aim is, first, to explore how these words are handled by a WSD-informed SMT system (the system using the local language models) compared to the baseline system that does not exploit any semantic information; and, second, to investigate whether their disambiguation influences the translation of surrounding non-disambiguated words.

Table 3 reports the percentage of words correctly translated by the semantically-informed system within each content word class: consistent gains in translation quality are observed for all parts-of-speech compared to the baseline, and the best results are obtained for nouns.

	baseline				WSD			
	w_{-2}	w_{-1}	w_{+1}	w_{+2}	w_{-2}	w_{-1}	w_{+1}	w_{+2}
Nouns	64.01	68.69	75.17	64.6	65.47	70.46	76.3	66.6
Verbs	68.67	67.58	63	62.19	69.98	68.89	64.85	64.25
Adjectives	63.1	64.39	64.28	66.55	64.09	65.65	64.76	69.33
Adverbs	70.8	69.44	68.67	66.38	71	71.21	70	67.22

Table 4: Impact of WSD prediction on the surrounding words

Table 4 shows how the words surrounding a disambiguated word w (noun, verb, adjective or adverb) in the text are handled by the two systems. More precisely, we look at the translation of words in the immediate context of w, i.e. at positions w_{-2}, w_{-1}, w_{+1} and w_{+2}. The left column reports the percentage of correct translations produced by the baseline system (without disambiguation) for words in these positions; the right column shows the positive impact that the disambiguation of a word has on the translation of its neighbors. Note that this time we look at disambiguated words and their context without evaluating the correctness of the WSD predictions. Nevertheless, even in this case, consistent gains are observed when WSD information is exploited. For instance, when a noun is disambiguated, 70.46% and 76.3% of the immediately preceding (w_{-1}) and following (w_{+1}) words, respectively, are correctly translated, versus 68.69% and 75.17% of correct translations produced by the baseline system.

6 Conclusion and future work

The preliminary results presented in this paper on integrating cross-lingual WSD into a state-of-the-art SMT system are encouraging. Both adopted approaches (n-best rescoring and local language modeling) benefit from the predictions of the proposed cross-lingual WSD classifier. The contrastive evaluation results further show that WSD improves not only the translation of disambiguated words, but also the translation of neighboring words in the input texts.

We consider various ways for extending this work. First, future experiments will involve the use of more abstract representations of senses than individual translations, by applying a cross-lingual word sense induction method to the training corpus prior to disambiguation. We will also experiment with disambiguation at the level of lemmas, to reduce sparseness issues, and with different ways for handling lemmatized predictions by the SMT systems. Furthermore, we intend to extend the coverage of the WSD method by exploring other filtering methods for cleaning the alignment lexicons, and by addressing the disambiguation of words of all PoS.

Acknowledgments

This work was partly funded by the European Union under the FP7 project META-NET (T4ME), Contract No. 249119, and by OSEO, the French agency for innovation, as part of the Quaero Program.

References

Marianna Apidianaki. 2008. Translation-oriented Word Sense Induction Based on Parallel Corpora. In *Proceedings of the Sixth International Conference on Language Resources and Evaluation (LREC'08)*, Marrakech, Morocco.

Marianna Apidianaki. 2009. Data-driven Semantic Analysis for Multilingual WSD and Lexical Selection in Translation. In *Proceedings of the 12th Conference of the European Chapter of the Association for Computational Linguistics (EACL-09)*, pages 77–85, Athens, Greece.

Marine Carpuat and Dekai Wu. 2005. Word Sense Disambiguation vs. Statistical Machine Translation. In *Proceedings of the 43rd Annual Meeting of the Association for Computational Linguistics (ACL'05)*, pages 387–394, Ann Arbor, Michigan.

Marine Carpuat and Dekai Wu. 2007. Improving Statistical Machine Translation using Word Sense Disambiguation. In *Proceedings of the Joint EMNLP-CoNLL Conference*, pages 61–72, Prague, Czech Republic.

Yee Seng Chan, Hwee Tou Ng, and David Chiang. 2007. Word Sense Disambiguation Improves Statistical Machine Translation. In *Proceedings of the 45th Annual Meeting of the Association for Computational Linguistics (ACL-07)*, pages 33–40, Prague, Czech Republic.

Josep Maria Crego, Aurélien Max, and François Yvon. 2010. Local lexical adaptation in Machine Translation through triangulation: SMT helping SMT. In *Proceedings of the 23rd International Conference on Computational Linguistics (Coling 2010)*, pages 232–240, Beijing, China.

Gregory Grefenstette. 1994. *Explorations in Automatic Thesaurus Discovery*. Kluwer Academic Publishers, Norwell, MA.

Rejwanual Haque, Sudip Naskar, Yanjun Ma, and Andy Way. 2009. Using supertags as source language context in SMT. In *Proceedings of the 13th Annual Meeting of the European Association for Machine Translation (EAMT 2009)*, pages 234–241, Barcelona, Spain.

Rejwanul Haque, Sudip Kumar Naskar, Antal Van Den Bosch, and Andy Way. 2010. Supertags as source language context in hierarchical phrase-based SMT. In *Proceedings of AMTA 2010: The Ninth Conference of the Association for Machine Translation in the Americas*, pages 210–219, Denver, CO.

N. Ide and Y. Wilks. 2007. Making Sense About Sense. In E. Agirre and P. Edmonds, editors, *Word Sense Disambiguation, Algorithms and Applications*, pages 47–73. Springer.

Philipp Koehn, Hieu Hoang, Alexandra Birch, Chris Callison-Burch, Marcello Federico, Nicola Bertoldi, Brooke Cowan, Wade Shen, Christine Moran, Richard Zens, Chris Dyer, Ondrej Bojar, Alexandra Constantin, and Evan Herbst. 2007. Moses: Open source toolkit for statistical machine translation. In *Proceedings of the 45th Annual ACL Meeting, Companion Volume Proceedings of the Demo and Poster Sessions*, pages 177–180, Prague, Czech Republic.

Els Lefever and Veronique Hoste. 2010. SemEval-2010 Task 3: Cross-lingual Word Sense Disambiguation. In *Proceedings of the 5th International Workshop on Semantic Evaluations (SemEval-2), ACL 2010*, pages 15–20, Uppsala, Sweden.

Arne Mauser, Saša Hasan, and Hermann Ney. 2009. Extending statistical machine translation with discriminative and trigger-based lexicon models. In *Proceedings of the Conference on Empirical Methods in Natural Language Processing (EMNLP)*, pages 210–217, Singapore, August.

Aurélien Max, Josep Maria Crego, and François Yvon. 2010. Contrastive Lexical Evaluation of Machine Translation. In *Proceedings of the Seventh International Conference on Language Resources and Evaluation (LREC'10)*, Valletta, Malta.

Rada Mihalcea, Ravi Sinha, and Diana McCarthy. 2010. SemEval-2010 Task 2: Cross-Lingual Lexical Substitution. In *Proceedings of the 5th International Workshop on Semantic Evaluations (SemEval-2), ACL 2010*, pages 9–14, Uppsala, Sweden.

Franz Josef Och and Hermann Ney. 2003. A Systematic Comparison of Various Statistical Alignment Models. *Computational Linguistics*, 29(1):19–51.

Franz Josef Och, Daniel Gildea, Sanjeev Khudanpur, Anoop Sarkar, Kenji Yamada, Alex Fraser, Shankar Kumar, Libin Shen, David Smith, Katherine Eng, Viren Jain, Zhen Jin, and Dragomir Radev. 2004. A smorgasbord of features for statistical machine translation. In *Proceedings of HLT-NAACL 2004*, pages 161–168, Boston, Massachusetts, USA.

Alexandre Patry and Philippe Langlais. 2011. Going beyond word cooccurrences in global lexical selection for statistical machine translation using a multilayer perceptron. In *Proceedings of 5th International Joint Conference on Natural Language Processing*, pages 658–666, Chiang Mai, Thailand, November.

Helmut Schmid. 1994. Probabilistic Part-of-Speech Tagging Using Decision Trees. In *Proceedings of the International Conference on New Methods in Language Processing*, pages 44–49, Manchester, UK.

Lucia Specia, Baskaran Sankaran, and Maria Das Graças Volpe Nunes. 2008. n-Best Reranking for the Efficient Integration of Word Sense Disambiguation and Statistical Machine Translation. In *Proceedings of the 9th international conference on Computational linguistics and intelligent text processing*, CICLing'08, pages 399–410, Berlin, Heidelberg. Springer-Verlag.

Lucia Specia. 2006. A Hybrid Relational Approach for WSD - First Results. In *Proceedings of the COLING/ACL 2006 Student Research Workshop*, pages 55–60, Sydney, Australia.

David Vickrey, Luke Biewald, Marc Teyssier, and Daphne Koller. 2005. Word-Sense Disambiguation for Machine Translation. In *Proceedings of the Joint Conference on Human Language Technology / Empirical Methods in Natural Language Processing (HLT-EMNLP)*, pages 771–778, Vancouver, Canada.

Linguistically-Enriched Models for Bulgarian-to-English Machine Translation

Rui Wang
Language Technology Lab
DFKI GmbH
Saarbrücken, Germany
ruiwang@dfki.de

Petya Osenova and Kiril Simov
Linguistic Modelling Department, IICT
Bulgarian Academy of Sciences
Sofia, Bulgaria
{petya,kivs}@bultreebank.org

Abstract

In this paper, we present our linguistically-enriched Bulgarian-to-English statistical machine translation model, which takes a statistical machine translation (SMT) system as backbone various linguistic features as factors. The motivation is to take advantages of both the robustness of the SMT system and the rich linguistic knowledge from morphological analysis as well as the hand-crafted grammar resources. The automatic evaluation has shown promising results and our extensive manual analysis confirms the high quality of the translation the system delivers. The whole framework is also extensible for incorporating information provided by different sources.

1 Introduction

Incorporating linguistic knowledge into statistical models is an everlasting topic in natural language processing. The same story happens in the machine translation community. Along with the success of statistical machine translation (SMT) models (summarized by Koehn (2010)), various approaches have been proposed to include linguistic information, ranging from early work by Wu (1997) to recent work by Chiang (2010), from deep transfer-based models (Graham and van Genabith, 2008) to mapping rules at the syntactic level (Galley et al., 2004; Liu et al., 2006; Zhang et al., 2008). Although the purely data-driven approaches achieve significant results as shown in the evaluation campaigns (Callison-Burch et al., 2011), according to the human evaluation, the final outputs of the SMT systems are still far from satisfactory.

Koehn and Hoang (2007) proposed a factored SMT model as an extension of the traditional phrase-based SMT model, which opens up an easy way to incorporate linguistic knowledge at the token level. Birch et al. (2007) and Hassan et al. (2007) have shown the effectiveness of adding supertags on the target side, and Avramidis and Koehn (2008) have focused on the source side, translating a morphologically-poor language (English) to a morphologically-rich language (Greek). However, all of them attempt to enrich the English part of the language pairs being translated. For the language pairs like Bulgarian-English, there has not been much study on it, mainly due to the lack of resources, including corpora, preprocessors, etc, on the Bulgarian part. There was a system published by Koehn et al. (2009), which was trained and tested on the European Union law data, but not on other popular domains like news. They reported a very high BLEU score (Papineni et al., 2002) on the Bulgarian-English translation direction (61.3).

Apart from being morphologically-rich, Bulgarian has a number of challenging linguistic phenomena to consider, including free word order, long distance dependency, coreference relations, clitic doubling, etc. For instance, the following two sentences:

(1) Momcheto j go dava buketa na momicheto.
Boy-the her-dat it-acc gives bouquet-the to girl-the.
The boy gives the bouquet to the girl.

(2) Momcheto j go dava.
Boy-the her-dat it-acc gives.
The boy gives it to her.

are difficult for the traditional phrase-based SMT system, because the clitic in the first sentence must not be translated, while in the second case it is obligatory. Via the semantic analysis (e.g., Minimal Recursion Semantics), the clitic information will be incorporated in the representation of the corresponding arguments.

In this work, we rely on the linguistic processing to cope with some of these phenomena and improve the correspondences between the two languages: 1) The lemmatization factors out the difference between word forms and ensures better coverage of the Bulgarian-English lexicon. 2) The dependency parsing helps to identify the grammatical functions such as subject, object in sentences with a non-standard word order. 3) The semantic analysis provides a further abstraction which hides some of the language specific features. Example of the last is the case of clitic doubling.

As for the Bulgarian-to-English translation model, we basically 'annotate' the SMT baseline with various linguistic features derived from the preprocessing and hand-crafted grammars. There are three contributions of this work:

- The models trained on a decent amount of parallel corpora output **surprisingly good results**, in terms of automatic evaluation metrics.
- The enriched models give us more space for experimenting with **different linguistic features** without losing the 'basic' robustness.
- According to our **extensive manual analyses**, the approach has shown promising results for future integration of more knowledge from the continued advances of the deep grammars.

The rest of the paper will be organized as follows: Section 2 briefly introduces some background of the hand-crafted grammar resources we use and also some previous related work on transfer-based MT. Section 3 describes the linguistic analyses we perform on the Bulgarian text, whose output is used in the factored SMT model. We show our experiments in Section 4 as well as both automatic and detailed manual evaluation of the results. We summarize this paper in Section 5 and point out several directions for future work.

2 Machine Translation with Deep Grammars

Our work is also enlightened by another line of research, transfer-based MT models using deep linguistic knowledge, which are seemingly different but actually very related. In this section, before we describe our model of incorporating linguistic knowledge from the hand-crafted grammars, we firstly introduce the background of such resources as well as some previous work on MT using them.

Our usage of Minimal Recursion Semantic (MRS) analysis of Bulgarian text is inspired by the work on MRS and RMRS (Robust Minimal Recursion Semantic) (see (Copestake, 2003) and (Copestake, 2007)) and the previous work on transfer of dependency analyses into RMRS structures described in (Spreyer and Frank, 2005) and (Jakob et al., 2010). Although being a semantic representation, MRS is still quite close to the syntactic level, which is not fully language independent. This requires a *transfer* at the MRS level, if we want to do translation from the source language to the target language. The transfer is usually implemented in the form of rewriting rules. For instance, in the Norwegian LOGON project (Oepen et al., 2004), the transfer rules were hand-written (Bond et al., 2005; Oepen et al., 2007), which included a large amount of manual work. Graham and van Genabith (2008) and Graham et al. (2009) explored the automatic rule induction approach in a transfer-based MT setting involving two lexical functional grammars (LFGs)[1], which was still restricted by the performance of both the parser and the generator. Lack of robustness for target side generation is one of the main issues, when various ill-formed or fragmented structures come out after transfer. Oepen et al. (2007) used their generator to generate text fragments instead of full sentences, in order to increase the robustness.

In our approach, we want to make use of the grammar resources while keeping the robustness, therefore, we experiment with another way of transfer involving information derived from the grammars. In particular, we take a robust SMT system as our 'backbone' and then we augment it with deep linguistic knowledge. In general, what we are doing

[1]Although their grammars are automatically induced from treebanks, the formalism supports rich linguistic information.

is still along the lines of previous work utilizing deep grammars, but we build a more 'light-weighted' but yet extensible *statistical transfer* model.

3 Factor-based SMT Model

Our translation model is built on top of the factored SMT model proposed by Koehn and Hoang (2007), as an extension of the traditional phrase-based SMT framework. Instead of using only the word form of the text, it allows the system to take a vector of factors to represent each token, both for the source and target languages. The vector of factors can be used for different levels of linguistic annotations, like lemma, part-of-speech, or other linguistic features, if they can be (somehow) represented as annotations to each token.

The process is quite similar to supertagging (Bangalore and Joshi, 1999), which assigns "rich descriptions (supertags) that impose complex constraints in a local context". In our case, all the linguistic features (factors) associated with each token form a supertag to that token. Singh and Bandyopadhyay (2010) had a similar idea of incorporating linguistic features, while they worked on Manipuri-English bidirectional translation. Our approach is slightly different from (Birch et al., 2007) and (Hassan et al., 2007), who mainly used the supertags on the target language side, English. Instead, we primarily experiment with the source language side, Bulgarian. This potentially huge feature space provides us with various possibilities of using our linguistic resources developed within and out of our project.

Firstly, the data was processed by the NLP pipe for Bulgarian (Savkov et al., 2012) including a morphological tagger, GTagger (Georgiev et al., 2012), a lemmatizer and a dependency parser[2]. Then we consider the following factors on the source language side (Bulgarian):

- WF – word form is just the original text token.
- LEMMA is the lexical invariant of the original word form. We use the lemmatizer, which operates on the output from the POS tagging. Thus, the 3rd person, plural, imperfect tense verb form 'varvyaha' ('walking-were', They were walking) is lemmatized as the 1st person, present tense verb 'varvya'.
- POS – part-of-speech of the word. We use the positional POS tag set of the BulTreeBank, where the first letter of the tag indicates the POS itself, while the next letters refer to semantic and/or morphosyntactic features, such as: Dm - where 'D' stands for 'adverb', and 'm' stand for 'modal'; Ncmsi - where 'N' stand for 'noun', 'c' means 'common', 'm' is 'masculine', 's' is 'singular',and 'i' is 'indefinite'.
- LING – other linguistic features derived from the POS tag in the BulTreeBank tagset.
- DEPREL is the dependency relation between the current word and the parent node.
- HLEMMA is the lemma of the parent node.
- HPOS is the POS tag of the parent node.

Here is an example of a processed sentence. The sentence is "spored odita v elektricheskite kompanii politicite zloupotrebyavat s dyrzhavnite predpriyatiya." The glosses for the words in the Bulgarian sentence are: spored (*according*) odita (*audit-the*) v (*in*) elektricheskite (*electrical-the*) kompanii (*companies*) politicite (*politicians-the*) zloupotrebyavat (*abuse*) s (*with*) dyrzhavnite (*state-the*) predpriyatiya (*enterprises*). The translation in the original source is : "electricity audits prove politicians abusing public companies." The result from the linguistic processing are presented in Table 1.

As for the deep linguistic knowledge, we also extract features from the semantic analysis — Minimal Recursion Semantics (MRS). MRS is introduced as an underspecified semantic formalism (Copestake et al., 2005). It is used to support semantic analyses in the English HPSG grammar ERG (Copestake and Flickinger, 2000), but also in other grammar formalisms like LFG. The main idea is that the formalism avoids spelling out the complete set of readings resulting from the interaction of scope bearing operators and quantifiers, instead providing a single underspecified representation from which the complete set of readings can be constructed. Here we will present only basic definitions from (Copestake et al., 2005). For more details the cited publication should be consulted.

An MRS structure is a tuple $\langle GT, R, C \rangle$, where GT is the top handle, R is a bag of EPs (elementary predicates) and C is a bag of handle constraints, such that there is no handle h that outscopes GT. Each elementary predicate contains exactly four components: 1) a handle which is the label of

[2]We have trained the MaltParser[3] (Nivre et al., 2007) on the dependency version of BulTreeBank: `http://www.bultreebank.org/dpbtb/`. The trained model achieves 85.6% labeled parsing accuracy.

No	WF	Lemma	POS	Ling	DepRel	HLemma	HPOS
1	spored	spored	R	_	adjunct	zloupotrebyavam	VP
2	odita	odit	Nc	npd	prepcomp	spored	R
3	v	v	R	_	mod	odit	Nc
4	elektricheskite	elektricheski	A	pd	mod	kompaniya	Nc
5	kompanii	kompaniya	Nc	fpi	prepcomp	v	R
6	politicite	politik	Nc	mpd	subj	zloupotrebyavam	Vp
7	zloupotrebyavat	zloupotrebyavam	Vp	tir3p	root	-	-
8	s	s	R	_	indobj	zloupotrebyavam	Vp
9	dyrzhavnite	dyrzhaven	A	pd	mod	predpriyatie	Nc
10	predpriyatiya	predpriyatie	Nc	npi	prepcomp	s	R

Table 1: The sentence analysis with added head information — HLemma and HPOS.

No	EP	EoV	EP_1/POS_1	EP_2/POS_2	EP_3/POS_3
1	spored_r	e	zloupotrebyavam_v/Vp	odit_n/Nc	-
2	odit_n	v	-	-	-
3	v_r	e	odit_n/Nc	kompaniya_n/Nc	-
4	elekticheski_a	e	kompaniya_n/Nc	-	-
5	kompaniya_n	v	-	-	-
6	politik_n	v	-	-	-
7	zloupotrebyavam_v	e	politik_n/Nc	-	s_r/R
8	s_r	e	zloupotrebyavam_v/Vp	predpriyatie_n/Nc	-
9	dyrzhaven_a	e	predpriyatie_n/Nc	-	-
10	predpriyatie_n	v	-	-	-

Table 2: Representation of MRS factors for each wordform in the sentence.

the EP; 2) a relation; 3) a list of zero or more ordinary variable arguments of the relation; and 4) a list of zero or more handles corresponding to scopal arguments of the relation (i.e., holes).

Robust MRS (RMRS) is introduced as a modification of MRS which captures the semantics resulting from the shallow analysis. Here the following assumption is taken into account: the shallow processor does not have access to a lexicon. Thus it does not have access to the arity of the relations in EPs. Therefore, the representation has to be underspecified with respect to the number of arguments of the relations. The names of relations are constructed on the basis of the lemma for each wordform in the text and the main argument for the relation is specified. This main argument could be of two types: *referential index* for nouns and *event* for the other parts of speech. Because in this work we are using only the RMRS relation and the type of the main argument as features to the translation model, we will skip here the explanation of the full RMRS structures and how they are constructed.

As for the factors, we firstly do a match between the surface tokens and the MRS elementary predicates (EPs) and then extract the following features as extra factors:

- EP – the name of the elementary predicate, which usually indicates an event or an entity semantically.
- EoV indicates the current EP is either an event or a reference variable.
- ARG_nEP indicates the elementary predicate of the argument which belongs to the predicate. n is usually from 1 to 3.
- ARG_nPOS indicates the POS tag of the argument which belongs to the predicate.

Notice that we do not take all the information provided by the MRS, e.g., we throw away the scopal information and the other arguments of the relations. Those kinds of information is not straightforward to be represented in such 'tagging'-style models, which will be tackled in the future.

The extra information for the example sentence is represented in Table 2. All these factors encoded within the corpus provide us with a rich selection of features for different experiments.

4 Experiments

To run the experiments, we use the phrase-based translation model provided by the open-source statistical machine translation system, Moses[4] (Koehn et al., 2007). For training the translation model, the SETIMES parallel corpus has been used, which is part of the OPUS parallel corpus[5]. As for the choice of the datasets, the language is more diverse in the news articles, compared with other corpora in more controlled settings, e.g., the JRC-Acquis corpus[6] used by Koehn et al. (2009).

We split the corpus into the training set and the test set by 150,000 and 1,000 sentence pairs respectively[7]. Both datasets are preprocessed with the tokenizer and lowercase converter provided by Moses. Then the procedure is quite standard: We run GIZA++ (Och and Ney, 2003) for bi-directional word alignment, and then obtain the lexical translation table and phrase table. A tri-gram language model is estimated using the SRILM toolkit (Stolcke, 2002). For the rest of the parameters we use the default setting provided by Moses.

Notice that, since on the target language side (i.e., English) we do not have any other factors than the word form, the factor-based models we use here only differentiate from each other in the translation phase, i.e., there is no 'generation' models involved.

4.1 Automatic Evaluation Metrics

The baseline results (non-factored model) under the standard evaluation metrics are shown in the first row of Table 3 in terms of BLEU (Papineni et al., 2002) and METEOR (Denkowski and Lavie, 2011). We then design various configurations to test the effectiveness of different linguistic annotations described in Section 3. The detailed configurations we considered are shown in the first column of Table 3.

The first impression is that the BLEU scores in general are high. These models can be roughly grouped into six categories (separated by double lines): word form with linguistic features; lemma with linguistic features; models with dependency features; MRS elementary predicates (EP) and the type of the main argument of the predicate (EOV); EP features without word forms; and EP features with MRS ARG_n features.

In terms of the resulting scores, POS and Lemma seem to be effective features, as Model 2 has the highest BLEU score and Model 4 the best METEOR score. Model 3 indicates that linguistic features also improve the performance. Model 4-6 show the necessity of including the word form as one of the factors. Incorporating HLEMMA feature largely decreases the results due to the vastly increasing vocabulary, i.e., aligning and translating bi-grams instead of tokens. Therefore, we did not include the results in the table. After replacing the HLEMMA with HPOS, the result is close to the others (Model 8). Model 9 may also indicate that increasing the number of factors does not guarantee performance enhancement. The experiments with predicate features (EP and EOV) from the MRS analyses (Model 10-12) show improvements over the baseline consistently and using only the MRS features (Model 13-14) also delivers descent results. Concerning the MRS ARG_n features, the models with $\mathrm{ARG}_n\mathrm{EP}$ again suffer from the sparseness problem as the dependency HLEMMA features, but the models with $\mathrm{ARG}_n\mathrm{POS}$ (Model 15-16) achieve better performance than those with dependency HPOS features. This is mainly because the dependency information is encoded together with the (syntactically) dependent word, while the MRS arguments are grouped around the semantic heads.

So far, incorporating additional linguistic knowledge has not shown huge improvement in terms of statistical evaluation metrics. However, this does not mean that the translations delivered are the same. In order to fully evaluate the system, manual analysis is absolutely necessary. We are still far from drawing a conclusion at this point, but the automatic evaluation scores already indicate that the system can deliver decent translation quality consistently.

4.2 Manual Evaluation

We manually validated the output for all the models mentioned in Table 3. The guideline includes two

[4]`http://www.statmt.org/moses/`

[5]OPUS — an open source parallel corpus, `http://opus.lingfil.uu.se/`

[6]`http://optima.jrc.it/Acquis/`

[7]We did not preform MERT (Och, 2003), as it is quite computationally heavy for such various configurations.

ID	Model	BLEU	1-gram	2-gram	3-gram	4-gram	METEOR
1	WF (Baseline)	38.61	**69.9**	44.6	31.5	22.7	0.3816
2	WF, POS	**38.85**	**69.9**	**44.8**	**31.7**	**23.0**	0.3812
3	WF, LEMMA, POS, LING	38.84	**69.9**	44.7	**31.7**	**23.0**	0.3803
4	LEMMA	37.22	68.8	43.0	30.1	21.5	**0.3817**
5	LEMMA, POS	37.49	68.9	43.2	30.4	21.8	0.3812
6	LEMMA, POS, LING	38.70	69.7	44.6	31.6	22.8	0.3800
7	WF, DEPREL	36.87	68.4	42.8	29.9	21.1	0.3627
8	WF, DEPREL, HPOS	36.21	67.6	42.1	29.3	20.7	0.3524
9	WF, LEMMA, POS, LING, DEPREL	36.97	68.2	42.9	30.0	21.3	0.3610
10	WF, POS, EP	38.74	69.8	44.6	31.6	22.9	0.3807
11	WF, EP, EOV	38.74	69.8	44.6	31.6	22.9	0.3807
12	WF, POS, LING, EP, EOV	38.76	69.8	44.6	**31.7**	22.9	0.3802
13	EP, EOV	37.22	68.5	42.9	30.2	21.6	0.3711
14	EP, EOV, LING	38.38	69.3	44.2	31.3	22.7	0.3691
15	EP, EOV, ARG$_n$POS	36.21	67.4	41.9	29.2	20.9	0.3577
16	WF, EP, EOV, ARG$_n$POS	37.37	68.4	43.2	30.3	21.8	0.3641

Table 3: Results of the factor-based model (Bulgarian-English, SETIMES 150,000/1,000)

aspects of the quality of the translation: *Grammaticality* and *Content*. *Grammaticality* can be evaluated solely on the system output and *Content* by comparison with the reference translation. We use a 1-5 score for each aspect as follows:

Grammaticality

1. The translation is not understandable.
2. The evaluator can somehow guess the meaning, but cannot fully understand the whole text.
3. The translation is understandable, but with some efforts.
4. The translation is quite fluent with some minor mistakes or re-ordering of the words.
5. The translation is perfectly readable and grammatical.

Content

1. The translation is totally different from the reference.
2. About 20% of the content is translated, missing the major content/topic.
3. About 50% of the content is translated, with some missing parts.
4. About 80% of the content is translated, missing only minor things.
5. All the content is translated.

For the missing lexicons or not-translated Cyrillic tokens, we ask the evaluators to score 2 for one Cyrillic token and score 1 for more than one tokens in the output translation. We have two annotators achieving the inter-annotator agreement according to Cohen's Kappa (Cohen, 1960) $\kappa = 0.73$ for grammaticality and $\kappa = 0.75$ for content, both of which are *substantial* agreement. For the conflict cases, we take the average value of both annotators and rounded the final score up or down in order to have an integer.

The current results from the manual validation are on the basis of randomly sampled 150 sentence pairs. The numbers shown in Table 4 are the number of sentences given the corresponding scores. The 'Sum' column shows the average score of all the output sentences by each model and the 'Final' column shows the average of the two 'Sum' scores.

The results show that linguistic and semantic analyses definitely improve the quality of the translation. Exploiting the linguistic processing on word level — LEMMA, POS and LING — produces the best result. However, the model with only EP and EOV features also delivers very good results, which indicates the effectiveness of the MRS features from the deep hand-crafted grammars, although incorporating the MRS ARG$_n$ features shows similar performance drops as dependency features. Including more factors in general reduces the results because of the sparseness effect over the dataset, which is consistent with the automatic evaluation. The last two rows are shown

ID	Model	Grammaticality						Content						Final
		1	2	3	4	5	Sum	1	2	3	4	5	Sum	
1	WF (Baseline)	20	47	5	32	**46**	3.25	20	46	5	23	56	3.33	3.29
2	WF, POS	20	48	5	37	40	3.19	20	48	5	24	53	3.28	3.24
3	WF, Lemma, POS, Ling	20	47	6	34	43	3.22	20	47	1	24	58	3.35	3.29
4	Lemma	**15**	34	11	46	44	**3.47**	15	32	5	**33**	**65**	**3.67**	**3.57**
5	Lemma, POS	**15**	38	12	**51**	34	**3.34**	15	35	9	32	59	**3.57**	**3.45**
6	Lemma, POS, Ling	20	48	5	34	43	3.21	20	48	5	22	55	3.29	3.25
7	WF, DepRel	32	48	3	29	38	2.95	32	49	4	14	51	3.02	2.99
8	WF, DepRel, HPOS	45	41	7	23	34	2.73	45	41	2	21	41	2.81	2.77
9	WF, Lemma, POS, Ling, DepRel	34	47	5	30	34	2.89	34	48	3	20	45	2.96	2.92
10	WF, POS, EP	19	49	4	34	44	3.23	19	49	3	20	59	3.34	3.29
11	WF, EP, EoV	20	49	2	41	38	3.19	19	50	4	16	61	3.33	3.26
12	WF, POS, Ling, EP, EoV	19	49	5	37	40	3.20	19	50	3	24	54	3.29	3.25
13	EP, EoV	**15**	41	10	44	40	**3.35**	**14**	38	7	31	60	**3.57**	**3.46**
14	EP, EoV, Ling	20	49	7	38	36	3.14	19	49	7	20	55	3.29	3.21
15	EP, EoV, ARG_nPOS	23	49	9	34	35	3.06	23	47	8	**33**	39	3.12	3.09
16	WF, EP, EoV, ARG_nPOS	34	47	10	30	29	2.82	34	47	10	20	39	2.89	2.85
*	Google	0	2	20	52	76	4.35	1	0	9	42	98	4.57	4.46
*	Reference	0	0	5	51	94	4.59	1	0	5	37	107	4.66	4.63

Table 4: Manual evaluation of the grammaticality and the content

for reference. 'Google' shows the results of using the online translation service provided by `http://translate.google.com/` on 06.02.2012. The high score (very close to the reference translation) may be because our test data are not excluded from their training data. In future we plan to do the same evaluation with a larger dataset.

Concerning the impact from the linguistic processing pipeline to the final translation results, Lemma and MRS elementary predicates help at the level of rich morphology. For example, the baseline model correctly translates the adjective 'Egyptian' in 'Egyptian Scientists' (plural), but not in 'Egyptian Government, as in the second phrase the adjective has a neutral gender. Model 4 and Model 13 are correct for both.

Generally speaking, if we roughly divide the linguistic processing pipeline in two categories: statistical processing (POS tagger and dependency parser) and rule-based processing (lemmatizer and MRS construction), the latter category (almost perfect) highly relies on the former one. For example, the lemma depends on the word form and the tag, and the result is unambiguous in more than 98% of the morphological lexicon and in text this is almost 100% (because the ambiguous cases are very rare). The errors come mainly from new words and errors in the tagger. Similarly, the RMRS rules are good when the parser is correct. Here, the main problems are duplications of the ROOT elements and the subject elements, which we plan to fix using heuristics in the future.

4.3 Question-Based Evaluation

Although the reported manual evaluation in the previous section demonstrates that linguistic knowledge improves the translation, we notice that the evaluators tend to give marks at the two ends of scale, and less in the middle. Generally, this is because the measurement is done on the basis of the content that the evaluators extract from the Bulgarian sentence using there own cognitive capacity. Then they start to overestimate or underestimate the translation, knowing in advance what has to be translated. In order to avoid this subjectivity, we design a different manual evaluation in which the evaluator does not know the original Bulgarian sentences. Then the evaluation is based only on the content represented within the English translation.

In order to do this, we represent the content of the Bulgarian sentences as a set of questions that have a list of possible answers, assigned to them. During the judgement of the content transfer, the evaluators need to answer these questions. As the list of answers also contains false answers, the evaluators are forced to select the right answer which can be inferred from the English translation.

The actual questions are created semi-automatically from the dependency analysis of the sentences. We defined a set of rules for generation of the questions on the basis of the dependency relations. For example, if a sentence has only a subject relation presented within the analysis, the question will be about who is doing the event. If the analysis presents subject and direct object, the question will be about who is doing something with what/whom. These automatically generated questions are manually investigated and, if necessary, edited. Also, additional answers are formulated on the basis of general language knowledge. The main idea is that the possible answers are conceptually close to each other, but not in a hypernymy relation. Always there is an answer "none".

Then the questions are divided into small groups and distributed to be answered by three evaluators in such a way that each question is answered by two evaluators, but no evaluator answers the whole set of questions for a given sentence. In this way, we try to minimize the influence of one question to the answers of the next questions. The answers are compared to the true answers of the questions for each given sentence. We evaluated 192 questions for each model and sum up the scores (correctly answered questions) in Table 5.

This evaluation is more expensive, but we expect them to be more objective. As for a related work, (Yuret et al., 2010) used textual entailment to evaluate different parser outputs. The way they constructed the *hypotheses* is similar to our creation of questions (based on dependency relations). However, they focused on the automatic evaluation and we adopt it for the manual evaluation.

ID	Model	Score
1	WF (Baseline)	127
2	WF, POS	126
3	WF, LEMMA, POS, LING	131
4	LEMMA	**133**
5	LEMMA, POS	**133**
6	LEMMA, POS, LING	128
7	WF, DEPREL	131
8	WF, DEPREL, HPOS	120
9	WF, LEMMA, POS, LING, DEPREL	124
10	WF, POS, EP	125
11	WF, EP, EOV	126
12	WF, POS, LING, EP, EOV	128
13	EP, EOV	**138**
14	EP, EOV, LING	122
15	EP, EOV, ARG$_n$POS	130
16	WF, EP, EOV, ARG$_n$POS	121

Table 5: Question-based evaluation

5 Conclusion and Future Work

In this paper, we report our work on building a linguistically-enriched statistical machine translation model from Bulgarian to English. Based on our observations of the previous approaches on transfer-based MT models, we decide to build a factored model by feeding an SMT system with deep linguistic features. We perform various experiments on several configurations of the system (with different linguistic knowledge). The high BLEU score shows the high quality of the translation delivered by the SMT baseline; and various manual analyses confirm the consistency of the system.

There are various aspects of the current approach we can improve: 1) The MRSes are not fully explored yet, although we have considered the most important predicate and argument features. 2) We would like to add factors on the target language side (English) as well to fulfill a 'complete' transfer. 3) Incorporating reordering rules on the Bulgarian side may help the alignment and larger language models on the English side should also help improving the translation results. 4) Due to the morphological complexity of the Bulgarian language, the other translation direction, from Bulgarian to English, is also worth investigation in this framework.

Acknowledgements

This work was partially supported by the EuroMatrixPlus project (IST-231720) funded by the European Community's Seventh Framework Programme. The authors would like to thank Laska Laskova, Stanislava Kancheva and Ivaylo Radev for doing the human evaluation of the data.

References

Eleftherios Avramidis and Philipp Koehn. 2008. Enriching morphologically poor languages for statistical machine translation. In *Proceedings of ACL*.

Srinivas Bangalore and Aravind K. Joshi. 1999. Supertagging: an approach to almost parsing. *Computational Linguistics*, 25(2), June.

Alexandra Birch, Miles Osborne, and Philipp Koehn. 2007. Ccg supertags in factored statistical machine translation. In *Proceedings of the Second Workshop on Statistical Machine Translation*, pages 9–16, Prague, Czech Republic, June.

Francis Bond, Stephan Oepen, Melanie Siegel, Ann Copestake, and Dan Flickinger. 2005. Open source machine translation with DELPH-IN. In *Proceedings of the Open-Source Machine Translation Workshop at the 10th Machine Translation Summit*, pages 15 – 22, Phuket, Thailand, September.

Chris Callison-Burch, Philipp Koehn, Christof Monz, and Omar F. Zaidan. 2011. Findings of the 2011 workshop on statistical machine translation. In *Proceedings of the 6th Workshop on SMT*.

David Chiang. 2010. Learning to translate with source and target syntax. In *Proceedings of ACL*, pages 1443–1452.

J. Cohen. 1960. A Coefficient of Agreement for Nominal Scales. *Educational and Psychological Measurement*, 20(1):37.

Ann Copestake and Dan Flickinger. 2000. An open source grammar development environment and broad-coverage english grammar using hpsg. In *Proceedings of the 2nd International Conference on Language Resources and Evaluation*, Athens, Greece.

Ann Copestake, Dan Flickinger, Carl Pollard, and Ivan Sag. 2005. Minimal recursion semantics: An introduction. *Research on Language & Computation*, 3(4):281–332.

Ann Copestake. 2003. Robust minimal recursion semantics (working paper).

Ann Copestake. 2007. Applying robust semantics. In *Proceedings of the 10th Conference of the Pacific Assocation for Computational Linguistics (PACLING)*, pages 1–12.

Michael Denkowski and Alon Lavie. 2011. Meteor 1.3: Automatic Metric for Reliable Optimization and Evaluation of Machine Translation Systems. In *Proceedings of the EMNLP 2011 Workshop on Statistical Machine Translation*.

Michel Galley, Mark Hopkins, Kevin Knight, and Daniel Marcu. 2004. What's in a translation rule? In *Proceedings of HLT-NAACL*, Boston, Massachusetts, USA, May.

G. Georgiev, V. Zhikov, P. Osenova, K. Simov, and P. Nakov. 2012. Feature-rich part-of-speech tagging for morphologically complex languages: Application to bulgarian. In *EACL 2012*.

Yvette Graham and Josef van Genabith. 2008. Packed rules for automatic transfer-rule induction. In *Proceedings of the European Association of Machine Translation Conference (EAMT 2008)*, pages 57–65, Hamburg, Germany, September.

Y. Graham, A. Bryl, and J. van Genabith. 2009. F-structure transfer-based statistical machine translation. In *Proceedings of the Lexical Functional Grammar Conference*, pages 317–328, Cambridge, UK. CSLI Publications, Stanford University, USA.

Hany Hassan, Khalil Sima'an, and Andy Way. 2007. Supertagged phrase-based statistical machine translation. In *Proceedings of ACL*, Prague, Czech Republic, June.

Max Jakob, Markéta Lopatková, and Valia Kordoni. 2010. Mapping between dependency structures and compositional semantic representations. In *Proceedings of the 7th International Conference on Language Resources and Evaluation (LREC 2010)*, pages 2491–2497.

Philipp Koehn and Hieu Hoang. 2007. Factored translation models. In *Proceedings of EMNLP*.

Philipp Koehn, Hieu Hoang, Alexandra Birch, Chris Callison-Burch, Marcello Federico, Nicola Bertoldi, Brooke Cowan, Wade Shen, Christine Moran, Richard Zens, Chris Dyer, Ondrej Bojar, Alexandra Constantin, and Evan Herbst. 2007. Moses: Open source toolkit for statistical machine translation. In *Proceedings of ACL (demo session)*.

P. Koehn, A. Birch, and R. Steinberger. 2009. 462 machine translation systems for europe. In *Proceedings of MT Summit XII*.

Philipp Koehn. 2010. *Statistical Machine Translation*. Cambridge University Press, January.

Yang Liu, Qun Liu, and Shouxun Lin. 2006. Tree-to-string alignment template for statistical machine translation. In *Proceedings of COLING-ACL*, pages 609–616.

Joakim Nivre, Jens Nilsson, Johan Hall, Atanas Chanev, Gülsen Eryigit, Sandra Kübler, Svetoslav Marinov, and Erwin Marsi. 2007. Maltparser: a language-independent system for data-driven dependency parsing. *Natural Language Engineering*, 13(1):1–41.

Franz Josef Och and Hermann Ney. 2003. A systematic comparison of various statistical alignment models. *Computational Linguistics*, 29(1).

Franz Josef Och. 2003. Minimum error rate training in statistical machine translation. In *Proceedings of ACL*.

Stephan Oepen, Helge Dyvik, Jan Tore Lønning, Erik Velldal, Dorothee Beermann, John Carroll, Dan

Flickinger, Lars Hellan, Janne Bondi Johannessen, Paul Meurer, Torbjørn Nordgård, , and Victoria Rosén. 2004. Som å kapp-ete med trollet? towards MRS-based norwegian to english machine translation. In *Proceedings of the 10th International Conference on Theoretical and Methodological Issues in Machine Translation*, Baltimore, MD.

Stephan Oepen, Erik Velldal, Jan Tore Lønning, Paul Meurer, Victoria Rosén, and Dan Flickinger. 2007. Towards hybrid quality-oriented machine translation — on linguistics and probabilities in MT. In *Proceedings of the 11th Conference on Theoretical and Methodological Issues in Machine Translation (TMI-07)*, Skovde, Sweden.

K. Papineni, S. Roukos, T. Ward, and W. J. Zhu. 2002. Bleu: a method for automatic evaluation of machine translation. In *Proceedings of ACL*.

Aleksandar Savkov, Laska Laskova, Stanislava Kancheva, Petya Osenova, and Kiril Simov. 2012. Linguistic processing pipeline for bulgarian. In *Proceedings of LREC*, Istanbul, Turkey.

Thoudam Doren Singh and Sivaji Bandyopadhyay. 2010. Manipuri-english bidirectional statistical machine translation systems using morphology and dependency relations. In *Proceedings of the Fourth Workshop on Syntax and Structure in Statistical Translation*, pages 83–91, Beijing, China, August.

Kathrin Spreyer and Anette Frank. 2005. Projecting RMRS from TIGER Dependencies. In *Proceedings of the HPSG 2005 Conference*, pages 354–363, Lisbon, Portugal.

A. Stolcke. 2002. Srilm – an extensible language modeling toolkit. In *Proceedings of the International Conference on Spoken Language Processing*, volume 2.

Dekai Wu. 1997. Stochastic inversion transduction grammars and bilingual parsing of parallel corpora. *Computational Linguistics*, 23(3):377–404, September.

Deniz Yuret, Aydın Han, and Zehra Turgut. 2010. Semeval-2010 task 12: Parser evaluation using textual entailments. In *Proceedings of the SemEval-2010 Evaluation Exercises on Semantic Evaluation*.

Min Zhang, Hongfei Jiang, Aiti Aw, Haizhou Li, Chew Lim Tan, and Sheng Li. 2008. A tree sequence alignment-based tree-to-tree translation model. In *Proceedings of ACL-HLT*, pages 559–567.

Enriching Parallel Corpora for Statistical Machine Translation with Semantic Negation Rephrasing

Dominikus Wetzel
Department of Computational Linguistics
Saarland University
dwetzel@coli.uni-sb.de

Francis Bond
Linguistics and Multilingual Studies
Nanyang Technological University
bond@ieee.org

Abstract

This paper presents an approach to improving performance of statistical machine translation by automatically creating new training data for difficult to translate phenomena. In particular this contribution is targeted towards tackling the poor performance of a state-of-the-art system on negated sentences. The corpus expansion is achieved by high quality rephrasing of existing sentences to their negated counterparts making use of semantic transfer. The method is designed to work on both sides of the parallel corpus while preserving the alignment. Our results show an overall improvement of 0.16 BLEU points, with a statistically significant increase of 1.63 BLEU points when tested on only negated test data.

1 Introduction

Having large and good quality parallel corpora is vital for the quality of statistical machine translation (SMT) systems. However, these corpora are expensive to create. Furthermore, certain phenomena are not very frequent and hence underrepresented in existing parallel corpora, such as negated sentences, questions, etc. Due to the lack of such training data, the SMT systems do not perform as well as they could. Especially when it comes to negation, it is important that the basic semantics is preserved, i.e. a negated statement should not be translated as a positive one and vice versa.

Given a state-of-the-art baseline Japanese-English SMT system, a separate evaluation on the semantic level of negative only vs. positive only test data reveals the considerably poorer performance on the negative test set. This tendency and the importance of preserving a negated statement motivates experiments with improving performance on negative sentences.

Providing more training data for negative sentences should even out the discrepancy of the performance between the above mentioned negative and positive test data. We present a method where a large amount of negative training data is obtained by rephrasing the original training data. The rephrasing is performed on the semantic level to ensure high reliability and quality of the generated data. Simple rewriting based on the surface or syntactic level would require complex language specific rules, which is not desirable.

Working on the semantic structure exploits the fact that these representations abstract away from language specific structures. Thus, our approach can be easily implemented for other languages, provided there are grammars available for both languages involved in the desired parallel corpus. The DELPH-IN project[1] provides various such grammars.

This paper first describes related work in the following section. Section 3 presents a semantic analysis of the data with respect to negation and provides some distributional statistics. In Section 4 we elaborate on the functionality of our rephrasing system and present different methods for corpus expansion. The experimental setup and the results are in Section 5. A discussion and our conclusion are given in Section 6 and Section 7, respectively.

2 Related Work

There has been plenty of work on paraphrasing data in order to overcome the limitations that insufficiently large or underrepresented phenomena in par-

[1] www.delph-in.net

allel corpora impose on SMT.

Callison-Burch et al. (2006) tackle the problem of unseen phrases in SMT by adding source language paraphrases to the phrase table with appropriate probabilities. Both are obtained from additional parallel corpora, where the translations of the same foreign language phrase are considered paraphrases.

He et al. (2011) use a statistical framework for paraphrase generation of the source language. A log-linear model similar to the one used in phrase-based SMT provides paraphrases which are ranked based on novelty and fluency. The training corpus is then expanded by either adding the first best paraphrase, or n-best paraphrases. The target language is just copied to provide the required target side of the paraphrase.

Marton et al. (2009) and Gao and Vogel (2011) create new information by means of shallow semantic methods. The former present an approach to overcome the problem of unknown words in a low resource experiment. They base their monolingual paraphrasing on semantic similarity measures. In their setting they achieve significantly better translations. Gao and Vogel (2011) expand the parallel corpus by creating new information from existing data. With the use of a monolingual semantic role labeller one side of the parallel corpus is labelled. Role-to-word rules are extracted. In sentences containing the frames and semantic roles for which replacement rules exist, the corresponding words are substituted. A support vector machine is used for filtering the generated paraphrases.

An approach where paraphrases are obtained via generation from semantic structures is presented in Nichols et al. (2010). It exploits the fact that the generator produces multiple surface realizations. The basic set up is similar to our work, however our approach additionally manipulates, i.e. rephrases the semantics before generation. Furthermore, we implement parallel rephrasing, changing the meaning of both source and target text simultaneously.

There is, on the other hand, little work in phrase-based SMT especially targeting negated sentences. Collins et al. (2005) approach the problem of properly translating negation in their general reordering setting. Transformation rules are applied to syntactic trees, so that the source language word order has a closer resemblance to the target language word order. In particular, the German negation is moved towards the same position as the English one. This however presumes the existence of at least some negated training data.

3 Analysis of the Semantic Structure

The linguistic analysis is performed based on the Head-Driven Phrase Structure Grammar (HPSG) formalism established in the DELPH-IN project. In particular we consider the language pair Japanese-English. Hence, the broad-coverage grammar Jacy for Japanese (Bender and Siegel, 2004) and the English Resource Grammar (ERG) (Flickinger, 2000) are used respectively to parse the data and obtain the semantics for each sentence.

3.1 Negation in Minimal Recursion Semantics

The formalism that is used to represent the semantics in the DELPH-IN grammars is Minimal Recursion Semantics (MRS) (Copestake et al., 2005). Per definition, an MRS structure consists of a top handle, a bag of elementary predicates (EP) and a bag of constraints on handles. EPs represent verbs, their arguments, negations, quantifiers, among others. Furthermore, each EP has a handle with which it can be identified. Constraints on handles are used to restrict EPs such that they are outscoped by negations or quantifiers.

In a negated sentence, the negated verb is outscoped by the negation relation EP. Technically, the negation relation with handle h_n takes as its argument (ARG1) a handle (h_x) which is equal modulo quantifiers to the handle of the verb (h_v), written as the handle constraint: $h_x =_q h_v$. For visualization, an example is given, which shows the relevant parts of such a negated structure for the sentence *"This may not suit your taste."* (Figure 1). There, the negated verb has the handle h_8. The negation relation EP with handle h_{10} outscopes this via the constraint $h_{12} =_q h_8$.

The rephrasing we propose can be achieved with little or no knowledge about the specific implementation choices of the individual grammar. Collecting a few sample sentences that appear to be negated in the original data – by performing a simple surface string matching – is enough to reveal the principle of how negation is implemented. Because negation

```
< e2,
  { h8: _MAY_V_MODAL_REL( ARG0 e2, ARG1 h9 ),
    h10: NEG_REL( ARG0 e11, ARG1 h12),
    h13: _suit_v_1_rel( ARG0 e14, ARG1 x4, ARG2 x15),
    ... }
  { h6 =q h3,
    h12 =q h8,
    h9 =q h13,
    ... } >
```

Figure 1: A visualization of the English MRS structure from the sentence *"This may not suit your taste."*. The irrelevant parts have been omitted. The necessary parts in the corresponding Japanese MRS are the same.

	Japanese	
English	neg_rel	no neg_rel
neg_rel	8.5%	1.4%
no neg_rel	9.7%	80.4%

Table 1: Distribution of negation measured by the presence or absence of a negation relation (*neg_rel*) for those sentences with parses in both languages.

is represented at the semantic level, both the ERG and Jacy have very similar analyses, even though the syntactic realization is very different (negation in English involves a negative marker such as *not* and the use of an auxiliary verb such as *do*, while in Japanese it is realized by an auxiliary verb *nai*).

3.2 Data and Distribution of Negations

The data we use in this work is the Japanese-English parallel Tanaka corpus (Tanaka, 2001; Bond et al., 2008). We used the version distributed with Jacy, which has approximately 150,000 sentence pairs randomly ordered and divided into 100 profiles of 1,500 sentences each (the last one is a little short). We summarize the distribution of negated sentence pairs in Table 1. The data we consider for these statistics excludes development and test profiles (000–005). 84.5% of the input sentence pairs can be parsed successfully (110,759 out of 139,150).

The table also shows mixed cases where one language had a negation relation EP, whereas the other did not. Mixed cases are especially frequent when the Japanese side has a negation relation. These cases have two main causes: lexical negation such as "She missed the bus." being translated with the equivalent of "She did not catch the bus."; and idioms, such as *ikanakereba naranai* "I must go (lit: go-not-if not-become)" where the Japanese expression of modality includes a negation. Instances of the latter type form the majority, and should be handled in a newer version of the grammar, they are not considered further in this work.

4 Method: MRS Rephrasing & Corpus Expansion

The basic setup of the whole rephrasing system consists of parsing, MRS manipulation, generation and finally parallel corpus compilation. In the following sections, the individual processing modules are described in detail.

4.1 Parsing

Parsing is done using PET (Callmeier, 2000) a bottom-up chart parser for unification-based grammars using the English and Japanese Grammars ERG and Jacy. Since our approach builds on semantic rephrasing, only the MRS structure is required. We only use the best (first) parse returned by the parser.

4.2 Rephrasing

This module takes an MRS structure as input and rephrases it if possible by adding a negation relation EP to the highest scoping predicate. Adding the negation relation in our current form does not explore alternatives, where the negation has scope over other EPs in the MRS, nor are more refined changes from positive to negative polarity items considered.

Before inserting the negation relation EP into the existing MRS structure with its required handle constraint, we have to identify the EP we want to negate. The event that is introduced by the highest scoping verb is used. The event variable e_2 is directly accessible at the top of the MRS structure (cf. Figure 1). The corresponding EP that we want to negate has the event variable as value of its ARG0 attribute. This EP has a handle h_8 that has to be outscoped by the negation by means of a handle constraint. Hence, a new negation relation EP (in the example it got the handle h_{10}) is inserted with the following condition: Its ARG1 attribute value has to be token identical to the left side of a $=_q$ constraint. The right side is set to the just identified handle h_8 of the verb.

4.3 Generation

The same grammars used for parsing can also be used by the generator of the Lexical Knowledge Builder Environment (Copestake, 2002) to generate an n-best list of surface realizations given an MRS structure. However, we only consider the highest ranked realization. For the English generation, a generation ranking model is provided within the DELPH-IN project, thus providing a more confident n-best list. For the current Japanese grammar, no such model is available.

An example of a successful generation can be found in Table 2. On the English side, two surface variations are generated. The Japanese realizations show more variations in honorification and aspect.

We can only negate sentence pairs in both languages for 13.3% of the training data (18,727). This is mainly because of the brittleness of the Japanese generation (Goodman and Bond, 2009). Further, there are multiple ways of negating sentences and we do not always select the correct one.

4.4 Expanded Parallel Corpus Compilation

The method for assembling the expanded version of the parallel corpus for the use as training or development data directly influences translation quality. This is also demonstrated in Nichols et al. (2010), where various versions of padding out the data and preserving the word distribution are compared. The reported differences in performance suggest the importance of the method. Therefore, we have experimented with the following versions:

- **Append**: The obtained negated sentence pairs are added to the original corpus. Only the highest ranked realization per sentence for each language is considered. Thus they are aligned with each other. This leads to the addition of the following sentence pair where bilingual negation was successful:
`(en_original, jp_original)`
`(en_negated_1, jp_negated_1)` added
- **Padding**: In order to preserve the word distribution as mentioned above, we additionally padded out the sentence pairs by copying, where no bilingual negation was possible:
`(en_original, jp_original)`
`(en_original, jp_original)` added
- **Replace**: For emphasizing the impact of negated sentences, a variant of *Append* was compiled. Instead of adding the original pair of a successful bilingual negation the former was replaced by the latter:
`(en_negated_1, jp_negated_1)` substituted

Another way of testing the quality of the generated rephrases is to include them in the language model training. The expectation is that when the rephrases are of good quality, then the language model will be better and in turn should have positive result on the overall SMT.

5 Experiments & Evaluation

We experiment with the phrase-based statistical machine translation toolkit Moses (Koehn et al., 2007) in order to train a Japanese - English system and to show the influence of the expanded parallel corpora obtained with negation rephrasing on translation performance.

5.1 Data

The Tanaka corpus is used as a basis for our experiments. We tokenize and truecase the English side, the Japanese side is already tokenized and there are no case distinctions. Sentences longer than 40 tokens are removed. For evaluation, the English part is recased and detokenized.

	English	Japanese
original	I aim to be a writer.	私は 作家 を 目指し て いる 。
negated	I don't aim to be a writer.	私は 作家 を 目指し て い ない
	I do not aim to be a writer.	私は 作家 を 目指し て い ませ ん
		私は 作家 を 目指し ませ ん
		私は 作家 を 目指さ ない
		作家 を 私は 目指し ませ ん
		作家 を 私は 目指さ ない

Table 2: English and Japanese generations of a successfully rephrased sentence pair.

The sentence and token statistics for the original Tanaka corpus and our various extensions are listed in Table 3. The original corpus version acts as baseline data with profiles 006–100 as training and 000–002 as development data. For the extended systems, the training data as described in Section 4.4 is used. The same methods are applied on the development portion of the Tanaka corpus for tuning. The full test data has 42,305 English and 53,242 Japanese tokens and 4,500 sentences and is equal to the Tanaka corpus profiles 003–005.

The language model training data is in almost all cases equal to the original English Tanaka training data. Only in the *Append + neg LM* experiment, the training data for the language model is equal to the *Append* training data, except that it is slightly larger, since long sentences have not been filtered out. The expanded language model training data consists of 1,476,231 tokens and 160,069 sentences.

5.2 Different Test Sets

In order to find out the performance of the baseline and the extended systems on negative sentences, the test data has to be split up into several subsets, most notably *neg-strict* and *pos-strict*. The former only contains negated sentences, the latter only positive sentences. The definition of both is based on the existence of a negation relation EP in the semantics of the sentence. In order to obtain the semantic structure, the sentence pairs have to be parsed successfully. This also means, we will have some sentence pairs for which we cannot make a decision. Therefore, we provide a third test subset *biparse*, which contains all the parsable sentence pairs. This set reveals the big jump of BLEU score compared to the fourth test set *all*, which is the regular test set of the Tanaka corpus. A combined dataset with *pos-strict-neg-strict* is provided, which is the union of the first two sets.

5.3 Setup

We use Moses (SVN revision 4293) with Giza++ (Och and Ney, 2003) and the SRILM toolkit 1.5.12 (Stolcke, 2002). The language model is trained as a 5-order model with Kneser-Ney discounting. The Giza++ alignment heuristic *grow-diag-final-and* is used. All systems are tuned with MERT (Och, 2003). Several tunings for each system are run, the best performing ones are reported here.

5.4 Results

The results of our experiments can be seen in Table 4. The baseline is outperformed by our two best variations *Append* and *Append + neg LM* with respect to the entire test set. The differences in BLEU points are 0.14 and 0.16, which are not statistically significant according to the paired bootstrap resampling method (Koehn, 2004).

When looking at the test set *neg-strict* that only contains negated sentences, our improvement is much more apparent. The gain of our best performing model *Append + neg LM* compared to the baseline is at 1.63 BLEU points, which is statistically significant ($p < 0.05$). On the other hand there is a statistically insignificant drop of 0.30 with *pos-strict*.

The model with the expanded language model training data (*Append + neg LM*) always performs

	Tokens		Sentences	
	train	dev	train	dev
Baseline	1,300,821 / 1,641,591	42,248 / 52,822	141,147	4,500
Append	1,469,569 / 1,841,139	47,905 / 59,400	159,874	5,121
Padding	2,628,757 / 3,293,246	85,422 / 105,952	282,294	9,000
Replace	1,327,936 / 1,651,655	43,174 / 53,130	141,147	4,500

Table 3: Counts of tokens and sentences of the original Tanaka corpus and our expanded versions. Tokens are split up in English/Japanese counts.

better than the model under the same conditions except language model training data (*Append*).

When padding out the original data to preserve the word distribution in *Padding*, the effect of the additional negated training pairs is not strong enough. Both scores on the entire test set, as well as on the negation specific test set drop below the baseline. This version performs slightly better overall compared to *Replace*, however, on *neg-strict* it is a lot worse.

We manually checked the *neg-strict* test data set of our best performing system *Append + neg LM* versus the baseline, checking only whether the negation was translated or not (ignoring the overall quality). For 146 sentences, both systems correctly translated the negation. For 76 sentences both systems failed to translate the negation. For 33 sentences *Append + neg LM* translated the negation where the baseline system did not, and for 30 sentences the baseline system translated the negation but *Append + neg LM* did not. Overall, we reduced the number of critical negation errors from 99 to 96. Some example sentences are given in Figure 2.

6 Discussion

For identifying the performance of a state-of-the-art baseline system on negated sentences, we have split the test data into several distinct sets. The translation quality drops considerably by about 3 BLEU points when looking at the negative data compared to the parsable test data *biparse*. This big decline and the difference between performance on negative vs. positive test data shows that there is great potential to improve SMT systems by tackling this problem. Our approach is successful in handling negations better and thus diminishing the discrepancy of the two sets.

As the results show, there is only a small decrease of BLEU score points on the positive test data. And on the negative test data, the increase is substantially higher. Nevertheless, the overall performance in terms of BLEU only reflects this high increase to a certain degree. This can be attributed to the fact that the test data has a similar distribution to that of the training data, i.e. the proportion of negative sentences is low. Thus, the big increase gets diluted in the overall test data.

The results further show that improvement on the negative test data set comes at the cost of a slight degradation of performance on the positive data set and hence also on the full test set. This behaviour is not surprising due to the fact that a positive and its negative correspondent only vary very little when looking at the surface structure. The models trained with our extended data are aimed at providing one model which provides a balance between this gain and the loss.

This notion suggests that one would benefit from providing two separate translation models, one for negated input data and one for positive data. In this setting, the ample amount of negative training data that we generated through rephrasing could be exploited even more. A yet higher increase of BLEU score is expected. This of course requires a preprocessing step that confidently splits up the data accordingly. However, since we have the grammars at hand that can reliably determine whether there is a semantic negation relation in the input, this step can be solved easily. One small disadvantage with this idea is that a decision can only be made if the gram-

Test data sets	all	biparse	neg-strict	pos-strict	pos-strict-neg-strict
Sentence counts	4500	3399	285	2684	2969
Baseline	22.87	25.76	22.77	**26.60**	26.25
Append	23.01	25.78	24.04	26.22	26.25
Append + neg LM	**23.03**	**25.88**	**24.40**	26.30	**26.28**
Padding	22.74	25.54	22.62	26.35	26.06
Replace	22.55	25.35	23.36	26.00	25.84

Table 4: Japanese-English translation evaluation results of the baseline and our extended systems.

mar of the input language produces a parse for the input sentence. This however can be circumvented by backing off to the well balanced model presented in this work. In other words, we use a positive model for positive sentences, a negative model for negative sentences and a balanced model if we are not sure.

Our method depends on two large-scale deep semantic grammars. However, developing such grammars has been made much more efficient with the emergence of the Grammar Matrix (Bender et al., 2002). There is is already a large collection of working grammars, which can readily be tried out. In addition to the ERG and Jacy, there are grammars for German, French, Korean, Modern Greek, Norwegian, Spanish, Portuguese, and more, with varying levels of coverage.[2]

Because parsing, rephrasing and generation do not have 100% coverage, we cannot produce negated versions of all sentences. The rephrasing can only work when both sides of a sentence pair are parsable. Furthermore, not every rephrased sentence pair can be successfully realized. However, we still manage to build far more negated training data than is otherwise available: more than doubling the amount. This could be further increased by a little more work on the generation, especially for Jacy. In addition, we have not made use of all the generated data, i.e. lower ranked realizations have been discarded even though they may still be useful.

Furthermore, we have shown in the experiment results that using our expanded version for language model training is also of great benefit, since we could achieve not only an overall increase, but especially one on negated test data.

[2] `moin.delph-in.net/GrammarCatalogue`

7 Conclusion & Future Work

We have presented an approach which alleviates the negation translation difficulties of phrase-based SMT. We have tackled the problem by automatically expanding the training data with negated sentence pairs. The additional data has been obtained by rephrasing existing data based on the semantic structure of the input.

Our experiments with the phrase-based SMT system Moses show small improvements over the baseline considering the entire test data. A more distinct look at only negated sentences in the test data shows a statistically significant improvement of 1.63 BLEU points. The best performing model represents a good balance of a high BLEU score increase on the negated test data vs. a statistically insignificant decrease on the positive test data, yet achieving a small overall improvement. Furthermore, it was shown, that expanding not only the translation training data, but also the language model training data boosts performance even more.

Our method works on the semantic level and can be easily adapted to other languages. Having access to a deep semantic structure opens possible extensions along our idea. On the one hand negation rephrasing could be refined in order to have a higher generation rate. On the other hand, other phenomena could also be tackled in the same way: e.g. rephrasing declarative statements to interrogatives.

Just for negation, the corpora expanded with our high quality negations could be combined with the syntactic reordering strategies presented in Section 2 such that the negation reordering rule has more training data and thus a bigger influence on the overall performance.

Acknowledgements

This research was supported in part by the Erasmus Mundus Action 2 program MULTI of the European Union, grant agreement number 2009-5259-5.

References

Bender, E. M., Flickinger, D., and Oepen, S. (2002). The grammar matrix: An open-source starter-kit for the rapid development of cross-linguistically consistent broad-coverage precision grammars. In *Proceedings of the Workshop on Grammar Engineering and Evaluation at the 19th International Conference on Computational Linguistics*, pages 8–14, Taipei, Taiwan.

Bender, E. M. and Siegel, M. (2004). Implementing the syntax of Japanese numeral classifiers. In *Proceedings of the IJC-NLP-2004*.

Bond, F., Kuribayashi, T., and Hashimoto, C. (2008). Construction of a free Japanese treebank based on HPSG. In *14th Annual Meeting of the Association for Natural Language Processing*, pages 241–244, Tokyo. (in Japanese).

Callison-Burch, C., Koehn, P., and Osborne, M. (2006). Improved statistical machine translation using paraphrases. In *Proceedings of the Human Language Technology Conference of the NAACL, Main Conference*, pages 17–24, New York City, USA. Association for Computational Linguistics.

Callmeier, U. (2000). PET - a platform for experimentation with efficient HPSG processing techniques. *Natural Language Engineering*, 6(1):99–108.

Collins, M., Koehn, P., and Kucerova, I. (2005). Clause Restructuring for Statistical Machine Translation. In *Proceedings of the 43rd Annual Meeting of the ACL*, Ann Arbor, Michigan. ACL.

Copestake, A. (2002). *Implementing Typed Feature Structure Grammars*. CSLI Publications.

Copestake, A., Flickinger, D., Pollard, C., and Sag, I. A. (2005). Minimal Recursion Semantics – An Introduction. *Research on Language and Computation*, 3:281–332.

Flickinger, D. (2000). On building a more efficient grammar by exploiting types. *Natural Language Engineering*, 6(1):15–28. (Special Issue on Efficient Processing with HPSG).

Gao, Q. and Vogel, S. (2011). Corpus expansion for statistical machine translation with semantic role label substitution rules. In *Proceedings of the 49th Annual Meeting of the Association for Computational Linguistics: Human Language Technologies*, pages 294–298, Portland, Oregon, USA. Association for Computational Linguistics.

Goodman, M. W. and Bond, F. (2009). Using generation for grammar analysis and error detection. In *Joint conference of the 47th Annual Meeting of the Association for Computational Linguistics and the 4th International Joint Conference on Natural Language Processing of the Asian Federation of Natural Language Processing*, pages 109–112, Singapore.

He, W., Zhao, S., Wang, H., and Liu, T. (2011). Enriching smt training data via paraphrasing. In *Proceedings of 5th International Joint Conference on Natural Language Processing*, pages 803–810, Chiang Mai, Thailand. Asian Federation of Natural Language Processing.

Koehn, P. (2004). Statistical Significance Tests for Machine Translation Evaluation. In *Proceedings of EMNLP 2004*, pages 388–395, Barcelona, Spain. Association for Computational Linguistics.

Koehn, P., Hoang, H., Birch, A., Callison-Burch, C., Federico, M., Bertoldi, N., Cowan, B., Shen, W., Moran, C., Zens, R., Dyer, C., Bojar, O., Constantin, A., and Herbst, E. (2007). Moses: Open Source Toolkit for Statistical Machine Translation. In *Annual Meeting of the ACL*.

Marton, Y., Callison-Burch, C., and Resnik, P. (2009). Improved statistical machine translation using monolingually-derived paraphrases. In *Proceedings of the 2009 Conference on Empirical Methods in Natural Language Processing*, pages 381–390, Singapore. Association for Computational Linguistics.

Nichols, E., Bond, F., Appling, D. S., and Matsumoto, Y. (2010). Paraphrasing Training Data for Statistical Machine Translation. *Journal of Natural Language Processing*, 17(3):101–122.

Och, F. J. (2003). Minimum Error Rate Training in Statistical Machine Translation. In *Proceedings of the 41st Annual Meeting of ACL*, pages 160–167.

Och, F. J. and Ney, H. (2003). A Systematic Comparison of Various Statistical Alignment Models. *Computational Linguistics*, 29:19–51.

Stolcke, A. (2002). SRILM – An Extensible Language Modeling Toolkit. In *Proc. Intl. Conf. on Spoken Language Processing*, volume 2, pages 901–904, Denver.

Tanaka, Y. (2001). Compilation of a multilingual parallel corpus. In *Proceedings of PACLING 2001*, pages 265–268, Kyushu.

Japanese	昨日 彼ら は テニス を し なかっ た 。
Baseline	They played tennis yesterday.
Append + neg LM	They do not play tennis yesterday.
Reference	Yesterday they didn't play tennis, because it rained.

(a) Baseline fails to translate the negation.

Japanese	彼 は 約束 を 破る こと は し ない と 確信 し て いる ん です が 。
Baseline	He is sure to break your promise, I'm sure.
Append + neg LM	He never breaks his word, I'm sure.
Reference	I'm sure he won't fail to keep his word.

(b) Correct translation by our system with valid variation of wording.

Japanese	私 が 家 に 帰っ た 時 は 彼 は 眠っ て い ませ ん でし た 。
Baseline	I was when I came home, he was asleep.
Append + neg LM	I came home when he is not asleep.
Reference	He wasn't sleeping when I came home.

(c) Baseline omits the negation.

Japanese	お金 の もちあわせ が あり ませ ん 。
Baseline	Money with me.
Append + neg LM	I don't have any money with me.
Reference	I don't have any money with me.

(d) Baseline omits subject, verb and negation.

Japanese	南十字星 は 日本 で は 見る こと が でき ない 。
Baseline	The 南十字星 in Japan, I cannot see it.
Append + neg LM	The 南十字星 in Japan.
Reference	The Southern Cross is not to be seen in Japan.

(e) Our system does not translate a part of the sentence.

Japanese	大声 で 話し て は いけ ない 。
Baseline	Don't speak in a loud voice.
Append + neg LM	You must speak in a loud voice.
Reference	You must not speak loudly.

(f) Our system omits the negation.

Japanese	彼女 は 友達 が い ない 。
Baseline	She has no friends.
Append + neg LM	She is a friend of mine.
Reference	She doesn't have a boy friend.

(g) Our system does not produce a negation. The object is incorrectly translated in both systems.

Figure 2: Sentences from the *neg-strict* test set showing differences between the baseline and our best performing system *Append + neg LM*. Examples in (a–d) show improvements, (e–g) show degradations.

Towards a Predicate-Argument Evaluation for MT

Ondřej Bojar[α], **Dekai Wu**[β]
[α] Charles University in Prague, Faculty of Mathematics and Physics
Institute of Formal and Applied Linguistics
[β] *HKUST*, Human Language Technology Center,
Department of Computer Science and Engineering
Hong Kong University of Science and Technology
bojar@ufal.mff.cuni.cz, dekai@cs.ust.hk

Abstract

HMEANT (Lo and Wu, 2011a) is a manual MT evaluation technique that focuses on predicate-argument structure of the sentence. We relate HMEANT to an established linguistic theory, highlighting the possibilities of reusing existing knowledge and resources for interpreting and automating HMEANT. We apply HMEANT to a new language, Czech in particular, by evaluating a set of English-to-Czech MT systems. HMEANT proves to correlate with manual rankings at the sentence level better than a range of automatic metrics. However, the main contribution of this paper is the identification of several issues of HMEANT annotation and our proposal on how to resolve them.

1 Introduction

Manual evaluation of machine translation output is a tricky enterprise. It has been long recognized that different evaluation techniques lead to different outcomes, e.g. Blanchon et al. (2004) mention an evaluation carried out in 1972 where the very same Russian-to-English MT outputs were scored 4.5 out of the maximum 5 points by prospective users of the system but only 1 out of 5 by teachers of English. Throughout the years, many techniques were explored with more or less of a success.

The two-scale scoring for adequacy and fluency used in NIST evaluation has been abandoned by some evaluation campaigns, most notably the WMT shared task series, see Koehn and Monz (2006) through Callison-Burch et al. (2012)[1]. Since 2008, WMT uses a simple relative ranking of MT outputs as its primary manual evaluation technique: the annotator is presented with up to 5 MT outputs for a given input sentence and the task is to rank them from best to worst (ties allowed) on whatever criteria he or she deems appropriate. While this single-scale relative ranking is perhaps faster to annotate and reaches a higher inter- and intra-annotator agreement than the (absolute) fluency and adequacy (Callison-Burch et al., 2007), the technique and its evaluation are still far from satisfactory. Bojar et al. (2011) observe several discrepancies in the interpretation of the rankings, partly due to the high load on human annotators (the comparison of several long sentences at once, among other issues) but partly also due to technicalities of the calculation.

Lo and Wu (2011a) present an interesting evaluation technique called MEANT (or HMEANT if carried out by humans), the core of which lies in assessing whether the key elements in the predicate-argument structure of the sentence have been preserved. In other words, lay annotators are checking, if they recognize *who did what* to *whom*, *when*, *where* and *why* from the MT outputs and whether the respective role fillers convey the same meaning as in the reference translation. HMEANT has been shown to correlate reasonably well with manual adequacy and ranking evaluations. It is relatively fast and should lend itself to full automatization. On the other hand, HMEANT was so far tested only on translation into English and with just three competing MT systems.

[1] `http://www.statmt.org/wmt06` till `wmt12`

In this work, we extend the application of HMEANT to evaluating MT into Czech, a morphologically rich language with relatively free word order. The paper is structured as follows: Section 2 presents the technical details of HMEANT and relates HMEANT to an established linguistic theory that underlies the Prague dependency treebanks (Hajič et al., 2006; Hajič et al., 2012) and several other works. We also suggest possible benefits of this coupling such as the reuse of tools. In Section 3, we describe the setup and results of our HMEANT experiment. Since this is the first time HMEANT is applied to a new language, Section 4 constitutes the main contribution of this work. We point out at several problems of HMEANT and propose a remedy, the empirical evaluation of which however remains for future work. Section 5 concludes our observations.

Semantic frames summarize a sentence using a simple event structure that captures essential parts of the meaning like "who did what to whom, when, where, why and how".
Phrases or clauses that express meanings can be identified as playing a particular semantic role in the sentence. In other words, semantic frames are the systematic abstraction of the meanings in a sentence.
The following is the list of the semantic roles to be used in HMEANT evaluation:

Agent (who)	Action (did)
Experiencer or Patient (what)	Benefactive (whom)
Temporal (when)	Locative (where)
Purpose (why)	Manner (how)
Degree or Extent (how)	Modal (how) [may, should, ...]
Negation (how) [not]	Other adverbial argument (how)

You may consider the Action predicate to be the central event, while the other roles modify the Action to give a more detailed description of the event. Each semantic frame contains exactly one Action and any number of other roles.
Please note that the Action predicate must be exactly ONE single word.
There may be multiple semantic frames in one sentence, because a sentence may be constructed to describe multiple events and each semantic frame captures only one event.

Figure 1: Semantic role labeling guidelines of HMEANT.

2 Relating HMEANT and Valency Theory of FGD

2.1 HMEANT Annotation Procedure

HMEANT is designed to be simple and fast. The annotation consists of two steps: (1) semantic role labelling, SRL in the sequel, and (2) alignment of roles between the hypothesis and the reference.

The annotation guidelines are deliberately minimalistic, so that even inexpert people can learn them quickly. The complete guidelines for SRL are given in Figure 1 and it takes less than 15 minutes to train an unskilled person.

In the alignment task, the annotators first indicate which frames in the reference and the hypothesis correspond to each other. In the second step, they align all matching role fillers to each other and also mark the translation as "Correct" or "Partial".

The HMEANT calculation then evaluates the f-score of the predicates and their role fillers in a given sentence. An important aspect of the calculation is that unmatched predicates with all their role fillers are excluded from the calculation.

2.2 Functional Generative Description

The core ideas of HMEANT follow the case grammar (Fillmore, 1968) or PropBank (Palmer et al., 2005) and can be also directly related to an established linguistic theory which was primarily developed for Czech, namely the Functional Generative Description (Sgall, 1967; Sgall et al., 1986). The theory defines so-called "tectogrammatical" layer (t-layer). At the t-layer, each sentence is represented as a dependency tree with just content words as separate nodes. All auxiliary words are "hidden" into attributes of the corresponding t-nodes. Moreover, ellipsis is restored to some extent, so e.g. dropped subject pronouns do have a corresponding t-node.

An important element of FGD is the valency theory (Panevová, 1980) which introduces empirical linguistic tests to distinguish between what other theories would call complements vs. adjuncts and postulates the relationship between the set of verb modifiers as observed in the sentence and the set of valency slots that should be listed in a valency dictionary. This aspect could provide a further refinement of HMEANT, e.g. weighing complements and adjuncts differently.

FGD has been thoroughly tested and refined during the development of the Prague Dependency Treebank (Hajič et al., 2006)[2] and the parallel Prague Czech-English Dependency Treebank (Hajič

[2] `http://ufal.mff.cuni.cz/pdt2.0/`

et al., 2012)[3]. Note that the latter is a translation of all the 49k sentences of the Penn Treebank WSJ section. Both English and Czech sentences are manually annotated at the tectogrammatical layer, where the English layer is based on the Penn annotation and manually adapted for t-layer. Both languages include their respective valency lexicons and the work on a bilingual valency lexicon is being developed (Šindlerová and Bojar, 2010).

A range of automatic tools to convert plain text up to the t-layer exist for both English and Czech. Most of them are now part of the Treex platform (Popel and Žabokrtský, 2010)[4] and they were successfully used in automatic annotation of 15 million parallel sentences (Bojar et al., 2012)[5] as well as other NLP tasks including English-to-Czech MT. Recently, significant effort was also invested in parsing not quite correct output of MT systems into Czech for the purposes of rule-based grammar correction (Rosa et al., 2012). Establishing the automatic pipeline for MEANT should be relatively easy with these tools at hand.

2.3 HMEANT vs. FGD Valency

The formulation of HMEANT in terms of FGD is straightforward: it is the f-score of matched t-nodes for predicates and the subtrees of their immediate dependents in the t-trees of the hypothesis and the reference.

HMEANT uses a simple web-based annotation interface which operates on the surface form of the sentence. Annotators mark the predicate and their complementations as contiguous spans in the sentence. While this seems natural when we want lay people to annotate, it brings some problems, see Section 4. A linguistically adequate interface would allow to mark tectogrammatical nodes and subtrees in the t-layer, however, the customizable editor TrEd[6] used for manual annotation of t-layer is too heavy for our purposes both in terms of speed and complexity of user interface.

Perhaps the best option we plan to investigate in future research is a mixed approach: the interface would display only the text version of the sentence but it would internally know the (automatic) t-layer structure. Selecting any word that corresponds to the t-node of a verb would automatically extend the selection to all other belongings of the t-node, i.e. all auxiliaries of the verb. For role fillers, selecting any word from the role filler would select the whole t-layer subtree. In order to handle errors in the automatic t-layer annotation, the interface would certainly need to allow manual selection and deselection of words, providing valuable feedback to the automatic tools.

[3] http://ufal.mff.cuni.cz/pcedt2.0/
[4] http://ufal.mff.cuni.cz/treex/
[5] http://ufal.mff.cuni.cz/czeng/
[6] http://ufal.mff.cuni.cz/tred/

HMEANT	0.2833
METEOR	0.2167
WER	0.1708
CDER	0.1375
NIST	0.1167
TER	0.1167
PER	0.0208
BLEU	0.0125

Table 1: Kendall's τ for sentence-level correlation with human rankings.

3 An Experiment in English-Czech MT Evaluation

In this first study, we selected 50 sentences from the English-to-Czech WMT12 manual evaluation. The sentences were chosen to overlap with the standard WMT ranking procedure (see Section 3.1) as much as possible.

In total, 13 MT systems participated in this translation direction. We allocated 14 annotators (one annotator for the SRL of the reference) so that nobody saw the same sentence translated by more systems. The hypotheses were shuffled so every annotator got samples from all systems as well as the reference. Unfortunately, time constraints and the large number of MT systems prevented us from collecting overlapping annotations, so we cannot evaluate inter-annotator agreement.

Following Lo and Wu (2011a) and Callison-Burch et al. (2012), we report Kendall's τ rank correlation coefficients for sentence-level rankings as provided by a range of automatic metrics and our HMEANT. The gold standard are the manual WMT rankings. See Table 1.

We see that HMEANT achieves a better correlation than all the tested automatic metrics, although in absolute terms, the correlation is not very high. Lo and Wu (2011b) report τ for HMEANT of up to 0.49 and Lo and Wu (2011a) observe τ in the range 0.33 to 0.43. These figures are not comparable to our result for several reasons: we evaluated 13 and not just 3 MT systems, the gold standard for us are overall system rankings, not just adequacy judgments as for Lo and Wu (2011b), and we evaluate translation to Czech, not English. Callison-Burch et al. (2012) report τ for several automatic metrics on the whole WMT12 English-to-Czech dataset, the best of which correlates at $\tau = 0.18$. The only common metric is METEOR and it reaches 0.16 on the whole WMT12 set.[7] In line with our observation, Czech-to-English correlations reported by Callison-Burch et al. (2012) are higher: the best metric achieves 0.28 and averages 0.25 across four source languages.

The overall low sentence-level correlation of our HMEANT and WMT12 rankings is obviously caused to some extent by the problems we identified, see Section 4 below. On the other hand, it is quite possible that the WMT-style rankings taken as the gold standard are of a disputable quality themselves, see Section 3.1 or the detailed report on inter-annotator agreement and a long discussion on interpreting the rankings in Callison-Burch et al. (2012). Last but not least, it is likely that HMEANT and manual ranking simply measure different properties of MT outputs. The Kendall's τ is thus not an ultimate meta-evaluation metric for us.

3.1 WMT-Style Rankings

This section illustrates some issues with the WMT rankings when used for system-level evaluation. Obviously, at the sentence level, the rankings can behave differently but the system-level evaluation benefits from a large number of manual labels.

In the WMT-style rankings, humans are provided with no more than 5 system outputs for a given sentence at once. The task is to rank these 5 systems relatively to each other, ties allowed.

Following Bojar et al. (2011), we report three possible evaluation regimes (or "interpretations") of these 5-fold rankings to obtain system-level scores. The first step is shared: all *pairwise* comparisons implied by the 5-fold ranking are extracted. For each system, we then report the percentage of cases where the system won the pairwise comparison. Our default interpretation is to exclude all ties from the calculation, labelled "Ties Ignored", i.e. $\frac{\text{wins}}{\text{wins + losses}}$. The former WMT interpretation (up to 2011) was to include ties in both the numerator and the denominator, i.e. $\frac{\text{wins + ties}}{\text{wins+ties+losses}}$ denoted "$\geq$ Others". WMT summary paper also reports "$>$ Others" where the ties are included in the denominator only, thus giving credit to systems that are different.

As we see in Table 2, each of the interpretations leads to different rankings of the systems. More importantly, the underlying set of sentences also affects the result. For instance, the system ONLINEA jumps to the second position in "Ties Ignored" if we consider only the 50 sentences used in our HMEANT evaluation. To some extent, the differences are caused by the lower number of observations. While "All-No Ties" is based on 2893$\pm$134 pairwise comparisons per system, "50-No Ties" is based on just 186$\pm$30 observations. Moreover, not all systems came up among the 5 ranked systems for a given sentence. In our 50 sentences, only 7.3$\pm$2.1 systems were compared per sentence. On the full set of sentences, this figure drops to 5.9$\pm$1.7.

4 Problems of HMEANT Annotation

We asked our annotators to take notes and report any problems. On the positive side, some annotators familiar with the WMT ranking evaluation felt that in both phases of HMEANT, they "knew what they were doing and why". In the ranking task, it is unfortunately quite common that the annotator is asked to rank incomparably bad hypotheses. In such cases, the annotator probably tries to follow some subjective and unspoken criteria, which often leads to a lower in inter- and intra-annotator agreement.

On the negative side, we observed many problems of the current version of HMEANT, and we propose a remedy for all of them. We disregard minor technical issues of the annotation interface and focus on the design decisions. The only technical limitation worth mentioning was the inability to return to previous sentences. In some cases, this even caused the

[7]It is possible that Callison-Burch et al. (2012) use somewhat different METEOR settings apart from the different subset of the data.

Interpretation	Ties Ignored		≥ Others		> Others	
Sentences	All	50	All	50	All	50
cu-depfix	66.4	72.5	73.0	77.5	53.3	59.4
onlineB	63.0	61.4	70.5	69.3	50.3	49.0
uedin-wmt12	55.8	60.3	63.6	66.3	46.0	≀ 51.1
cu-tamch-boj	55.6	54.6	≀ 64.7	62.1	44.2	45.7
cu-bojar_2012	54.3	53.2	≀ 64.1	≀ 62.2	42.6	43.0
CU_TectoMT	53.1	≀ 54.9	60.5	59.8	≀ 44.6	≀ 49.0
onlineA	52.9	≀ 61.4	≀ 60.8	≀ 66.7	≀ 44.0	≀ 53.0
pctrans2010	47.7	≀ 54.1	55.1	≀ 60.1	40.9	≀ 47.1
commercial2	46.0	51.3	54.6	59.5	38.7	42.7
cu-poor-comb	44.1	41.6	≀ 54.7	50.5	35.7	35.2
uk-dan-moses	43.5	33.2	53.4	44.2	≀ 35.9	27.7
SFU	36.1	31.0	46.8	43.0	30.0	25.6
jhu-hiero	32.2	26.7	43.2	36.0	27.0	23.3

Table 2: WMT12 system-level ranking results in three different evaluation regimes evaluated either on all sentences or just the 50 sentences that were subject to our HMEANT annotation. The table is sorted along the first column and the symbol "≀" in other columns marks items out of sequence.

annotators to skip parts of the annotation altogether, because they clicked Next Sentence instead of the Next Frame button.

Note that the impact of the problems on the final HMEANT reliability varies. What causes just minor hesitations in the SRL phase can lead to complete annotation failures in the Alignment phase and vice versa. We list the problems in decreasing severity, based on our observations as well as the number of annotators who complained about the given issue.

4.1 Vague SRL Guidelines

The first group of problems is caused by the SRL guidelines being (deliberately) too succinct and developed primarily for English.

Complex predicates. Out of the many possible cases where predicates are described using several words, SRL guidelines mention just modal verbs and reserve a label for them (assuming that the main verb will be chosen as the Action, i.e. the predicate itself). This goes against the syntactic properties of Czech and other languages, where the modal verb is the one that conjugates and it is only complemented by the content verb in infinitive. Some annotators thus decided to mark such cases as a pair of nested frames.

The problem becomes more apparent for other classes of verbs, such as phasic verbs (e.g. "to begin"), which naturally lead to nested frames.

A specific problem for Czech mentioned by almost all annotators, was the copula verb "to be". Here, the meaning-bearing element is actually the adjective that follows (e.g. "to be glad to …"). HMEANT forced the annotators to use e.g. the Experiencer slot for the non-verbal part of this complex predicate. In the negated form, "není (is not)", some annotators even marked the copula as Negation and the non-verbal part as the Action.

No verb at all. HMEANT does not permit to annotate frames with no predicate. There are however at least two frequent cases that deserve this option: (1) the whole sentence can be a nominal construction such as the title of a section, and (2) an MT system may erroneously omit the verb, while the remaining slot fillers are understandable and the whole meaning of the sentence can be also guessed. Giving no credit to such a sentence at all seems too strict. In some cases, it was possible for the annotators to find a substitute word for the Action role, e.g. a noun that should have been translated as the verb.

A related issue was caused by the uncertainty to what extent the frame annotation should go. There are many nouns derived from verbs that also bear valency. FGD acknowledges this and valency lexicons for Czech do include also many of such nouns. If the

Reference	Oblečky	musíme	vystříhat	z časopisů
Gloss	clothes	we-must	cut	from magazines
Roles	Experiencer	Modal	Action	Locative
Meaning	We must cut the clothes (assuming paper toys) from magazines			
Hypothesis	Musíme	vyříznout	oblečení z časopisů	
Gloss	We-must	cut	clothes from magazines	
Roles	Modal	Action	Experiencer	

Figure 2: An example of PP-attachment mismatch. While it is (almost) obvious from the word order of the reference that the preposition phrase "z časopisů" is a separate filler, it was marked as part of the Experiencer role in the hypothesis. In the alignment phase, there is no way to align the single Experiencer slot of the hypothesis onto the two slots (Experiencer, Locative) if the reference.

instructions are not clear in this respect, it is quite possible that one annotator creates frames for such nouns and the other does not, causing a mismatch in the Alignment phase.

PP-attachment. The problem of attaching prepositional phrases to verbs or to other noun phrases is well acknowledged in many languages including English and Czech. See an example in Figure 2.

A complete solution of the problem in the SRL phase will never be possible, because there are naturally ambiguous cases where each annotator can prefer a different reading. However, the Alignment phase should be somehow prepared for the inevitable mismatches.

Unclear role labels. Insufficient role labels. The set of role labels of HMEANT is very simple compared to the set of edge labels (called "functors") in the tectogrammatical annotation. Several annotators mentioned that the HMEANT roleset is hard to use especially for passive constructions or verbs with a secondary object.

Because the final HMEANT calculation requires aligned fillers to match in their role labels, the agreement on role labels is important. We suggest experimenting also with a variant of HMEANT that would disregard the labels altogether.

Other problematic cases are sentences where several role fillers appear to belong to the same type, e.g. Locative: "Byl převezen (He was transported) | do nemocnice (to the hospital) | v záchranném vrtulníku (in a helicopter)". While it is semantically obvious that the hospital is not in the helicopter, so this is not a PP-attachment problem, some annotators still mark both Locatives jointly as a single slot, causing the same slot mismatch. It is also possible that the annotator has actually assigned the Locative label twice but the annotation interface interpreted all the words as belonging to one filler only.

Coreference. The SRL guidelines are not specific on handling of slot fillers realized as pronouns (or even dropped pronouns). If we consider a sentence like "It is the man who wins", it is not clear which words should be marked as the Agent of the Action "wins". There are three candidates, all equally correct from the purely semantic point of view: "it", "the man" and "who".

A natural choice would be to select the closest word referring to the respective object, however, in constructions of complex verbs or in pro-drop languages the object may not be explicitly stated in the syntactically closest position. Depending on the annotators' decisions, this can lead to a mismatch in the number of slots in the subsequent Alignment phase.

Other problems. Some annotators mentioned a few other problems. One of them were paratactic constructions: the frame-labelling procedure does not allow to distinguish between sentences like "It is windy and it rains" vs. "It is windy but it rains", because neither "and" nor "but" are a slot filler. Similarly, expressions like "for example" do not seem to constitute a slot filler but still somehow refine the meaning of the sentence and should be preserved in the translation.

One annotator suggested that the importance of the SRL phase should be emphasized and the annotators should be pushed towards annotating as much as they can, e.g. also by highlighting all verbs in the sentence, in order to provide enough frames and fillers to align in the second phase.

Reference	Opilý řidič	těžce	zraněn
Gloss	A drunken driver	seriously	injured
Roles	Agent	Extent	Action
Meaning	A drunken driver is seriously injured.		
Hypothesis	Opilý řidič	vážně	zranil
Gloss	A drunken driver	seriously	injured (active form)
Roles	Agent	Extent	Action
Meaning	A drunken driver seriously injured (someone).		

Figure 3: A mismatch of the meanings of the predicates. Other roles in the frames match perfectly.

The following sections describe problems of the Alignment phase.

4.2 Correctness of the Predicate

HMEANT alignment phase allows the annotators to either align or not align a pair of frames. There is no option to indicate that the match of the predicates themselves is somewhat incorrect. Once the predicates are aligned, the user can only match individual fillers, possibly penalizing partial mismatches.

Figure 3 illustrates this issue on a real example from our data. Once the annotator decides to align the frames, there is no way to indicate that the meaning was reversed by the translation.

What native speakers of Czech also feel is that the MT output in Figure 3 is incomplete, an Experiencer is missing. A similar example from the data is the hypothesis "Svědek oznámil policii. (The witness informed/announced the police.)" The verb "oznámit (inform/announce)" in Czech requires the message (perhaps the Experiencer in the HMEANT terminology), similarly to the English "announce" but unlike "inform". The valency theory of FGD formally describes the problem as a missing slot filler and given a valency dictionary, such errors can be even identified automatically.

On the other hand, it should be noted that a mismatch in the predicate alone does not mean that the translation is incorrect. An example in our data was the phrase "dokud se současné umění nedočkalo ve Vídni nového stánku" vs. "než současné umění ve Vídni dostalo nový domov". Both versions mean "until contemporary art in Vienna was given a new home" but due to the different conjunction chosen ("dokud/než, till/until"), one of the verbs has to be negated.

4.3 Need for M:N Frame Alignment

The majority of our annotators complained that complex predicates such as phasal verbs or copula constructions as well as muddled MT output with no verb often render the frame matching impossible. If the reference and the hypothesis differ in the number of frames, then it is also almost certain that the role fillers observed in the two sentences will be distributed differently among the frames, prohibiting filler alignment.

A viable solution would be allow merging of frames during the Alignment phase, which is equivalent to allowing many-to-many alignment of frames. The sets of role fillers would be simply unioned, improving the chance for filler alignment.

4.4 Need for M:N Slot Alignment

Inherent ambiguities like PP-attachment or spurious differences in SRL prevent from 1-1 slot alignment rather frequently. A solution would be to allow many-to-many alignments of slot fillers.

4.5 Partial Adequacy vs. Partial Fluency

The original HMEANT Alignment guidelines say to mark an aligned slot pair as Correct or Partial match. (Mismatching slots should not be aligned at all.) A Partial match is described as:

> Role fillers in MT express part of the meaning of the aligned role fillers in the reference translation. Do NOT penalize extra meaning unless it belongs in other role fillers in the reference translation.

The second sentence of the instructions is probably aimed at cases where the MT expresses *more* than the reference does, which is possible because the translator may have removed part of the content or because the source and the reference are both not quite literal translations from a third language. A clarifying example of this case in the instructions is highly desirable.

What our annotators noticed were cases where the translation was semantically adequate but contained e.g. an agreement mismatch or another grammar error. The instructions should exemplify, if this is to be treated as a Correct or Partial match. Optionally, the Partial match could be split into three separate cases: partially inadequate, partially disfluent, and partially inadequate and disfluent.

4.6 Summary of Suggested HMEANT Fixes

To summarize the observations above, our experience with HMEANT was overall positive, but we propose several changes in the design to improve the reliability of the annotations:

SRL Phase:

- The SRL guidelines should be kept as simple as they are, but more examples and especially examples of incorrect MT output should be provided.
- The Action should be allowed to consist of several words, including non-adjacent ones.
- The possibility of using automatic t-layer annotation tools should be explored, at least to pre-annotate which words form a multi-word predicate or role filler.

Alignment Phase:

- The annotator must be able to indicate a partial or incorrect match of the predicates themselves.
- Both frames as well as fillers should support M:N alignment to overcome a range of naturally appearing as well as spurious mismatches in the two SRL annotations.
- Examples of anaphoric expressions should be included in the guidelines, stressing that any element of the anaphora chain should be treated as an appropriate representant of the role filler.
- The Partial match could distinguish between an error in adequacy or fluency, or rather, the Alignment guidelines should explicitly provide examples of both types and ask the annotators to disregard the difference.

Technical Changes:

- The annotators need to be able to go back within each phase. (The division between the SRL and Alignment phases should be preserved.)

We do not expect any of the proposed changes to negatively impact annotation time. Actually, some speedup may be obtained from the suggested pre-annotation and also from a reduced hesitation of the annotators in the alignment phase thanks to the M:N alignment possibility.

5 Conclusion

We applied HMEANT, a technique for manual evaluation of MT quality based on predicate-argument structure, to a new language, Czech. The experiment confirmed that HMEANT is applicable in this setting, outperforming automatic metrics in sentence-level correlation with manual rankings.

During our annotation, we identified a range of problems in the current HMEANT design. We thus propose a few modifications to the technique and also suggest backing HMEANT with a linguistic theory of deep syntax, opening the avenue to automating the metric using available tools.

Acknowledgments

We would like to thank our annotators for all the comments and also Chi-kiu Lo, Karteek Addanki, Anand Karthik Tumuluru, and Avishek Kumar Thakur for administering the annotation interface. This work was supported by the project EuroMatrixPlus (FP7-ICT-2007-3-231720 of the EU and 7E09003+7E11051 of the Czech Republic) and the Czech Science Foundation grants P406/11/1499 and P406/10/P259 (Ondřej Bojar); and by the Defense Advanced Research Projects Agency (DARPA) under BOLT contract no. HR0011-12-C-0016, and GALE contract nos. HR0011-06-C-0022 and HR0011-06-C-0023; by the European Union under the FP7 grant agreement no. 287658; and by the Hong Kong Research Grants Council (RGC) research grant GRF621008 (Dekai Wu). Any opinions, findings and conclusions or recommendations expressed in this material are those of the authors and do not necessarily reflect the views of the RGC, EU, or DARPA.

References

Hervé Blanchon, Christian Boitet, and Laurent Besacier. 2004. Spoken Dialogue Translation Systems Evaluation: Results, New Trends, Problems and Proposals. In *Proceedings of International Conference on Spoken Language Processing ICSLP 2004*, Jeju Island, Korea, October.

Ondřej Bojar, Miloš Ercegovčević, Martin Popel, and Omar Zaidan. 2011. A Grain of Salt for the WMT Manual Evaluation. In *Proceedings of the Sixth Workshop on Statistical Machine Translation*, pages 1–11, Edinburgh, Scotland, July. Association for Computational Linguistics.

Ondřej Bojar, Zdeněk Žabokrtský, Ondřej Dušek, Petra Galuščáková, Martin Majliš, David Mareček, Jiří Maršík, Michal Novák, Martin Popel, and Aleš Tamchyna. 2012. The Joy of Parallelism with CzEng 1.0. In *Proceedings of the Eighth International Language Resources and Evaluation Conference (LREC'12)*, Istanbul, Turkey, May. ELRA, European Language Resources Association. In print.

Chris Callison-Burch, Cameron Fordyce, Philipp Koehn, Christof Monz, and Josh Schroeder. 2007. (Meta-) Evaluation of Machine Translation. In *Proceedings of the Second Workshop on Statistical Machine Translation*, pages 136–158, Prague, Czech Republic, June. Association for Computational Linguistics.

Chris Callison-Burch, Philipp Koehn, Christof Monz, Matt Post, Radu Soricut, and Lucia Specia. 2012. Findings of the 2012 workshop on statistical machine translation. In *Proceedings of the Seventh Workshop on Statistical Machine Translation*, Montreal, Canada, June. Association for Computational Linguistics.

Charles J. Fillmore. 1968. The Case for Case. In E. Bach and R. Harms, editors, *Universals in Linguistic Theory*, pages 1–90. New York.

Jan Hajič, Eva Hajičová, Jarmila Panevová, Petr Sgall, Ondřej Bojar, Silvie Cinková, Eva Fučíková, Marie Mikulová, Petr Pajas, Jan Popelka, Jiří Semecký, Jana Šindlerová, Jan Štěpánek, Josef Toman, Zdeňka Urešová, and Zdeněk Žabokrtský. 2012. Announcing Prague Czech-English Dependency Treebank 2.0. In *Proceedings of the Eighth International Language Resources and Evaluation Conference (LREC'12)*, Istanbul, Turkey, May. ELRA, European Language Resources Association. In print.

Jan Hajič, Jarmila Panevová, Eva Hajičová, Petr Sgall, Petr Pajas, Jan Štěpánek, Jiří Havelka, Marie Mikulová, Zdeněk Žabokrtský, and Magda Ševčíková Razímová. 2006. Prague Dependency Treebank 2.0. LDC2006T01, ISBN: 1-58563-370-4.

Philipp Koehn and Christof Monz. 2006. Manual and automatic evaluation of machine translation between european languages. In *Proceedings on the Workshop on Statistical Machine Translation*, pages 102–121, New York City, June. Association for Computational Linguistics.

Chi-kiu Lo and Dekai Wu. 2011a. Meant: An inexpensive, high-accuracy, semi-automatic metric for evaluating translation utility based on semantic roles. In *Proceedings of the 49th Annual Meeting of the Association for Computational Linguistics: Human Language Technologies*, pages 220–229, Portland, Oregon, USA, June. Association for Computational Linguistics.

Chi-kiu Lo and Dekai Wu. 2011b. Structured vs. flat semantic role representations for machine translation evaluation. In *Proceedings of the Fifth Workshop on Syntax, Semantics and Structure in Statistical Translation*, SSST-5, pages 10–20, Stroudsburg, PA, USA. Association for Computational Linguistics.

Martha Palmer, Daniel Gildea, and Paul Kingsbury. 2005. The Proposition Bank: An Annotated Corpus of Semantic Roles. *Computational Linguistics*, 31(1):71–106.

Jarmila Panevová. 1980. *Formy a funkce ve stavbě české věty [Forms and functions in the structure of the Czech sentence]*. Academia, Prague, Czech Republic.

Martin Popel and Zdeněk Žabokrtský. 2010. TectoMT: Modular NLP Framework. In Hrafn Loftsson, Eirikur Rögnvaldsson, and Sigrun Helgadottir, editors, *Lecture Notes in Artificial Intelligence, Proceedings of the 7th International Conference on Advances in Natural Language Processing (IceTAL 2010)*, volume 6233 of *Lecture Notes in Computer Science*, pages 293–304, Berlin / Heidelberg. Iceland Centre for Language Technology (ICLT), Springer.

Rudolf Rosa, David Mareček, and Ondřej Dušek. 2012. DEPFIX: A System for Automatic Correction of Czech MT Outputs. In *Proceedings of the Seventh Workshop on Statistical Machine Translation*, Montreal, Canada, June. Association for Computational Linguistics. Submitted.

Petr Sgall, Eva Hajičová, and Jarmila Panevová. 1986. *The Meaning of the Sentence and Its Semantic and Pragmatic Aspects*. Academia/Reidel Publishing Company, Prague, Czech Republic/Dordrecht, Netherlands.

Petr Sgall. 1967. *Generativní popis jazyka a česká deklinace*. Academia, Prague, Czech Republic.

Jana Šindlerová and Ondřej Bojar. 2010. Building a Bilingual ValLex Using Treebank Token Alignment: First Observations. In *Proceedings of the Seventh International Language Resources and Evaluation (LREC'10)*, pages 304–309, Valletta, Malta, May. ELRA, European Language Resources Association.

Using Parallel Features in Parsing of Machine-Translated Sentences for Correction of Grammatical Errors *

Rudolf Rosa, Ondřej Dušek, David Mareček, and Martin Popel
Charles University in Prague, Faculty of Mathematics and Physics
Institute of Formal and Applied Linguistics
{rosa,odusek,marecek,popel}@ufal.mff.cuni.cz

Abstract

In this paper, we present two dependency parser training methods appropriate for parsing outputs of statistical machine translation (SMT), which pose problems to standard parsers due to their frequent ungrammaticality. We adapt the MST parser by exploiting additional features from the source language, and by introducing artificial grammatical errors in the parser training data, so that the training sentences resemble SMT output.

We evaluate the modified parser on DEPFIX, a system that improves English-Czech SMT outputs using automatic rule-based corrections of grammatical mistakes which requires parsed SMT output sentences as its input. Both parser modifications led to improvements in BLEU score; their combination was evaluated manually, showing a statistically significant improvement of the translation quality.

1 Introduction

The machine translation (MT) quality is on a steady rise, with mostly statistical systems (SMT) dominating the area (Callison-Burch et al., 2010; Callison-Burch et al., 2011). Most MT systems do not employ structural linguistic knowledge and even the state-of-the-art MT solutions are unable to avoid making serious grammatical errors in the output, which often leads to unintelligibility or to a risk of misinterpretations of the text by a reader.

This problem is particularly apparent in target languages with rich morphological inflection, such as Czech. As Czech often conveys the relations between individual words using morphological agreement instead of word order, together with the word order itself being relatively free, choosing the correct inflection becomes crucial.

Since the output of phrase-based SMT shows frequent inflection errors (even in adjacent words) due to each word belonging to a different phrase, a possible way to address the grammaticality problem is a combination of statistical and structural approach, such as SMT output post-editing (Stymne and Ahrenberg, 2010; Mareček et al., 2011).

In this paper, we focus on improving SMT output parsing quality, as rule-based post-editing systems rely heavily on the quality of SMT output analysis. Parsers trained on gold standard parse trees often fail to produce the expected result when applied to SMT output with grammatical errors. This is partly caused by the fact that when parsing highly inflected free word-order languages the parsers have to rely on morphological agreement, which, as stated above, is often erroneous in SMT output.

Training a parser specifically by creating a manually annotated treebank of MT systems' outputs would be very expensive, and the application of such treebank to other MT systems than the ones used for its generation would be problematic. We address this issue by two methods of increasing the quality of SMT output parsing:

- a different application of previous works on bitext parsing – exploiting additional features from the source language (Section 3), and

*This research has been supported by the EU Seventh Framework Programme under grant agreement n° 247762 (Faust), and by the grants GAUK116310 and GA201/09/H057.

- introducing artificial grammatical errors in the target language parser training data, so that the sentences resemble the SMT output in some ways (Section 4). This technique is, to our knowledge, novel with regards to its application to SMT and the statistical error model.

We test these two techniques on English-Czech MT outputs using our own reimplementation of the MST parser (McDonald et al., 2005) named RUR[1] parser. and evaluate their contribution to the SMT post-editing quality of the DEPFIX system (Mareček et al., 2011), which we outline in Section 5. We describe the experiments carried out and present the most important results in Section 6. Section 7 then concludes the paper and indicates more possibilities of further improvements.

2 Related Work

Our approach to parsing with parallel features is similar to various works which seek to improve the parsing accuracy on parallel texts ("bitexts") by using information from both languages. Huang et al. (2009) employ "bilingual constraints" in shift-reduce parsing to disambiguate difficult syntactic constructions and resolve shift-reduce conflicts. Chen et al. (2010) use similar subtree constraints to improve parser accuracy in a dependency scenario. Chen et al. (2011) then improve the method by obtaining a training parallel treebank via SMT. In recent work, Haulrich (2012) experiments with a setup very similar to ours: adding alignment-projected features to an originally monolingual parser.

However, the main aim of all these works is to improve the parsing accuracy on correct parallel texts, i.e. human-translated. This paper applies similar methods, but with a different objective in mind – increasing the ability of the parser to process ungrammatical SMT output sentences and, ultimately, improve rule-based SMT post-editing.

Xiong et al. (2010) use SMT parsing in translation quality assessment, providing syntactic features to a classifier detecting erroneous words in SMT output, yet they do not concentrate on improving parsing accuracy – they employ a link grammar parser, which is robust, but not tuned specifically to process ungrammatical input.

There is also another related direction of research in parsing of parallel texts, which is targeted on parsing under-resourced languages, e.g. the works by Hwa et al. (2005), Zeman and Resnik (2008), and McDonald et al. (2011). They address the fact that parsers for the language of interest are of low quality or even non-existent, whereas there are high-quality parsers for the other language. They exploit common properties of both languages and delexicalization. Zhao et al. (2009) uses information from word-by-word translated treebank to obtain additional training data and boost parser accuracy.

This is different from our situation, as there exist high performance parsers for Czech (Buchholz and Marsi, 2006; Nivre et al., 2007; Hajič et al., 2009). Boosting accuracy on correct sentences is not our primary goal and we do not intend to *replace* the Czech parser by an English parser; instead, we aim to increase the robustness of an already *existing* Czech parser by adding knowledge from the corresponding English source, parsed by an English parser.

Other works in bilingual parsing aim to parse the parallel sentences directly using a grammar formalism fit for this purpose, such as Inversion Transduction Grammars (ITG) (Wu, 1997). Burkett et al. (2010) further include ITG parsing with word-alignment in a joint scenario. We concentrate here on using dependency parsers because of tools and training data availability for the examined language pair.

Regarding treebank adaptation for parser robustness, Foster et al. (2008) introduce various kinds of artificial errors into the training data to make the final parser less sensitive to grammar errors. However, their approach concentrates on mistakes made by humans (such as misspellings, word repetition or omission etc.) and the error models used are handcrafted. Our work focuses on morphology errors often encountered in SMT output and introduces statistical error modelling.

3 Parsing with Parallel Features

This section describes our SMT output parsing setup with features from analyzed *source* sentences. We

[1]The abbreviation "RUR" parser stands for "Rudolph's Universal Robust" parser.

explain our motivation for the inclusion of parallel features in Section 3.1, then provide an account of the parsers used (including our RUR parser) in Section 3.2, and finally list all the monolingual and parallel features included in the parser training (in Sections 3.3 and 3.4, respectively).

3.1 Motivation

An advantage of SMT output parsing over general dependency parsing is that one can also make use of *source* – English sentences in our case. Moreover, although SMT output is often in many ways ungrammatical, *source* is usually grammatical and therefore easier to process (in our case especially to tag and parse). This was already noticed in Mareček et al. (2011), who use the analysis of *source* sentence to provide additional information for the DEPFIX rules, claiming it to be more reliable than the analysis of SMT output sentence.

We have carried this idea further by having devised a simple way of making use of this information in parsing of the SMT output sentences: We parse the *source* sentence first and include features computed over the parsed *source* sentence in the set of features used for parsing SMT output. We first align the *source* and SMT output sentences on the word level and then use alignment-wise local features – i.e. for each SMT output word, we add features computed over its aligned *source* word, if applicable (cf. Section 3.4 for a listing).

3.2 Parsers Used

We have reimplemented the MST parser (McDonald et al., 2005) in order to provide for a simple insertion of the parallel features into the models.

We also used the original implementation of the MST parser by McDonald et al. (2006) for comparison in our experiments. To distinguish the two variants used, we denote the original MST parser as MCD parser,[2] and the new reimplementation as RUR parser.

We trained RUR parser in a first-order non-projective setting with single-best MIRA. Dependency labels are assigned in a second stage by a MIRA-based labeler, which has been implemented according to McDonald (2006) and Gimpel and Cohen (2007).

We used the Prague Czech-English Dependency Treebank[3] (PCEDT) 2.0 (Bojar et al., 2012) as the training data for RUR parser – a parallel treebank created from the Penn Treebank (Marcus et al., 1993) and its translation into Czech by human translators. The dependency trees on the English side were converted from the manually annotated phrase-structure trees in Penn Treebank, the Czech trees were created automatically using MCD. Words of the Czech and English sentences were aligned by GIZA++ (Och and Ney, 2003).

We apply RUR parser only for SMT output parsing; for *source* parsing, we use MCD parser trained on the English CoNLL 2007 data (Nivre et al., 2007), as the performance of this parser is sufficient for this task.

3.3 Monolingual Features

The set of monolingual features used in RUR parser follows those described by McDonald et al. (2005). For parsing, we use the features described below. The individual features are computed for both the parent node and the child node of an edge and conjoined in various ways. The *coarse morphological tag* and *lemma* are provided by the Morče tagger (Spoustová et al., 2007).

- *coarse morphological tag* – Czech two-letter coarse morphological tag, as described in (Collins et al., 1999),[4]
- *lemma* – morphological lemma,
- context features: *preceding coarse morphological tag*, *following coarse morphological tag* – coarse morphological tag of a neighboring node,
- *coarse morphological tags in between* – bag of coarse morphological tags of nodes positioned between the parent node and the child node,

[2] MCD uses k-best MIRA, does first- and second-order parsing, both projectively and non-projectively, and can be obtained from http://sourceforge.net/projects/mstparser.

[3] http://ufal.mff.cuni.cz/pcedt

[4] The first letter is the main POS (12 possible values), the second letter is either the morphological case field if the main POS displays case (i.e. for nouns, adjectives, pronouns, numerals and prepositions; 7 possible values), or the detailed POS if it does not (22 possible values).

- *distance* – signed bucketed distance of the parent and the child node in the sentence (in # of words), using buckets 1, 2, 3, 4, 5 and 11.

To assign dependency labels, we use the same set as described above, plus the following features (called "non-local" by McDonald (2006)), which make use of the knowledge of the tree structure.

- *is first child, is last child* – a boolean indicating whether the node appears in the sentence as the first/last one among all the child nodes of its parent node,

- *child number* – the number of syntactic children of the current node.

3.4 Parallel Features

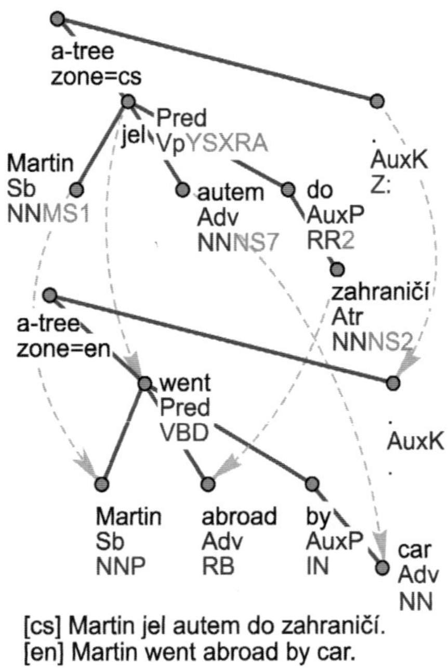

Figure 1: Example sentence for parallel features illustration (see Table 1).

In RUR parser we use three types of parallel features, computed for the parent and child node of an edge, which make use of the *source* English nodes aligned to the parent and child node.

- *aligned tag*: morphological tag following the Penn Treebank Tagset (Marcus et al., 1993) of the English node aligned to the Czech node

Feature	Feature value on parent node	Feature value on child node
word form	jel	Martin
aligned tag	VBD	NNP
aligned dep. label	Pred	Sb
aligned edge existence	true	
word form	jel	autem
aligned tag	VBD	NN
aligned dep. label	Pred	Adv
aligned edge existence	false	
word form	do	zahraničí
aligned tag	—	RB
aligned dep. label	—	Adv
aligned edge existence	—	
word form	#root#	.
aligned tag	#root#	.
aligned dep. label	AuxS	AuxK
aligned edge existence	true	

Table 1: Parallel features for several edges in Figure 1.

- *aligned dependency label*: dependency label of the English node aligned to the Czech node in question, according to the PCEDT 2.0 label set (Bojar et al., 2012)

- *aligned edge existence*: a boolean indicating whether the English node aligned to the Czech parent node is also the parent of the English node aligned to the Czech child node

The parallel features are conjoined with the monolingual *coarse morphological tag* and *lemma* features in various ways.

If there is no *source* node aligned to the parent or child node, the respective feature cannot be computed and is skipped.

An example of a pair of parallel sentences is given in Figure 1 with the corresponding values of parallel features for several edges in Table 1.

4 Worsening Treebanks to Simulate Some of the SMT Frequent Errors

Addressing the issue of great differences between the gold standard parser training data and the actual analysis input (SMT output), we introduced artificial inconsistencies into the training treebanks, in order to make the parsers more robust in the face of grammar errors made by SMT systems. We have concentrated solely on modeling incorrect word flection, i.e. the dependency trees retained their original correct structures and word lemmas remained fixed, but the individual inflected word forms have been modified according to an error model trained on real SMT output. We simulate thus, with respect to morphology, a treebank of parsed MT output sentences.

In Section 4.1 we describe the steps we take to prepare the worsened parser training data. Section 4.2 contains a description of our monolingual greedy alignment tool which is needed during the process to map SMT output to reference translations.

4.1 Creating the Worsened Parser Training Data

The whole process of treebank worsening consists of five steps:

1. We translated the English side of PCEDT[5] to Czech using SMT (we chose the Moses system (Koehn et al., 2007) for our experiments) and tagged the resulting translations using the Morče tagger (Spoustová et al., 2007).

2. We aligned the Czech side of PCEDT, now serving as a reference translation, to the SMT output using our Monolingual Greedy Aligner (see Section 4.2).

3. Collecting the counts of individual errors, we estimated the Maximum Likelihood probabilities of changing a correct fine-grained morphological tag (of a word from the reference) into a possibly incorrect fine-grained morphological tag of the aligned word (from the SMT output).

4. The tags on the Czech side of PCEDT were randomly sampled according to the estimated "fine-grained morphological tag error model". In those positions where fine-grained morphological tags were changed, new word forms were generated using the Czech morphological generator by Hajič (2004).[6]

We use the resulting "worsened" treebank to train our parser described in Section 3.2.

4.2 The Monolingual Greedy Aligner

Our monolingual alignment tool, used in treebank worsening to tie reference translations to MT output (see Section 4.1), scores all possible alignment links and then greedily chooses the currently highest scoring one, creating the respective alignment link from word A (in the reference) to word B (in the SMT output) and deleting all scores of links from A or to B, so that one-to-one alignments are enforced. The process is terminated when no links with a score higher than a given threshold are available; some words may thus remain unaligned.

The score is computed as a linear combination of the following four features:

- word form (or lemma if available) similarity based on Jaro-Winkler distance (Winkler, 1990),
- fine-grained morphological tag similarity,
- similarity of the relative position in the sentence,
- and an indication whether the word following (or preceding) A was already aligned to the word following (or preceding) B.

Unlike bilingual word aligners, this tool needs no training except for setting weights of the four features and the threshold.[7]

5 The DEPFIX System

The DEPFIX system (Mareček et al., 2011) applies various rule-based corrections to Czech-English SMT output sentences, especially of morphological agreement. It also employs the parsed *source* sentences, which must be provided on the input together with the SMT output sentences.

The corrections follow the rules of Czech grammar, e.g. requiring that the clause subject be in the

[5]This approach is not conditioned by availability of parallel treebanks. Alternatively, we might translate any text for which reference translations are at hand. The model learned in the third step would then be applied (in the fourth step) to a different text for which parse trees are available.

[6]According to the "fine-grained morphological tag error model", about 20% of fine-grained morphological tags were changed. In 4% of cases, no word form existed for the new fine-grained morphological tag and thus it was not changed.

[7]The threshold and weights were set manually using just ten sentence pairs. The resulting alignment quality was found sufficient, so no additional weights tuning was performed.

nominative case or enforcing subject-predicate and noun-attribute agreements in morphological gender, number and case, where applicable. Morphological properties found violating the rules are corrected and the corresponding word forms regenerated.

The *source* sentence parse, word-aligned to the SMT output using GIZA++ (Och and Ney, 2003), is used as a source of morpho-syntactic information for the correction rules. An example of a correction rule application is given in Figure 2.

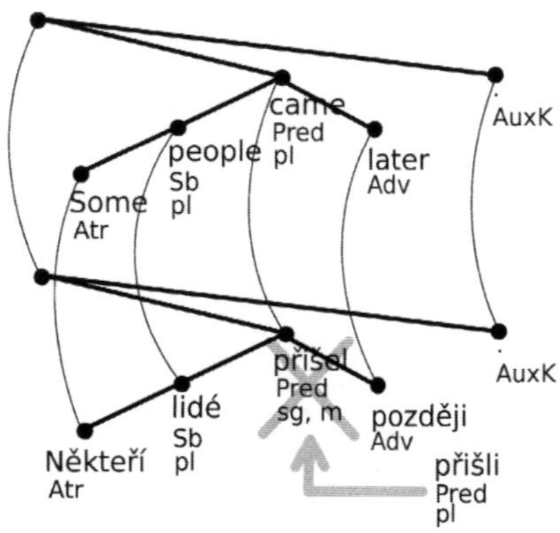

Figure 2: Example of fixing subject-predicate agreement. The Czech word *přišel [he came]* has a wrong morphological number and gender. Adapted from Mareček et al. (2011).

The system is implemented within the TectoMT/Treex NLP framework (Popel and Žabokrtský, 2010). Mareček et al. (2011) feed the DEPFIX system with analyses by the MCD parser trained on gold-standard treebanks for parsing of English *source* sentences as well as Czech SMT output.

6 Experiments and Results

We evaluate RUR parser indirectly by using it in the DEPFIX system and measuring the performance of the whole system. This approach has been chosen instead of direct evaluation of the SMT output parse trees, as the task of finding a correct parse tree of a possibly grammatically incorrect sentence is not well defined and considerably difficult to do.

We used WMT10, WMT11 and WMT12 English to Czech translation test sets, `newssyscombtest2010`, `newssyscombtest2011` and `newstest2012`,[8] (denoted as WMT10, WMT11 and WMT12) for the automatic evaluation. The data sets include the source (English) text, its reference translation and translations produced by several MT systems. We used the outputs of three SMT systems: GOOGLE,[9] UEDIN (Koehn et al., 2007) and BOJAR (Bojar and Kos, 2010).

For the manual evaluation, two sets of 1000 randomly selected sentences from WMT11 and from WMT12 translated by GOOGLE were used.

6.1 Automatic Evaluation

Table 2 shows BLEU scores (Papineni et al., 2002) for the following setups of DEPFIX:

- SMT output: output of an SMT system without applying DEPFIX
- MCD: parsing with MCD
- RUR: parsing with RUR (Section 3.2)
- RUR+PARA: parsing with RUR using parallel features (Section 3.4)
- RUR+WORS: parsing with RUR trained on worsened treebank (Section 4)
- RUR+WORS+PARA: parsing with RUR trained on worsened treebank and using parallel features

It can be seen that both of the proposed ways of adapting the parser to parsing of SMT output often lead to higher BLEU scores of translations post-processed by DEPFIX, which suggests that they both improve the parsing accuracy.

We have computed 95% confidence intervals on 1000 bootstrap samples, which showed that the BLEU score of RUR+WORS+PARA was significantly higher than that of MCD and RUR parser in 4 and 3 cases, respectively (results where RUR+WORS+PARA achieved a significantly higher score are marked with '*'). On the other hand, the score of neither RUR+WORS+PARA nor RUR+WORS and RUR+PARA was ever significantly lower than the score of MCD or RUR parser. This leads us to believe that the two proposed methods are able to produce slightly better SMT output parsing results.

[8] `http://www.statmt.org/wmt10`, `http://www.statmt.org/wmt11`, `http://www.statmt.org/wmt12`

[9] `http://translate.google.com`

Test set	WMT10			WMT11			WMT12		
SMT system	BOJAR	GOOGLE	UEDIN	BOJAR	GOOGLE	UEDIN	BOJAR	GOOGLE	UEDIN
SMT output	*15.85	*16.57	*15.91	*16.88	*20.26	*17.80	14.36	16.25	*15.54
MCD	16.09	16.95	*16.35	*17.02	20.45	*18.12	14.35	**16.32**	*15.65
RUR	16.08	*16.85	*16.29	17.03	20.42	*18.09	14.37	16.31	15.66
RUR+PARA	**16.13**	*16.90	*16.35	17.05	20.47	18.19	14.35	16.31	15.72
RUR+WORS	16.12	16.96	*16.45	17.06	**20.53**	18.21	**14.40**	16.31	15.71
RUR+WORS+PARA	**16.13**	**17.03**	**16.54**	**17.12**	**20.53**	**18.25**	14.39	16.30	**15.74**

Table 2: Automatic evaluation using BLEU scores for the unmodified SMT output (output of BOJAR, GOOGLE and UEDIN systems on WMT10, WMT11 and WMT12 test sets), and for SMT output parsed by various parser setups and processed by DEPFIX. The score of RUR+WORS+PARA is significantly higher at 95% confidence level than the scores marked with '*' on the same data.

6.2 Manual Evaluation

Performance of RUR+WORS+PARA setup was manually evaluated by doing a pairwise comparison with other setups – SMT output, MCD and RUR parser. The evaluation was performed on both the WMT11 (Table 4) and WMT12 (Table 5) test set. 1000 sentences from the output of the GOOGLE system were randomly selected and processed by DEPFIX, using the aforementioned SMT output parsers. The annotators then compared the translation quality of the individual variants in differing sentences, selecting the better variant from a pair or declaring two variants "same quality" (indefinite). They were also provided with the *source* sentence and a reference translation. The evaluation was done as a blind test, with the sentences randomly shuffled.

The WMT11 test set was evaluated by two independent annotators. (The WMT12 test set was evaluated by one annotator only.) The inter-annotator agreement and Cohen's kappa coefficient (Cohen and others, 1960), shown in Table 3, were computed both including all annotations ("with indefs"), and disregarding sentences where at least one of the annotators marked the difference as indefinite ("without indefs") – we believe a disagreement in choosing the better translation to be more severe than a disagreement in deciding whether the difference in quality of the translations allows to mark one as being better.

For both of the test sets, RUR+WORS+PARA significantly outperforms both MCD and RUR baseline, confirming that a combination of the proposed modifications of the parser lead to its better performance. Statistical significance of the results was

RUR+WORS+PARA	with indefs		without indefs	
compared to	IAA	Kappa	IAA	Kappa
SMT output	77%	0.54	92%	0.74
MCD	79%	0.66	95%	0.90
RUR	75%	0.60	94%	0.85

Table 3: Inter-annotator agreement on WMT11 data set translated by GOOGLE

confirmed by a one-sided pairwise t-test, with the following differences ranking: RUR+WORS+PARA better = 1, baseline better = -1, indefinite = 0.

6.3 Inspection of Parser Modification Benefits

For a better understanding of the benefits of using our modified parser, we inspected a small number of parse trees, produced by RUR+WORS+PARA, and compared them to those produced by RUR. In many cases, the changes introduced by RUR+WORS+PARA were clearly positive. We provide two representative examples below.

Subject Identification

Czech grammar requires the subject to be in nominative case, but this constraint is often violated in SMT output and a parser typically fails to identify the subject correctly in such situations. By worsening the training data, we make the parser more robust in this respect, as the worsening often switches the case of the subject; by including parallel features, especially the *aligned dependency label* feature, RUR+WORS+PARA parser can often identify the subject as the node aligned to the *source* subject.

Annotator	Baseline	Differing sentences	Out of the differing sentences					
			RUR+WORS+PARA better		baseline better		indefinite	
			count	percent	count	percent	count	percent
A	SMT output	422	301	71%	79	19%	42	10%
	McD	211	120	57%	65	31%	26	12%
	RUR	217	123	57%	64	29%	30	14%
B	SMT output	422	284	67%	69	16%	69	16%
	McD	211	107	51%	56	26%	48	23%
	RUR	217	118	54%	53	24%	46	21%

Table 4: Manual comparison of RUR+WORS+PARA with various baselines, on 1000 sentences from WMT11 data set translated by GOOGLE, evaluated by two independent annotators.

Annotator	Baseline	Differing sentences	Out of the differing sentences					
			RUR+WORS+PARA better		baseline better		indefinite	
			count	percent	count	percent	count	percent
A	SMT output	420	270	64%	88	21%	62	15%
	McD	188	86	45%	64	34%	38	20%
	RUR	187	96	51%	57	30%	34	18%

Table 5: Manual comparison of RUR+WORS+PARA with various baselines, on 1000 sentences from WMT12 data set translated by GOOGLE.

Governing Noun Identification

A parser for Czech typically relies on morphological agreement between an adjective and its governing noun (in morphological number, gender and case), which is often violated in SMT output. Again, RUR+WORS+PARA is more robust in this respect, *aligned edge existence* now being the crucial feature for the correct identification of this relation.

7 Conclusions and Future Work

We have studied two methods of improving the parsing quality of Machine Translation outputs by providing additional information to the parser.

In Section 3, we propose a method of integrating additional information known *at runtime*, i.e. the knowledge of the source sentence (*source*), from which the sentence being parsed (SMT output) has been translated. This knowledge is provided by extending the parser feature set with new features from the source sentence, projected through word-alignment.

In Section 4, we introduce a method of utilizing additional information known *in the training phase*, namely the knowledge of the ways in which SMT output differs from correct sentences. We provide this knowledge to the parser by adjusting its training data to model some of the errors frequently encountered in SMT output, i.e. incorrect inflection forms.

We have evaluated the usefulness of these two methods by integrating them into the DEPFIX rule-based MT output post-processing system (Mareček et al., 2011), as MT output parsing is crucial for the operation of this system. When used with our improved parsing, the DEPFIX system showed better performance both in automatic and manual evaluation on outputs of several, including state-of-the-art, MT systems.

We believe that the proposed methods of improving MT output parsing can be extended beyond their current state. The parallel features used in our setup are very few and very simple; it thus remains to be examined whether more elaborate features could help utilize the additional information contained in the source sentence to a greater extent. Modeling other types of SMT output inconsistencies in parser training data is another possible step.

We also believe that the methods could be adapted for use in other applications, e.g. automatic classification of translation errors, confidence estimation or multilingual question answering.

References

Ondřej Bojar and Kamil Kos. 2010. 2010 Failures in English-Czech Phrase-Based MT. In *Proceedings of the Joint Fifth Workshop on Statistical Machine Translation and MetricsMATR*, pages 60–66, Uppsala, Sweden, July. Association for Computational Linguistics.

Ondřej Bojar, Jan Hajič, Eva Hajičová, Jarmila Panevová, Petr Sgall, Silvie Cinková, Eva Fučíková, Marie Mikulová, Petr Pajas, Jan Popelka, Jiří Semecký, Jana Šindlerová, Jan Štěpánek, Josef Toman, Zdeňka Urešová, and Zdeněk Žabokrtský. 2012. Announcing Prague Czech-English Dependency Treebank 2.0. In *Proceedings of LREC 2012*, Istanbul, Turkey, May. ELRA, European Language Resources Association. In print.

Sabine Buchholz and Erwin Marsi. 2006. CoNLL-X shared task on multilingual dependency parsing. In *Proceedings of the Tenth Conference on Computational Natural Language Learning*, pages 149–164. Association for Computational Linguistics.

David Burkett, John Blitzer, and Dan Klein. 2010. Joint parsing and alignment with weakly synchronized grammars. In *Human Language Technologies: The 2010 Annual Conference of the North American Chapter of the Association for Computational Linguistics*, pages 127–135. Association for Computational Linguistics.

Chris Callison-Burch, Philipp Koehn, Christof Monz, Kay Peterson, Mark Przybocki, and Omar Zaidan. 2010. Findings of the 2010 joint workshop on statistical machine translation and metrics for machine translation. In *Proceedings of the Joint Fifth Workshop on Statistical Machine Translation and MetricsMATR*, pages 17–53, Uppsala, Sweden, July. Association for Computational Linguistics.

Chris Callison-Burch, Philipp Koehn, Christof Monz, and Omar Zaidan. 2011. Findings of the 2011 workshop on statistical machine translation. In *Proceedings of the Sixth Workshop on Statistical Machine Translation*, pages 22–64, Edinburgh, Scotland, July. Association for Computational Linguistics.

Wenliang Chen, Jun'ichi Kazama, and Kentaro Torisawa. 2010. Bitext dependency parsing with bilingual subtree constraints. In *Proceedings of the 48th Annual Meeting of the Association for Computational Linguistics*, pages 21–29. Association for Computational Linguistics.

Wenliang Chen, Jun'ichi Kazama, Min Zhang, Yoshimasa Tsuruoka, Yujie Zhang, Yiou Wang, Kentaro Torisawa, and Haizhou Li. 2011. SMT helps bitext dependency parsing. In *EMNLP*, pages 73–83. ACL.

Jacob Cohen et al. 1960. A coefficient of agreement for nominal scales. *Educational and psychological measurement*, 20(1):37–46.

Michael Collins, Lance Ramshaw, Jan Hajič, and Christoph Tillmann. 1999. A statistical parser for Czech. In *Proceedings of the 37th annual meeting of the Association for Computational Linguistics on Computational Linguistics*, ACL '99, pages 505–512, Stroudsburg, PA, USA. Association for Computational Linguistics.

Jennifer Foster, Joachim Wagner, and Josef Van Genabith. 2008. Adapting a WSJ-trained parser to grammatically noisy text. In *Proceedings of the 46th Annual Meeting of the Association for Computational Linguistics on Human Language Technologies: Short Papers*, pages 221–224. Association for Computational Linguistics.

Kevin Gimpel and Shay Cohen. 2007. Discriminative online algorithms for sequence labeling- a comparative study.

Jan Hajič, Massimiliano Ciaramita, Richard Johansson, Daisuke Kawahara, Maria Antònia Martí, Lluís Màrquez, Adam Meyers, Joakim Nivre, Sebastian Padó, Jan Štěpánek, et al. 2009. The CoNLL-2009 shared task: Syntactic and semantic dependencies in multiple languages. In *Proceedings of the Thirteenth Conference on Computational Natural Language Learning: Shared Task*, pages 1–18. Association for Computational Linguistics.

Jan Hajič. 2004. *Disambiguation of rich inflection: computational morphology of Czech*. Karolinum.

Martin Haulrich. 2012. *Data-Driven Bitext Dependency Parsing and Alignment*. Ph.D. thesis.

Liang Huang, Wenbin Jiang, and Qun Liu. 2009. Bilingually-constrained (monolingual) shift-reduce parsing. In *Proceedings of the 2009 Conference on Empirical Methods in Natural Language Processing: Volume 3-Volume 3*, pages 1222–1231. Association for Computational Linguistics.

Rebecca Hwa, Philip Resnik, Amy Weinberg, Clara Cabezas, and Okan Kolak. 2005. Bootstrapping parsers via syntactic projection across parallel texts. *Nat. Lang. Eng.*, 11:311–325, September.

Philipp Koehn, Hieu Hoang, Alexandra Birch, Chris Callison-Burch, Marcello Federico, Nicola Bertoldi, Brooke Cowan, Wade Shen, Christine Moran, Richard Zens, Chris Dyer, Ondřej Bojar, Alexandra Constantin, and Evan Herbst. 2007. Moses: Open Source Toolkit for Statistical Machine Translation. In *ACL 2007, Proceedings of the 45th Annual Meeting of the Association for Computational Linguistics Companion Volume Proceedings of the Demo and Poster Sessions*, pages 177–180, Prague, Czech Republic, June. Association for Computational Linguistics.

Mitchell P. Marcus, Mary Ann Marcinkiewicz, and Beatrice Santorini. 1993. Building a large annotated corpus of English: The Penn Treebank. *Comput. Linguist.*, 19:313–330, June.

David Mareček, Rudolf Rosa, Petra Galuščáková, and Ondřej Bojar. 2011. Two-step translation with grammatical post-processing. In Chris Callison-Burch, Philipp Koehn, Christof Monz, and Omar Zaidan, editors, *Proceedings of the Sixth Workshop on Statistical Machine Translation*, pages 426–432, Edinburgh, UK. Association for Computational Linguistics.

Ryan McDonald, Fernando Pereira, Kiril Ribarov, and Jan Hajič. 2005. Non-projective dependency parsing using spanning tree algorithms. In *HLT '05: Proceedings of the conference on Human Language Technology and Empirical Methods in Natural Language Processing*, pages 523–530, Vancouver, British Columbia, Canada.

Ryan McDonald, Kevin Lerman, and Fernando Pereira. 2006. Multilingual dependency analysis with a two-stage discriminative parser. In *Proceedings of the Tenth Conference on Computational Natural Language Learning*, CoNLL-X '06, pages 216–220, Stroudsburg, PA, USA. Association for Computational Linguistics.

Ryan McDonald, Slav Petrov, and Keith Hall. 2011. Multi-source transfer of delexicalized dependency parsers. In *Proceedings of the Conference on Empirical Methods in Natural Language Processing*, pages 62–72. Association for Computational Linguistics.

Ryan McDonald. 2006. *Discriminative learning and spanning tree algorithms for dependency parsing*. Ph.D. thesis, Philadelphia, PA, USA. AAI3225503.

Joakim Nivre, Johan Hall, Sandra Kübler, Ryan McDonald, Jens Nilsson, Sebastian Riedel, and Deniz Yuret. 2007. The CoNLL 2007 shared task on dependency parsing. In *Proceedings of the CoNLL 2007 Shared Task. Joint Conf. on Empirical Methods in Natural Language Processing and Computational Natural Language Learning (EMNLP-CoNLL)*, June.

Franz Josef Och and Hermann Ney. 2003. A Systematic Comparison of Various Statistical Alignment Models. *Computational Linguistics*, 29(1):19–51.

Kishore Papineni, Salim Roukos, Todd Ward, and Wei-Jing Zhu. 2002. BLEU: a Method for Automatic Evaluation of Machine Translation. In *ACL 2002, Proceedings of the 40th Annual Meeting of the Association for Computational Linguistics*, pages 311–318, Philadelphia, Pennsylvania.

Martin Popel and Zdeněk Žabokrtský. 2010. TectoMT: modular NLP framework. In *Proceedings of the 7th international conference on Advances in natural language processing*, IceTAL'10, pages 293–304, Berlin, Heidelberg. Springer-Verlag.

Drahomíra Spoustová, Jan Hajič, Jan Votrubec, Pavel Krbec, and Pavel Květoň. 2007. The best of two worlds: Cooperation of statistical and rule-based taggers for Czech. In *Proceedings of the Workshop on Balto-Slavonic Natural Language Processing, ACL 2007*, pages 67–74, Praha.

Sara Stymne and Lars Ahrenberg. 2010. Using a grammar checker for evaluation and postprocessing of statistical machine translation. In *Proceedings of LREC*, pages 2175–2181.

William E. Winkler. 1990. String comparator metrics and enhanced decision rules in the Fellegi-Sunter model of record linkage. In *Proceedings of the Section on Survey Research Methods (American Statistical Association)*, pages 354–359.

Dekai Wu. 1997. Stochastic inversion transduction grammars and bilingual parsing of parallel corpora. *Computational Linguistics*, 23(3):377–403.

Deyi Xiong, Min Zhang, and Haizhou Li. 2010. Error detection for statistical machine translation using linguistic features. In *Proceedings of the 48th Annual Meeting of the Association for Computational Linguistics*, pages 604–611. Association for Computational Linguistics.

Daniel Zeman and Philip Resnik. 2008. Cross-language parser adaptation between related languages. *NLP for Less Privileged Languages*, page 35.

Hai Zhao, Yan Song, Chunyu Kit, and Guodong Zhou. 2009. Cross language dependency parsing using a bilingual lexicon. In *Proceedings of the Joint Conference of the 47th Annual Meeting of the ACL and the 4th International Joint Conference on Natural Language Processing of the AFNLP: Volume 1-Volume 1*, pages 55–63. Association for Computational Linguistics.

Unsupervised vs. supervised weight estimation for semantic MT evaluation metrics

Chi-kiu LO and **Dekai WU**
HKUST
Human Language Technology Center
Department of Computer Science and Engineering
Hong Kong University of Science and Technology
{jackielo,dekai}@cs.ust.hk

Abstract

We present an unsupervised approach to estimate the appropriate degree of contribution of each semantic role type for semantic translation evaluation, yielding a semantic MT evaluation metric whose correlation with human adequacy judgments is comparable to that of recent supervised approaches but without the high cost of a human-ranked training corpus. Our new unsupervised estimation approach is motivated by an analysis showing that the weights learned from supervised training are distributed in a similar fashion to the relative frequencies of the semantic roles. Empirical results show that even without a training corpus of human adequacy rankings against which to optimize correlation, using instead our relative frequency weighting scheme to approximate the importance of each semantic role type leads to a semantic MT evaluation metric that correlates comparable with human adequacy judgments to previous metrics that require far more expensive human rankings of adequacy over a training corpus. As a result, the cost of semantic MT evaluation is greatly reduced.

1 Introduction

In this paper we investigate an unsupervised approach to estimate the degree of contribution of each semantic role type in semantic translation evaluation in low cost without using a human-ranked training corpus but still yields a evaluation metric that correlates comparably with human adequacy judgments to that of recent supervised approaches as in Lo and Wu (2011a, b, c). The new approach is motivated by an analysis showing that the distribution of the weights learned from the supervised training is similar to the relative frequencies of the occurrences of each semantic role in the reference translation. We then introduce a relative frequency weighting scheme to approximate the importance of each semantic role type. With such simple weighting scheme, the cost of evaluating translation of languages with fewer resources available is greatly reduced.

For the past decade, the task of measuring the performance of MT systems has relied heavily on lexical n-gram based MT evaluation metrics, such as BLEU (Papineni *et al.*, 2002), NIST (Doddington, 2002), METEOR (Banerjee and Lavie, 2005), PER (Tillmann *et al.*, 1997), CDER (Leusch *et al.*, 2006) and WER (Nießen *et al.*, 2000) because of their support on fast and inexpensive evaluation. These metrics are good at ranking overall systems by averaging their scores over the entire document. As MT systems improve, the focus of MT evaluation changes from generally reflecting the quality of each system to assisting error analysis on each MT output in detail. The failure of such metrics in evaluating translation quality on sentence level are becoming more apparent. Though containing roughly the correct words, the MT output as a whole sentence is still quite incomprehensible and fails to express meaning that is close to the input. Lexical n-gram based evaluation metrics are surface-oriented and do not do so well at ranking translations according to adequacy and are particularly poor at reflecting significant translation quality improvements on more meaningful word sense or semantic frame choices which human judges can indicate clearly. Callison-Burch *et al.* (2006) and Koehn and Monz (2006) even reported cases where BLEU strongly disagrees with human judgment on translation quality.

Liu and Gildea (2005) proposed STM, a structural approach based on syntax to addresses the failure of lexical similarity based metrics in evaluating translation grammaticality. However, a grammatical translation can achieve a high syntax-based score but still contains meaning errors arising from confusion of semantic roles. On the other hand, despite the fact that non-automatic, manually evaluations, such as HTER (Snover *et al.*, 2006), are more adequacy oriented and show a high correlation with human adequacy judgment, the high labor cost prohibits their widespread use. There was also work on explicitly evaluating MT adequacy with aggregated linguistic features (Giménez and Màrquez, 2007, 2008) and textual entailment (Pado *et al.*, 2009).

In the work of Lo and Wu (2011a), MEANT and its human variants HMEANT were introduced and empirical experimental results showed that HMEANT, which can be driven by low-cost monolingual semantic roles annotators with high interannotator agreement, correlates as well as HTER and far superior than BLEU and other surfaced oriented evaluation metrics. Along with additional improvements to the MEANT family of metrics, Lo and Wu (2011b) detailed the studies of the impact of each individual semantic role to the metric's correlation with human adequacy judgments. Lo and Wu (2011c) further discussed that with a proper weighting scheme of semantic frame in a sentence, structured semantic role representation is more accurate and intuitive than flattened role representation for semantic MT evaluation metrics.

The recent trend of incorporating more linguistic features into MT evaluation metrics raise the discussion on the appropriate approach in weighting and combining them. ULC (Giménez and Màrquez, 2007, 2008) uses uniform weights to aggregate linguistic features. This approach does not capture the importance of each feature to the overall translation quality to the MT output. One obvious example of different semantic roles contribute differently to the overall meaning is that readers usually accept translations with errors in adjunct arguments as a valid translation but not those with errors in core arguments. Unlike ULC, Liu and Gildea (2007); Lo and Wu (2011a) approach the weight estimation problem by maximum correlation training which directly optimize the correlation with human adequacy judgments. However, the shortcomings of this approach is that it requires a human-ranked training corpus which is expensive, especially for languages with limited resource.

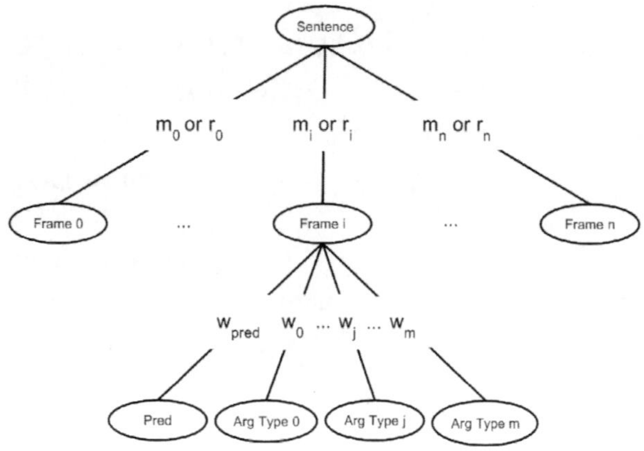

Figure 1: HMEANT structured role representation with a weighting scheme reflecting the degree of contribution of each semantic role type to the semantic frame. (Lo and Wu, 2011a,b,c).

We argue in this paper that for semantic MT evaluation, the importance of each semantic role type can easily be estimated using a simple unsupervised approach which leverage the relative frequencies of the semantic roles appeared in the reference translation. Our proposed weighting scheme is motivated by an analysis showing that the weights learned from supervised training are distributed in a similar fashion to the relative frequencies of the semantic roles. Our results show that the semantic MT evaluation metric using the relative frequency weighting scheme to approximate the importance of each semantic role type correlates comparably with human adequacy judgments to previous metrics that use maximum correlation training, which requires expensive human rankings of adequacy over a training corpus. Therefore, the cost of semantic MT evaluation is greatly reduced.

2 Semantic MT evaluation metrics

Adopting the principle that a good translation is one from which human readers may successfully understand at least the basic event structure-"who did what to whom, when, where and why" (Pradhan *et al.*, 2004)-which represents the most essential meaning of the source utterances, Lo and Wu (2011a,b,c) proposed HMEANT to evaluate translation utility based on semantic frames reconstructed by human reader of machine translation output. Monolingual (or bilingual) annotators must label the semantic roles in both the reference and machine translations, and then to align the semantic predicates and role fillers in the MT output to the reference translations. These annotations allow HMEANT to then look at the aligned role fillers, and aggregate the translation accuracy for each role. In the spirit of Occam's razor and representational transparency, the HMEANT score is defined simply in terms of a weighted f-score over these aligned predicates and role fillers. More precisely, HMEANT is defined as follows:

1. Human annotators annotate the shallow semantic structures of both the references and MT output.
2. Human judges align the semantic frames between the references and MT output by judging the correctness of the predicates.
3. For each pair of aligned semantic frames,
   (a) Human judges determine the translation correctness of the semantic role fillers.
   (b) Human judges align the semantic role fillers between the reference and MT output according to the correctness of the semantic role fillers.
4. Compute the weighted f-score over the matching role labels of these aligned predicates and role fillers.

$$m_i \equiv \frac{\text{\#tokens filled in frame i of MT}}{\text{total \#tokens in MT}}$$

$$r_i \equiv \frac{\text{\#tokens filled in frame i of REF}}{\text{total \#tokens in REF}}$$

$$M_{i,j} \equiv \text{total \# ARG j of PRED i in MT}$$

$$R_{i,j} \equiv \text{total \# ARG j of PRED i in REF}$$

$$C_{i,j} \equiv \text{\# correct ARG j of PRED i in MT}$$

$$P_{i,j} \equiv \text{\# partially correct ARG j of PRED i in MT}$$

$$\text{precision} = \frac{\sum_i m_i \frac{w_{\text{pred}} + \sum_j w_j (C_{i,j} + w_{\text{partial}} P_{i,j})}{w_{\text{pred}} + \sum_j w_j M_{i,j}}}{\sum_i m_i}$$

$$\text{recall} = \frac{\sum_i r_i \frac{w_{\text{pred}} + \sum_j w_j (C_{i,j} + w_{\text{partial}} P_{i,j})}{w_{\text{pred}} + \sum_j w_j R_{i,j}}}{\sum_i r_i}$$

$$\text{HMEANT} = \frac{2 * \text{precision} * \text{recall}}{\text{precision} + \text{recall}}$$

where m_{i} and r_{i} are the weights for frame,i, in the MT/REF respectively. These weights estimate the degree of contribution of each frame to the overall meaning of the sentence. $M_{i,j}$ and $R_{i,j}$ are the total counts of argument of type j in frame i in the MT/REF respectively. $C_{i,j}$ and $P_{i,j}$ are the count of the correctly and partial correctly translated argument of type j in frame i in the MT. w_{pred} is the weight for the predicate and w_{j} is the weights for the arguments of type j. These weights estimate the degree of contribution of different types of semantic roles to the overall meaning of the semantic frame they attached to. The frame precision/recall is the weighted sum of the number of correctly translated roles in a frame normalized by the weighted sum of the total number of all roles in that frame in the MT/REF respectively. The sentence precision/recall is the weighted sum of the frame precision/recall for all frames normalized by the weighted sum of the total number of frames in MT/REF respectively. Figure 1 shows the internal structure of HMEANT.

In the work of Lo and Wu (2011b), the correlation of all individual roles with the human adequacy judgments were found to be non-negative. Therefore, grid search was used to estimate the weights of each roles by optimizing the correlation with human adequacy judgments. This approach requires an expensive human-ranked training corpus which may not be available for languages with sparse resources.Unlike the supervised training approach, our proposed relative frequency weighting scheme does not require additional resource other than the SRL annotated reference translation.

3 Which roles contribute more in the semantic MT evaluation metric?

We begin with an investigation that suggests that the relative frequency of each semantic role (which can be estimated in unsupervised fashion without human rankings) approximates fairly closely its importance as determined by previous supervised optimization approaches. Since there is no ground truth on which

Role	Deviation (GALE-A)	Deviation (GALE-B)	Deviation (WMT12)
Agent	-0.09	-0.05	0.03
Experiencer	0.23	0.05	0.02
Benefactive	0.02	0.04	-0.01
Temporal	0.11	0.08	0.03
Locative	-0.05	-0.05	-0.07
Purpose	-0.01	0.03	-0.01
Manner	-0.01	0.00	-0.01
Extent	-0.02	0.00	-0.01
Modal	—	0.04	0.01
Negation	—	0.01	-0.01
Other	-0.12	0.05	-0.01

Table 1: Deviation of relative frequency from optimized weight of each semantic role in GALE-A, GALE-B and WMT12

semantic role contribute more to the overall meaning in a sentence for semantic MT evaluation, we first show that the unsupervised estimation are close to the weights obtained from the supervised maximum correlation training on a human-ranked MT evaluation corpus. More precisely, the weight estimation function is defined as follows:

$$c_j \equiv \text{\# count of ARG j in REF of the test set}$$

$$w_j = \frac{c_j}{\sum_j c_j}$$

3.1 Experimental setup

For our benchmark comparison, the evaluation data for our experiment is the same two sets of sentences, GALE-A and GALE-B that were used in Lo and Wu (2011b). The translation in GALE-A is SRL annotated with 9 semantic role types, while those in GALE-B are SRL annotated with 11 semantic role types (segregating the *modal* and the *negation* roles from the *other* role).

To validate whether or not our hypothesis is language independent, we also construct an evaluation data set by randomly selecting 50 sentences from WMT12 English to Czech (WMT12) translation task test corpus, in which 5 systems (out of 13 participating systems) were randomly picked for translation adequacy ranking by human readers. In total, 85 sets of translations (with translations from some source sentences appear more than once in different sets) were ranked. The translation in WMT12 are also SRL annotated with the tag set as GALE-B, i.e., 11 semantic role types.

The weights w_{pred}, w_j and w_{partial} were estimated using grid search to optimize the correlation against human adequacy judgments.

3.2 Results

Inspecting the distribution of the trained weights and the relative frequencies from all three data sets, as shown in table 1, we see that the overall pattern of weights from unsupervised estimation has a fairly small deviation from the those learned via supervised optimization. To visualize more clearly the overall pattern of the weights from the two estimation methods, we show the deviation of the unsupervised estimation from the supervised estimation. A deviation of 0 for all roles would mean that unsupervised and supervised estimation produce exactly identical weights. If the unsupervised estimation is higher than the supervised estimation, the deviation will be positive and vice versa.

What we see is that in almost all cases, the deviation between the trained weight and the relative frequency of each role is always within the range [-0.1, 0.1].

Closer inspection also reveals the following more detailed patterns:

- The weight of the less frequent adjunct arguments (e.g. purpose, manner, extent, modal and negation) from the unsupervised estimation is highly similar to that learned from the super-

PRED estimation	Deviation (GALE-A)	Deviation (GALE-B)	Deviation (WMT12)
Method (i)	0.16	0.16	0.31
Method (ii)	0.02	0.01	0.01

Table 2: Deviation from optimized weight in GALE-A, GALE-B and WMT12 of the predicate's weight as estimated by (i) frequency of predicates in frames, relative to predicates and arguments; and (ii) one-fourth of agent's weight.

vised maximum correlation training.

- The unsupervised estimation usually gives a higher weight to the temporal role than the supervised training would.
- The unsupervised estimation usually gives a lower weight to the locative role than the supervised training would but the two weights from the two approach are still high similar to each other, yielding a deviation within the range of [-0.07, 0.07].
- There is an obvious outlier found in GALE-A where the deviation of the relative frequency from the optimized weight is unusually high. This suggests that the optimized weights in GALE-A may be at the risk of over-fitting the training data.

4 Estimating the weight for the predicate

The remaining question left to be investigated is how we are to estimate the importance of the predicate in an unsupervised approach. One obvious approach is to treat the predicate the same way as the arguments. That is, just like with arguments, we could weight predicates by the relative frequency of how often predicates occur in semantic frames. However, this does not seem well motivated since predicates are fundamentally different from arguments: by definition, every semantic frame is defined by one predicate, and arguments are defined relative to the predicate.

On the other hand, inspecting the weights on the predicate obtained from the supervised maximum correlation training, we find that the weight of the predicate is usually around one-fourth of the weight of the agent role. More precisely, the two weight estimation functions are defined as follows:

$$c_{\text{pred}} \equiv \text{\# count of PRED in REF of the test set}$$

$$\text{Method (i)} = \frac{c_{\text{pred}}}{c_{\text{pred}} + \sum_j c_j}$$

$$\text{Method (ii)} = 0.25 \cdot w_{\text{agent}}$$

We now show that the supervised estimation of the predicate's weight is closely approximated by unsupervised estimation.

4.1 Experimental setup

The experimental setup is the same as that used in section 3.

4.2 Results

The results in table 2 show that the trained weight of the predicate and its unsupervised estimation of one-fourth of the agent role's weight are highly similar to each other. In all three data sets, the deviation between the trained weight and the heuristic of one-fourth of the agent's weight is always within the range [0.1, 0.2].

On the other hand, treating the predicate the same as arguments by estimating the unsupervised weight using relative frequency largely over-estimates and has a large deviation from the weight learned from supervised estimation.

5 Semantic MT evaluation using unsupervised weight estimates

Having seen that the weights of the predicate and semantic roles estimated by the unsupervised approach fairly closely approximate those learned from the supervised approach, we now show that the unsupervised approach leads to a semantic MT evaluation metric that correlates comparably with human adequacy judgments to one that is trained on a far more expensive human-ranked training corpus.

5.1 Experimental setup

Following the benchmark assessment in NIST MetricsMaTr 2010 (Callison-Burch *et al.*, 2010), we assess the performance of the semantic MT evaluation

Metrics	GALE-A	GALE-B	WMT12
HMEANT (supervised)	0.49	0.27	0.29
HMEANT (unsupervised)	0.42	0.23	0.20
NIST	0.29	0.09	0.12
METEOR	0.20	0.21	0.22
TER	0.20	0.10	0.12
PER	0.20	0.07	0.02
BLEU	0.20	0.12	0.01
CDER	0.12	0.10	0.14
WER	0.10	0.11	0.17

Table 3: Average sentence-level correlation with human adequacy judgments of HMEANT using supervised and unsupervised weight scheme on GALE-A, GALE-B and WMT12, (with baseline comparison of commonly used automatic MT evaluation metric.

metric at the sentence level using Kendall's rank correlation coefficient which evaluate the correlation of the proposed metric with human judgments on translation adequacy ranking. A higher the value for indicates a higher similarity to the ranking by the evaluation metric to the human judgment. The range of possible values of correlation coefficient is [-1,1], where 1 means the systems are ranked in the same order as the human judgment and -1 means the systems are ranked in the reverse order as the human judgment. For GALE-A and GALE-B, the human judgment on adequacy was obtained by showing all three MT outputs together with the Chinese source input to a human reader. The human reader was instructed to order the sentences from the three MT systems according to the accuracy of meaning in the translations. For WMT12, the human adequacy judgments are provided by the organizers.

The rest of the experimental setup is the same as that used in section 3.

5.2 Results

Table 3 shows that HMEANT with the proposed unsupervised semantic role weighting scheme correlate comparably with human adequacy judgments to that optimized with a more expensive human-ranked training corpus, and, outperforms all other commonly used automatic metrics (except for METEOR in Czech). The results from GALE-A, GALE-B and WMT12 are consistent. These encouraging results show that semantic MT evaluation metric could be widely applicable to languages other than English.

6 Conclusion

We presented a simple, easy to implement yet well-motivated weighting scheme for HMEANT to estimate the importance of each semantic role in evaluating the translation adequacy. Unlike the previous metrics, the proposed metric does not require an expensive human-ranked training corpus and still outperforms all other commonly used automatic MT evaluation metrics. Interestingly, the distribution of the optimal weights obtained by maximum correlation training, is similar to the relative frequency of occurrence of each semantic role type in the reference translation. HMEANT with the new weighting scheme showed consistent results across different language pairs and across different corpora in the same language pair. With the proposed weighting scheme, the semantic MT evaluation metric is ready to be used off-the-shelf without depending on a human-ranked training corpus. We believe that our current work reduces the barrier for semantic MT evaluation for resource scarce languages sufficiently so that semantic MT evaluation can be applied to most other languages.

Acknowledgments

We would like to thank Ondřej Bojar and all the annotators from the Charles University in Prague for participating in the experiments. This material is based upon work supported in part by the Defense Advanced Research Projects Agency (DARPA) under BOLT contract no. HR0011-12-C-0016, and GALE contract nos. HR0011-06-C-0022 and HR0011-06-C-0023; by the European Union under the FP7 grant agreement no. 287658; and by the Hong Kong Research Grants Council (RGC) research grants GRF621008, GRF612806, DAG03/04.EG09, RGC6256/00E, and RGC6083/99E. Any opinions, findings and conclusions or recommendations expressed in this material are those of the authors and do not necessarily reflect the views of the RGC, EU, or DARPA.

References

Satanjeev Banerjee and Alon Lavie. METEOR: An Automatic Metric for MT Evaluation with Improved Correlation with Human Judgments. In *Proceedings of the 43th Annual Meeting of the Association of Computational Linguistics (ACL-05)*, pages 65–72, 2005.

Chris Callison-Burch, Miles Osborne, and Philipp Koehn. Re-evaluating the role of BLEU in Machine Translation Research. In *Proceedings of the 13th Conference of the European Chapter of the Association for Computational Linguistics (EACL-06)*, pages 249–256, 2006.

Chris Callison-Burch, Philipp Koehn, Christof Monz, Kay Peterson, Mark Pryzbocki, and Omar Zaidan. Findings of the 2010 Joint Workshop on Statistical Machine Translation and Metrics for Machine Translation. In *Proceedings of the Joint 5th Workshop on Statistical Machine Translation and MetricsMATR*, pages 17–53, Uppsala, Sweden, 15-16 July 2010.

G. Doddington. Automatic Evaluation of Machine Translation Quality using N-gram Co-occurrence Statistics. In *Proceedings of the 2nd International Conference on Human Language Technology Research (HLT-02)*, pages 138–145, San Francisco, CA, USA, 2002. Morgan Kaufmann Publishers Inc.

Jesús Giménez and Lluís Màrquez. Linguistic Features for Automatic Evaluation of Heterogenous MT Systems. In *Proceedings of the 2nd Workshop on Statistical Machine Translation*, pages 256–264, Prague, Czech Republic, June 2007. Association for Computational Linguistics.

Jesús Giménez and Lluís Màrquez. A Smorgasbord of Features for Automatic MT Evaluation. In *Proceedings of the 3rd Workshop on Statistical Machine Translation*, pages 195–198, Columbus, OH, June 2008. Association for Computational Linguistics.

Philipp Koehn and Christof Monz. Manual and Automatic Evaluation of Machine Translation between European Languages. In *Proceedings of the Workshop on Statistical Machine Translation*, pages 102–121, 2006.

Gregor Leusch, Nicola Ueffing, and Hermann Ney. CDer: Efficient MT Evaluation Using Block Movements. In *Proceedings of the 13th Conference of the European Chapter of the Association for Computational Linguistics (EACL-06)*, 2006.

Ding Liu and Daniel Gildea. Syntactic Features for Evaluation of Machine Translation. In *Proceedings of the ACL Workshop on Intrinsic and Extrinsic Evaluation Measures for Machine Translation and/or Summarization*, page 25, 2005.

Ding Liu and Daniel Gildea. Source-Language Features and Maximum Correlation Training for Machine Translation Evaluation. In *Proceedings of the 2007 Conference of the North American Chapter of the Association of Computational Linguistics (NAACL-07)*, 2007.

Chi-kiu Lo and Dekai Wu. MEANT: An Inexpensive, High-Accuracy, Semi-Automatic Metric for Evaluating Translation Utility based on Semantic Roles. In *Proceedings of the Joint conference of the 49th Annual Meeting of the Association for Computational Linguistics : Human Language Technologies (ACL-HLT-11)*, 2011.

Chi-kiu Lo and Dekai Wu. SMT vs. AI redux: How semantic frames evaluate MT more accurately. In *Proceedings of the 22nd International Joint Conference on Artificial Intelligence (IJCAI-11)*, 2011.

Chi-kiu Lo and Dekai Wu. Structured vs. Flat Semantic Role Representations for Machine Translation Evaluation. In *Proceedings of the 5th Workshop on Syntax and Structure in Statistical Translation (SSST-5)*, 2011.

Sonja Nießen, Franz Josef Och, Gregor Leusch, and Hermann Ney. A Evaluation Tool for Machine Translation: Fast Evaluation for MT Research. In *Proceedings of the 2nd International Conference on Language Resources and Evaluation (LREC-2000)*, 2000.

Sebastian Pado, Michel Galley, Dan Jurafsky, and Chris Manning. Robust Machine Translation Evaluation with Entailment Features. In *Proceedings of the Joint conference of the 47th Annual Meeting of the Association for Computational Linguistics and the 4th International Joint Conference on Natural Language Processing of the Asian Federation of Natural Language Processing (ACL-IJCNLP-09)*, 2009.

Kishore Papineni, Salim Roukos, Todd Ward, and Wei-Jing Zhu. BLEU: A Method for Automatic Evaluation of Machine Translation. In *Proceedings of the 40th Annual Meeting of the Association for Computational Linguistics (ACL-02)*, pages 311–318, 2002.

Sameer Pradhan, Wayne Ward, Kadri Hacioglu, James H. Martin, and Dan Jurafsky. Shallow Semantic Parsing Using Support Vector Machines. In *Proceedings of the 2004 Conference on Human Language Technology and the North American Chapter of the Association for Computational Linguistics (HLT-NAACL-04)*, 2004.

Matthew Snover, Bonnie J. Dorr, Richard Schwartz, Linnea Micciulla, and John Makhoul. A Study of Translation Edit Rate with Targeted Human Annotation. In *Proceedings of the 7th Conference of the Association for Machine Translation in the Americas (AMTA-06)*, pages 223–231, 2006.

Christoph Tillmann, Stephan Vogel, Hermann Ney, Arkaitz Zubiaga, and Hassan Sawaf. Accelerated DP Based Search For Statistical Translation. In *Proceedings of the 5th European Conference on Speech Communication and Technology (EUROSPEECH-97)*, 1997.

Head Finalization Reordering for Chinese-to-Japanese Machine Translation

Han Dan[+] **Katsuhito Sudoh**[‡] **Xianchao Wu**[‡*]
Kevin Duh[‡†] **Hajime Tsukada**[‡] **Masaaki Nagata**[‡]
[+]The Graduate University For Advanced Studies, Tokyo, Japan
[‡]NTT Communication Science Laboratories, NTT Corporation
[+]handan@nii.ac.jp, [*]wuxianchao@baidu.com, [†]kevinduh@is.naist.jp
[‡]{sudoh.katsuhito, tsukada.hajime, nagata.masaaki}@lab.ntt.co.jp

Abstract

In Statistical Machine Translation, reordering rules have proved useful in extracting bilingual phrases and in decoding during translation between languages that are structurally different. Linguistically motivated rules have been incorporated into Chinese-to-English (Wang et al., 2007) and English-to-Japanese (Isozaki et al., 2010b) translation with significant gains to the statistical translation system. Here, we carry out a linguistic analysis of the Chinese-to-Japanese translation problem and propose one of the first reordering rules for this language pair. Experimental results show substantially improvements (from 20.70 to 23.17 BLEU) when head-finalization rules based on HPSG parses are used, and further gains (to 24.14 BLEU) were obtained using more refined rules.

1 Introduction

In state-of-the-art Statistical Machine Translation (SMT) systems, bilingual phrases are the main building blocks for constructing a translation given a sentence from a source language. To extract those bilingual phrases from a parallel corpus, the first step is to discover the implicit word-to-word correspondences between bilingual sentences (Brown et al., 1993). Then, a symmetrization matrix is built (Och and Ney, 2004) by using word-to-word alignments, and a wide variety of heuristics can be used to extract the bilingual phrases (Zens et al., 2002; Koehn et al., 2003).

This method performs relatively well when the source and the target languages have similar word order, as in the case of French, Spanish, and English. However, when translating between languages with very different structures, as in the case of English and Japanese, or Japanese and Chinese, the quality of extracted bilingual phrases and the overall translation quality diminishes.

In the latter scenario, a simple but effective strategy to cope with this problem is to reorder the words of sentences in one language so that it resembles the word order of another language (Wu et al., 2011; Isozaki et al., 2010b). The advantages of this strategy are two fold. The first advantage is at the decoding stage, since it enables the translation to be constructed almost monotonically. The second advantage is at the training stage, since automatically estimated word-to-word alignments are likely to be more accurate and symmetrization matrices reveal more evident bilingual phrases, leading to the extraction of better quality bilingual phrases and cleaner phrase tables.

In this work, we focus on Chinese-to-Japanese translation, motivated by the increasing interaction between these two countries and the need to improve direct machine translation without using a pivot language. Despite the countries' close cultural relationship, their languages significantly differ in terms of syntax, which poses a severe difficulty in statistical machine translation. The syntactic relationship of this language pair has not been carefully studied before in the machine translation

[*]Now at Baidu Japan Inc.

[†] Now at Nara Institute of Science and Technology (NAIST)

field, and our work aims to contribute in this direction as follows:

- We present a detailed syntactic analysis of several reordering issues in Chinese-Japanese translation using the information provided by an HPSG-based deep parser.
- We introduce novel reordering rules based on head-finalization and linguistically inspired refinements to make words in Chinese sentences resemble Japanese word order. We empirically show its effectiveness (e.g. 20.70 to 24.23 BLEU improvement).

The paper is structured as follows. Section 2 introduces the background and gives an overview of similar techniques related to this work. Section 3 describes the proposed method in detail. Experimental evaluation of the performance of the proposed method is described in section 4. There is an error analysis on the obtained results in section 5. Conclusions and a short description on future work derived from this research are given in the final section.

2 Background

2.1 Head Finalization

The structure of languages can be characterized by phrase structures. The head of a phrase is the word that determines the syntactic category of the phrase, and its modifiers (also called dependents) are the rest of the words within the phrase. In English, the head of a phrase can be usually found before its modifiers. For that reason, English is called a head-initial language (Cook and Newson, 1988). Japanese, on the other hand, is head-final language (Fukui, 1992), since the head of a phrase always appears after its modifiers.

In certain applications, as in the case of machine translation, word reordering can be a promising strategy to ease the task when working with languages with different phrase structures like English and Japanese. Head Finalization is a successful syntax-based reordering method designed to reorder sentences from a head-initial language to resemble the word order in sentences from a head-final language (Isozaki et al., 2010b). The essence of this rule is to move the syntactic heads to the end of its dependency by swapping child nodes in a phrase structure tree when the head child appears before the dependent child.

Isozaki et al. (2010b) proposed a simple method of Head Finalization, by using an HPSG-based deep parser for English (Miyao and Tsujii, 2008) to obtain phrase structures and head information. The score results from several mainstream evaluation methods indicated that the translation quality had been improved; the scores of Word Error Rate (WER) and Translation Edit Rate (TER) (Snover et al., 2006) had especially been greatly reduced.

2.2 Chinese Deep Parsing

Syntax-based reordering methods need parsed sentences as input. Isozaki et al. (2010b) used *Enju*, an HPSG-based deep parser for English, but they also discussed using other types of parsers, such as word dependency parsers and Penn Treebank-style parsers. However, to use word dependency parsers, they needed an additional heuristic rule to recover phrase structures, and Penn Treebank-style parsers are problematic because they output flat phrase structures (i.e. a phrase may have multiple dependents, which causes a problem of reordering within a phrase). Consequently, compared to different types of parsers, *Head-Final English* performs the best on the basis of English Enju's parsing result.

In this paper, we follow their observation, and use the HPSG-based parser for Chinese (*Chinese Enju*) (Yu et al., 2011) for Chinese syntactic parsing. Since Chinese Enju is based on the same parsing model as English Enju, it provides rich syntactic information including phrase structures and syntactic/semantic heads.

Figure 1 shows an example of an XML output from Chinese Enju for the sentence "`wo` (I) `qu` (go to) `dongjing` (Tokyo) `he` (and) `jingdu` (Kyoto)." The label `<cons>` and `<tok>` represent the non-terminal nodes and terminal nodes, respectively. Each node is identified by a unique "`id`" and has several attributes. The attribute "`head`" indicates which child node is the syntactic head. In this figure, **<head="c4" id="c3">** means that the node that has **id="c4"** is the syntactic head of the node that has **id="c3"**.

```
<cons cat="N" head="t0" id="c1">
  <tok id="t0"> wo (I) </tok>
</cons>
<cons cat="V" head="c3" id="c2" schema="head_mod">
 <cons cat="V" head="c4" id="c3">
  <cons cat="V" head="t1" id="c4">
   <tok id="t1"> qu (go to) </tok>
  </cons>
  <cons cat="N" head="c6" id="c5" schema="coord_left">
   <cons cat="N" head="t2" id="c6">
    <tok id="t2"> dongjing (Tokyo) </tok>
   </cons>
   <cons cat="COOD" head="c8" id="c7">
    <cons cat="CONJ" head="t3" id="c8">
     <tok id="t3"> he (and) </tok>
    </cons>
    <cons cat="N" head="t4" id="c9">
     <tok id="t4"> jingdu (Kyoto) </tok>
    </cons>
   </cons>
  </cons>
 </cons>
 <cons cat="PU" head="t5" id="c10">
  <tok id="t5"> ，</tok>
 </cons>
</cons>
```

Figure 1: An XML output for a Chinese sentence from Chinese Enju. For clarity, we only draw information related to the phrase structure and the heads.

2.3 Related Work

Reordering is a popular strategy for improving machine translation quality when source and target languages are structurally very different. Researchers have approached the reordering problem in multiple ways. The most basic idea is pre-ordering (Xia and McCord, 2004; Collins et al., 2005), that is, to do reordering during preprocessing time, where the source side of the training and development data and sentences from a source language that have to be translated are first reordered to ease the training and the translation, respectively. In (Xu et al., 2009), authors used a dependency parser to introduce manually created pre-ordering rules to reorder English sentences when translating into five different SOV(Subject-Object-Verb) languages. Other authors (Genzel, 2010; Wu et al., 2011) use automatically generated rules induced from parallel data. Tillmann (2004) used a lexical reordering model, and Galley et al. (2004) followed a syntactic-based model.

In this work, however, we are centered in the design of manual rules inspired by the Head Finalization (HF) reordering (Isozaki et al., 2010b). HF reordering is one of the simplest methods for pre-ordering that significantly improves word alignments and leads to a better translation quality. Although the method is limited to translation where the target language is head-final, it requires neither training data nor fine-tuning. To our knowledge, HF is the best method to reorder languages when translating into head-final languages like Japanese.

The implementation of HF method for English-to-Japanese translation appears to work well. A reasonable explanation for this is the close match between the concept of "head" in this language pair. However, for Chinese-to-Japanese, there are differences in the definitions of numbers of important syntactic concepts, including the definition of the syntactic head. We concluded that the difficulties we encountered in using HF to Chinese-to-Japanese translation were the result of these differences in the definition of "head". As we believe that such differences are also likely to be observed in other language pairs, the present work is generally important for head-initial to head-final translation as it shows a systematic linguistic analysis that consistently improves the effectivity of the HF method.

3 Syntax-based Reordering Rules

This section describes our method for syntax-based reordering for Chinese-to-Japanese translation. We start by introducing Head Finalization for Chinese (HFC), which is a simple adaptation of Isozaki et al. (2010b)'s method for English-to-Japanese translation. However, we found that this simple method has problems when applied to Chinese, due to peculiarities in Chinese syntax. In Section 3.2, we analyze several distinctive cases of the problem in detail. And following this analysis, Section 3.3 proposes a refinement of the original HFC, with a couple of exception rules for reordering.

3.1 Head Finalization for Chinese (HFC)

Since Chinese and English are both known to be head-initial languages[1], the reordering rule introduced in (Isozaki et al., 2010b) ideally would reorder Chinese sentences to follow the word order

[1] As Gao (2008) summarized, whether Chinese is a head-initial or a head-final language is open for debate. Nevertheless, we take the view that most Chinese sentence structures are head-initial since the written form of Chinese mainly behaves as an head-initial language.

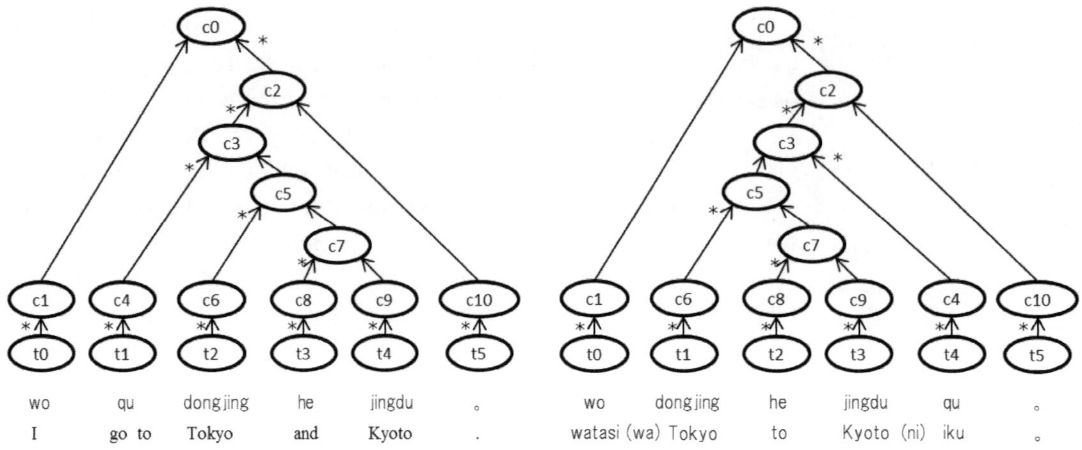

Figure 2: Simple example for Head-Final Chinese. The left figure shows the parsing tree of the original sentence and its English translation. The right figure shows the reordered sentence along with its Japanese translation. ("*" indicate the syntactic head).

of their Japanese counterparts.

Figure 2 shows an example of a head finalized Chinese sentence based on the output from Chinese Enju shown in Figure 1. Notice that the coordination exception rule described in (Isozaki et al., 2010b) also applies to Chinese reordering. This exception rule says that child nodes are not swapped if the node is a coordination[2]. Another exception rule is for punctuation symbols, which are also preserved in their original order. In this case, as can be seen in the example in Figure 2, the nodes of **c3**, **c6**, and **c8** had not been swapped with their dependency. In this account, only the verb "qu" had been moved to the end of the sentence, following the same word order as its Japanese translation.

3.2 Discrepancies in Head Definition

Head Finalization relies on the idea that head-dependent relations are largely consistent among different languages while word orders are different. However, in Chinese, there has been much debate on the definition of head[3], possibly because Chinese has fewer surface syntactic features than other languages like English and Japanese. This causes some discrepancies between the definitions of the head in Chinese and Japanese, which leads to undesirable reordering of Chinese sentences. Specifically, in preliminary experiments we observed unexpected reorderings that are caused by the differences in the head definitions, which we describe below.

3.2.1 Aspect Particle

Although Chinese has no syntactic tense marker, three aspect particles following verbs can be used to identify the tense semantically. They are "le0" (did), "zhe0" (doing), and "guo4" (done), and their counterparts in Japanese are "ta", "teiru", and "ta", respectively. Both the first word and third word can represent the past tense, but the third one is more often used in the past perfect.

The Chinese parser[4] treated aspect particles as dependents of verbs, whereas their Japanese counterparts are identified as the head. For example in Table 1[5], "qu" (go) and "guo" (done) aligned with "i" and "tta", respectively. However, since "guo" is treated as a dependent of "qu", by directly implementing the Head Final Chinese (HFC), the sentence will be reordered like

[2]Coordination is easily detected in the output of Enju; it is marked by the attributes `xcat="COOD"` or `schema="coord-left/right"` as shown in Figure 1.

[3]In this paper, we only consider the syntactic head.

[4]The discussions in this section presuppose the syntactic analysis done by Chinese Enju, but most of the analysis is consistent with the common explanation for Chinese syntax.

[5]English translation (En); Chinese original sentence (Ch); reordered Chinese by Head-Final Chinese (HFC); reordered Chinese by Refined Head-Final Chinese (R-HFC) and Japanese translation (Ja).

HFC in Table 1, which does not follow the word order of the Japanese (Ja) translation. In contrast, the reordered sentence from refined-HFC (R-HFC) can be translated monotonically.

En	I have been to Tokyo.
Ch	wo **qu** ***guo*** dongjing.
HFC	wo dongjing ***guo*** **qu**.
R-HFC	wo dongjing **qu** ***guo***.
Ja	watashi (wa) Tokyo (ni) **i tta**.

Table 1: An example for Aspect Particle. Best word alignment Ja-Ch (En): "watashi" – "wo"(I); "Tokyo" – "dongjing" (Tokyo); "i" – "qu" (been); "tta" – "guo" (have).

3.2.2 Adverbial Modifier '`bu4`'

Both in Chinese and Japanese, verb phrase modifiers typically occur in pre-verbal positions, especially when the modifiers are adverbs. Since adverbial modifiers are dependents in both Chinese and Japanese, head finalization works perfectly for them. However, there is an exceptional adverb, "`bu4`", which means negation and is usually translated into "`nai`", which is always at the end of the sentence in Japanese and thus is the head. For example in Table 2, the word "`kan`" (watch) will be identified as the head and the word "`bu`" is its dependent; on the contrary, in the Japanese translation (Ja), the word "`nai`", which is aligned with "`bu`", will be identified as the head. Therefore, the Head Final Chinese is not in the same order, but the reordered sentence by R-HFC obtained the same order with the Japanese translation.

En	I do not watch TV.
Ch	wo ***bu*** **kan** dianshi.
HFC	wo dianshi ***bu*** **kan**.
R-HFC	wo dianshi **kan** ***bu***.
Ja	watashi (wa) terebi (wo) **mi nai**.

Table 2: An example for Adverbial Modifier `bu4`. Best word alignment Ja-Ch (En): "watashi" – "wo" (I); "terebi" – "dianshi" (TV); "mi" – "kan" (watch); "nai" – "bu" (do not).

3.2.3 Sentence-final Particle

Sentence-final particles often appear at the end of a sentence to express a speaker's attitude: e.g. "`ba0, a0`" in Chinese, and "`naa, nee`" in Japanese. Although they appear in the same position in both Chinese and Japanese, in accordance with the differences of head definition, they are identified as the dependent in Chinese while they are the head in Japanese. For example in Table 3, since "`a0`" was identified as the dependent, it had been reordered to the beginning of the sentence while its Japanese translation "`nee`" is at the end of the sentence as the head. Likewise, by refining the HFC, we can improve the word alignment.

En	It is good weather.
Ch	tianqi zhenhao **a**.
HFC	**a** tianqi zhenhao.
R-HFC	tianqi zhenhao **a**.
Ja	ii tennki desu **nee**.

Table 3: An example for Sentence-final Particle. Best word alignment Ja-Ch (En): "tennki" – "tianqi" (weather); "ii" – "zhenhao" (good); "nee" – "a' (None).

3.2.4 *Et cetera*

In Chinese, there are two expressions for representing the meaning of "and other things" with one Chinese character: "`deng3`" and "`deng3 deng3`", which are both identified as dependent of a noun. In contrast, in Japanese, "`nado`" is always the head because it appears as the right-most word in a noun phrase. Table 4 shows an example.

En	Fruits include apples, etc.
Ch	shuiguo baokuo pingguo **deng**.
HFC	shuiguo **deng** pingguo baokuo.
R-HFC	shuiguo pingguo **deng** baokuo.
Ja	kudamono (wa) ringo **nado** (wo) fukunde iru.

Table 4: An example for Et cetera. Best word alignment Ja-Ch (En): "kudamono" – "shuiguo" (Fruits); "ringo" – "pingguo" (apples); "nado" – "deng" (etc.); "fukunde iru" – "baokuo" (include).

AS	Aspect particle
SP	Sentence-final particle
ETC	*et cetera* (i.e. deng3 and deng3 deng3)
IJ	Interjection
PU	Punctuation
CC	Coordinating conjunction

Table 5: The list of POSs for exception reordering rules

3.3 Refinement of HFC

In the preceding sections, we have discussed syntactic constructions that cause wrong application of Head Finalization to Chinese sentences. Following the observations, we propose a method to improve the original Head Finalization reordering rule to obtain better alignment with Japanese.

The idea is simple: we define a list of POSs, and when we find one of them as a dependent child of the node, we do not apply reordering. Table 5 shows the list of POSs we define in the current implementation[6]. While interjections are not discussed in detail, we should obviously not reorder to interjections because they are position-independent. The rules for PU and CC are basically equivalent to the exception rules proposed by (Isozaki et al., 2010b).

4 Experiments

The corpus we used as training data comes from the China Workshop on Machine Translation (CWMT) (Zhao et al., 2011). This is a Japanese-Chinese parallel corpus in the news domain, containing $281,322$ sentence pairs. We also collected another Japanese-Chinese parallel corpus from news containing $529,769$ sentences and merged it with the CWMT corpus to create an extended version of the CWMT corpus. We will refer to this corpus as "CWMT ext." We split an inverted multi-reference set into a development and a test set containing $1,000$ sentences each. In these two sets, the Chinese input was different, but the Japanese reference was identical. We think that this split does not pose any severe problem to the comparison fairness of the experiment, since no new phrases are added during tuning and the experimental conditions remain equal for all tested methods. Detailed Corpus statistics can be found in Table 6.

[6]The POSs are from Penn Chinese Treebank.

		Ch	Ja
CWMT	Sentences	282K	
	Run. words	2.5M	3.2M
	Avg. sent. leng.	8.8	11.5
	Vocabulary	102K	42K
CWMT ext.	Sentences	811K	
	Run. words	14.7M	17M
	Avg. sent. leng.	18.1	20.9
	Vocabulary	249K	95K
Dev.	Sentences	1000	
	Run. words	29.9K	35.7K
	Avg. sent. leng.	29.9	35.7
	OoV w.r.t. CWMT	485	106
	OoV w.r.t. CWMT ext.	244	53
Test	Sentences	1000	
	Run. words	25.8K	35.7K
	Avg. sent. leng.	25.8	35.7
	OoV w.r.t. CWMT	456	106
	OoV w.r.t. CWMT ext.	228	53

Table 6: Characteristics of CWMT and extended CWMT Chinese-Japanese corpus. Dev. stands for Development, OoV for "Out of Vocabulary" words, K for thousands of elements, and M for millions of elements. Data statistics were collected after tokenizing.

To parse Chinese sentences, we used Chinese Enju (Yu et al., 2010), an HPSG-based parser trained with the Chinese HPSG treebank converted from Penn Chinese Treebank. Chinese Enju requires segmented and POS-tagged sentences to do parsing. We used the Stanford Chinese segmenter (Chang et al., 2008) and Stanford POS-tagger (Toutanova et al., 2003) to obtain the segmentation and POS-tagging of the Chinese side of the training, development, and test sets.

The baseline system was trained following the instructions of recent SMT evaluation campaigns (Callison-Burch et al., 2010) by using the MT toolkit Moses (Koehn et al., 2007) in its default configuration. Phrase pairs were extracted from symmetrized word alignments and distortions generated by GIZA++ (Och and Ney, 2003) using the combination of heuristics "grow-diag-final-and" and "msd-bidirectional-fe". The language model was a 5-gram language model estimated on the target side of the parallel corpora by using the modified Kneser-Ney smoothing (Chen and Goodman, 1999) implemented in the SRILM (Stolcke, 2002) toolkit. The weights of the log-linear combination of feature functions were estimated by using MERT (Och, 2003) on the development set described in Table 6.

The effectiveness of the reorderings proposed in Section 3.3 was assessed by using two precision metrics and two error metrics on translation quality. The first evaluation metric is BLEU (Papineni et al., 2002), a very common accuracy metric in SMT that measures N-gram precision, with a penalty for too short sentences. The second evaluation metric was RIBES (Isozaki et al., 2010a), a recent precision metric used to evaluate translation quality between structurally different languages. It uses notions on rank correlation coefficients and precision measures. The third evaluation metric is TER (Snover et al., 2006), another error metric that computes the minimum number of edits required to convert translated sentences into its corresponding references. Possible edits include insertion, deletion, substitution of single words, and shifts of word sequences. The fourth evaluation metric is WER, an error metric inspired in the Levenshtein distance at word level. BLEU, WER, and TER were used to provide a sense of comparison but they do not significantly penalize long-range word order errors. For this reason, RIBES was used to account for this aspect of translation quality.

The baseline system was trained and tuned using the same configuration setup described in this section, but no reordering rule was implemented at the preprocessing stage.

Three systems have been run to translate the test set for comparison when the systems were trained using the two training data sets. They are the baseline system, the system consisting in the naïve implementation of HF reordering, and the system with refined HFC reordering rules. Assessment of translation quality can be found in Table 7.

As can be observed in Table 7, the translation quality, as measured by precision and error metrics, was consistently and significantly increased when the HFC reordering rule was used and was significantly improved further when the refinement proposed in this work was used. Specifically, the BLEU score increased from 19.94 to 20.79 when the CWMT corpus was used, and from 23.17 to 24.14 when the extended CWMT corpus was used.

AS	SP	ETC	IJ	PU	COOD
3.8%	0.8%	1.3%	0.0%*	21.0%	38.3%

Table 8: Weighted recall of each exception rule during reordering on CWMT ext. training data, dev data, and test data. (* actual value 0.0016%.)

Table 8 shows the recall of each exception rule listed in Section 3, and was computed by counting the times an exception rule was triggered divided by the number of times the head finalization rule applied. Data was collected for CWMT ext. training, dev and test sets. Although the exception rules related to aspect particles, *Et cetera*, sentence-final particles and interjections have a comparatively lower frequency of application than punctuation or coordination exception rules, the improvements they led to are significant.

5 Error Analysis

In Section 3 we have analyzed syntactic differences between Chinese and Japanese that led to the design of an effective refinement. A manual error analysis of the results of our refined reordering rules showed that some more reordering issues remain and, although they are not side effects of our proposed rule, they are worth mentioning in this separate section.

5.1 Serial Verb Construction

Serial verb construction is a phenomenon occurring in Chinese, where several verbs are put together as one unit without any conjunction between them. The relationship between these verbs can be progressive or parallel. Apparently, Japanese has a largely corresponding construction, which indicates that no reordering should be applied. An example to illustrate this fact in Chinese is "**weishi** (maintain) **shenhua** (deepen) `zhongriguanxi` (Japan-China relations) `de` (of) `gaishan` (improvement) `jidiao` (basic tone)."[7] The two verbs "`weishi`" (in Japanese, `iji`) and "`shenhua`" (in Japanese, `shinka`) are used together, and they follow the same order as in Japanese: "`nicchukankei` (Japan-China re-

[7]English translation: Maintain and deepen the improved basic tone of Japan-China relations.

	CWMT				CWMT ext.			
	BLEU	RIBES	TER	WER	BLEU	RIBES	TER	WER
baseline	16.74	71.24	70.86	77.45	20.70	74.21	66.10	72.36
HFC	19.94	73.49	65.19	71.39	23.17	75.35	61.38	67.74
refined HFC	**20.79**	**75.09**	**64.91**	**70.39**	**24.14**	**77.17**	**59.67**	**65.31**

Table 7: Evaluation of translation quality of a test set when CWMT and CWMT extended corpus were used for training. Results are given in terms of BLEU, RIBES, TER, and WER for baseline, head finalization, and proposed refinement of head finalization reordering rules.

lations) `no` (of) `kaizan` (improvement) `kityo` (basic tone) `wo` **iji** (maintain) **shinka** (deepen) `suru` (do)."

5.2 Complementizer

A "complementizer" is a particle used to introduce a complement. In English, a very common complementizer is the word "that" when making a clausal complement, while in Chinese it can denote other types of word, such as verbs, adjectives or quantifiers. The complementizer is identified as the dependent of the verb that it modifies. For instance, a Chinese sentence: "`wo` (I) **mang wan** `le` (have finished the work)." This can be translated into Japanese: "`watashi` (I) `wa` `shigoto` (work) `wo` **owa tta** (have finished)." In Chinese, the verb "`mang`" is the head while "`wan`" is the complementizer, and its Japanese counterpart "`owa tta`" has the same word order.

However, during the reordering, "`mang`" will be placed at the end of the sentence and "`wan`" in the beginning, leading to an inconsistency with respect to the Japanese translation where the complementizer "`tta`" is the head.

5.3 Verbal Nominalization and Nounal Verbalization

As discussed by Guo (2009), compared to English and Japanese, Chinese has little inflectional morphology, that is, no inflection to denote tense, case, etc. Thus, words are extremely flexible, making verb nominalization and noun verbalization appear frequently and commonly without any conjugation or declension. As a result, it is difficult to do disambiguation during POS tagging and parsing. For example, the Chinese word "`kaifa`" may have two syntactic functions: verb (develop) and noun (development). Thus, it is difficult to reliably tag without considering the context. In contrast, in Japanese, "`suru`" can be used to identify verbs. For example, "`kaihatu suru`" (develop) is a verb and "`kaihatu`" (development) is a noun. This ambiguity is prone to not only POS tagging error but also parsing error, and thus affects the identification of heads, which may lead to incorrect reordering.

5.4 Adverbial Modifier

Unlike the adverb "`bu4`" we discussed in Section 3.2, the ordinary adverbial modifier comes directly before the verb it modifies both in Chinese and Japanese, but not in English. Nevertheless, in accordance with the principle of identifying the head for Chinese, the adverb will be treated as the dependent and it will not be reordered following the verb it modified. As a result, the alignment between adverbs and verbs is non-monotonic. This can be observed in the Chinese sentence "`guojia` (country) **yanli** (severely) `chufa` (penalize) `jiage` (price) `weifa` (violation) `xingwei` (behavior)"[8], and its Japanese translation: "`kuni` (country) `wa` `kakaku` (price) `no ihou` (violation) `koui` (behavior) `wo` **kibisiku** (severely) `syobatu` (penalize)." Both in Chinese and Japanese, the adverbial modifier "`yanli`" and "`kibisiku`" are directly in front of the verb "`chufa`" and "`syobatu`", respectively. However, the verb in Chinese is identified as the head and will be reordered to the end of the sentence without the adverb.

[8]English translation: The country severely penalizes violations of price restrictions.

5.5 POS tagging and Parsing Errors

There were word reordering issues not caused solely by differences in syntactic structures. Here we summarize two that are difficult to remedy during reordering and that are hard to avoid since reordering rules are highly dependent on the tagger and parser.

- POS tagging errors

  In Chinese, for example, the word "`Iran`" was tagged as "`VV`" or "`JJ`" instead of "`NR`". This led to identifying "`Iran`" as a head in accordance with the head definition in Chinese, and it was reordered undesirably.

- Parsing errors

  For example, in the Chinese verb phrase "`touzi` (invest) `20 yi` (200 million) `meiyuan` (dollars)", "`20`" and "`yi`" were identified as dependent of "`touzi`" and "`meiyuan`", respectively, which led to an unsuitable reordering for posterior word alignment.

6 Conclusion and Future Work

In the present work, we have proposed novel Chinese-to-Japanese reordering rules inspired in (Isozaki et al., 2010b) based on linguistic analysis on Chinese HPSG and differences among Chinese and Japanese. Although a simple implementation of HF to reorder Chinese sentences performs well, translation quality was substantially improved further by including linguistic knowledge into the refinement of the reordering rules.

In Section 5, we found more patterns on reordering issues when reordering Chinese sentences to resemble Japanese word order. The extraction of those patterns and their effective implementation may lead to further improvements in translation quality, so we are planning to explore this possibility.

In this work, syntactic information from a deep parser has been used to reorder words better. We believe that using semantic information can further increase the expressive power of reordering rules. With that objective, Chinese Enju can be used since it provides the semantic head of nodes and can interpret sentences by using their semantic dependency.

Acknowledgments

This work was mainly developed during an internship at NTT Communication Science Laboratories. We would like to thank Prof. Yusuke Miyao for his invaluable support on this work.

References

P.F. Brown, S.A. Della Pietra, V.J. Della Pietra, and R.L. Mercer. 1993. The mathematics of machine translation. In *Computational Linguistics*, volume 19, pages 263–311, June.

Chris Callison-Burch, Philipp Koehn, Christof Monz, Kay Peterson, and Omar Zaidan, editors. 2010. *Proceedings of the joint 5th workshop on Statistical Machine Translation and MetricsMATR*. Association for Computational Linguistics, July.

Pi-Chuan Chang, Michel Galley, and Christopher D. Manning. 2008. Optimizing Chinese word segmentation for machine translation performance. In *Proceedings of the 3rd Workshop on SMT*, pages 224–232, Columbus, Ohio. Association for Computational Linguistics.

Stanley F. Chen and Joshua Goodman. 1999. An empirical study of smoothing techniques for language modeling. *Computer Speech and Language*, 4(13):359–393.

Michael Collins, Philipp Koehn, and Ivona Kučerová. 2005. Clause restructuring for statistical machine translation. In *Proceedings of the 43rd Annual Meeting on Association for Computational Linguistics*, ACL '05, pages 531–540, Stroudsburg, PA, USA. Association for Computational Linguistics.

Vivian James Cook and Mark Newson. 1988. *Chomsky's Universal Grammar: An introduction*. Oxford: Basil Blackwell.

Naoki Fukui. 1992. *Theory of Projection in Syntax*. CSLI Publisher and Kuroshio Publisher.

Michel Galley, Mark Hopkins, Kevin Knight, and Daniel Marcu. 2004. Whats in a translation rule? In *Proceedings of HLT-NAACL*.

Qian Gao. 2008. Word order in mandarin: Reading and speaking. In *Proceedings of the 20th North American Conference on Chinese Linguistics (NACCL-20)*, volume 2, pages 611–626.

Dmitriy Genzel. 2010. Automatically learning source-side reordering rules for large scale machine translation. In *Proceedings of the 23rd International Conference on Computational Linguistics*, COLING '10, pages 376–384, Stroudsburg, PA, USA. Association for Computational Linguistics.

Yuqing Guo. 2009. *Treebank-based acquisition of Chinese LFG resources for parsing and generation.* Ph.D. thesis, Dublin City University.

Hideki Isozaki, Tsutomu Hirao, Kevin Duh, Katsuhito Sudoh, and Hajime Tsukada. 2010a. Automatic evaluation of translation quality for distant language pairs. In *Proceedings of Empirical Methods on Natural Language Processing (EMNLP).*

Hideki Isozaki, Katsuhito Sudoh, Hajime Tsukada, and Kevin Duh. 2010b. Head finalization: A simple reordering rule for sov languages. In *Proceedings of WMTMetricsMATR*, pages 244–251.

P. Koehn, F. J. Och, and D. Marcu. 2003. Statistical phrase-based translation. In *Proceedings HLT/NAACL'03*, pages 48–54.

Philipp Koehn et al. 2007. Moses: Open source toolkit for statistical machine translation. In *Proceedings of the ACL Demo and Poster Sessions, 2007*, pages 177–180, June 25–27.

Yusuke Miyao and Jun'ichi Tsujii. 2008. Feature forest models for probabilistic hpsg parsing. *Computational Linguistics*, 34:35–80, March.

F. J. Och and H. Ney. 2003. A systematic comparison of various statistical alignment models. *Computational Linguistics*, 29(1):19–51.

Franz Josef Och and Hermann Ney. 2004. The alignment template approach to statistical machine translation. *Computational Linguistics.*

Franz J. Och. 2003. Minimum error rate training for statistical machine translation. In *Proceedings of the 41st annual conference of the Association for Computational Linguistics, 2003*, pages 160–167, July 7–12.

Kishore Papineni, Salim Roukos, Todd Ward, and Wei-Jing Zhu. 2002. Bleu: A method for automatic evaluation of machine translation. In *Proceedings of the 40th annual conference of the Association for Computational Linguistics, 2002*, pages 311–318, July 6–12.

Matthew Snover, Bonnie Dorr, Richard Schwartz, Linnea Micciulla, and John Makhoul. 2006. A study of translation edit rate with targeted human annotation. In *Proceedings of Association for Machine Translation in the Americas*, pages 223–231.

Andreas Stolcke. 2002. SRILM – an extensible language modeling toolkit. In *Proceedings of the 7th international conference on Spoken Language Processing, 2002*, pages 901–904, September 16–20.

Christoph Tillmann. 2004. A unigram orientation model for statistical machine translation. In *Proceedings of HLT-NAACL 2004: Short Papers*, HLT-NAACL-Short '04, pages 101–104, Stroudsburg, PA, USA. Association for Computational Linguistics.

Kristina Toutanova, Dan Klein, Christopher D. Manning, and Yoram Singer. 2003. Feature-rich part-of-speech tagging with a cyclic dependency network. In *Proceedings OF HLT-NAACL*, pages 252–259.

Chao Wang, Michael Collins, and Philipp Koehn. 2007. Chinese syntactic reordering for statistical machine translation. In *Proceedings of the 2007 Joint Conference on Empirical Methods in Natural Language Processing and Computational Natural Language Learning (EMNLP-CoNLL)*, pages 737–745, Prague, Czech Republic, June. Association for Computational Linguistics.

Xianchao Wu, Katsuhito Sudoh, Kevin Duh, Hajime Tsukada, and Masaaki Nagata. 2011. Extracting pre-ordering rules from predicate-argument structures. In *Proceedings of 5th International Joint Conference on Natural Language Processing*, pages 29–37, Chiang Mai, Thailand, November. Asian Federation of Natural Language Processing.

Fei Xia and Michael McCord. 2004. Improving a statistical mt system with automatically learned rewrite patterns. In *Proceedings of the 20th international conference on Computational Linguistics*, COLING '04, Stroudsburg, PA, USA. Association for Computational Linguistics.

Peng Xu, Jaeho Kang, Michael Ringgaard, and Franz Och. 2009. Using a dependency parser to improve smt for subject-object-verb languages. In *Proceedings of Human Language Technologies: The 2009 Annual Conference of the North American Chapter of the Association for Computational Linguistics*, NAACL '09, pages 245–253, Stroudsburg, PA, USA. Association for Computational Linguistics.

Kun Yu, Yusuke Miyao, Xiangli Wang, Takuya Matsuzaki, and Jun ichi Tsujii. 2010. Semi-automatically developing chinese hpsg grammar from the penn chinese treebank for deep parsing. In *COLING (Posters)'10*, pages 1417–1425.

Kun Yu, Yusuke Miyao, Takuya Matsuzaki, Xiangli Wang, and Junichi Tsujii. 2011. Analysis of the difficulties in chinese deep parsing. In *Proceedings of the 12th International Conference on Parsing Technologies*, pages 48–57.

R. Zens, F.J. Och, and H. Ney. 2002. Phrase-based statistical machine translation. In *Proceedings of KI'02*, pages 18–32.

Hong-Mei Zhao, Ya-Juan Lv, Guo-Sheng Ben, Yun Huang, and Qun Liu. 2011. Evaluation report for the 7th china workshop on machine translation (cwmt2011). *The 7th China Workshop on Machine Translation (CWMT2011).*

Extracting Semantic Transfer Rules from Parallel Corpora with SMT Phrase Aligners

Petter Haugereid and **Francis Bond**
Linguistics and Multilingual Studies
Nanyang Technological University
petterha@ntu.edu.sg bond@ieee.org

Abstract

This paper presents two procedures for extracting transfer rules from parallel corpora for use in a rule-based Japanese-English MT system. First a "shallow" method where the parallel corpus is lemmatized before it is aligned by a phrase aligner, and then a "deep" method where the parallel corpus is parsed by deep parsers before the resulting predicates are aligned by phrase aligners. In both procedures, the phrase tables produced by the phrase aligners are used to extract semantic transfer rules. The procedures were employed on a 10 million word Japanese English parallel corpus and 190,000 semantic transfer rules were extracted.

1 Introduction

Just like syntactic and semantic information finds its way into SMT models and contribute to improved quality of SMT systems, rule-based systems benefit from the inclusion of statistical models, typically in order to rank the output of the components involved. In this paper, we present another way of improving RBMT systems with the help of SMT tools. The basic idea is to learn transfer rules from parallel texts: first creating alignments of predicates with the help of SMT phrase aligners and then extracting semantic transfer rules from these. We discuss two procedures for creating the alignments. In the first procedure the parallel corpus is lemmatized before it is aligned with two SMT phrase aligners. Then the aligned lemmas are mapped to predicates with the help of the lexicons of the parsing grammar and the generating grammar. Finally, the transfer rules are extracted from the aligned predicates. In the second procedure, the parallel corpus is initially parsed by the parsing grammar and the generating grammar. The grammars produce semantic representations, which are represented as strings of predicates. This gives us a parallel corpus of predicates, about a third of the size of the original corpus, which we feed the phrase aligners. The resulting phrase tables with aligned predicates are finally used for extraction of semantic transfer rules.

The two procedures complement each other. The first procedure is more robust and thus learns from more examples although the resulting rules are less reliable. Here we extract 127,000 semantic transfer rules. With the second procedure, which is more accurate but less robust, we extract 113,000 semantic transfer rules. The union of the procedures gives a total of 190,000 unique rules for the Japanese English MT system Jaen.

2 Semantic Transfer

Jaen is a rule-based machine translation system employing semantic transfer rules. The medium for the semantic transfer is Minimal Recursion Semantics, MRS (Copestake et al., 2005). The system consists of the two HPSG grammars: JACY, which is used for the parsing of the Japanese input (Siegel and Bender, 2002) and the ERG, used for the generation of the English output (Flickinger, 2000). The third component of the system is the transfer grammar, which transfers the MRS representation produced by the Japanese grammar into an MRS representation that the English grammar can generate from: Jaen (Bond et al., 2011).

At each step of the translation process, the output

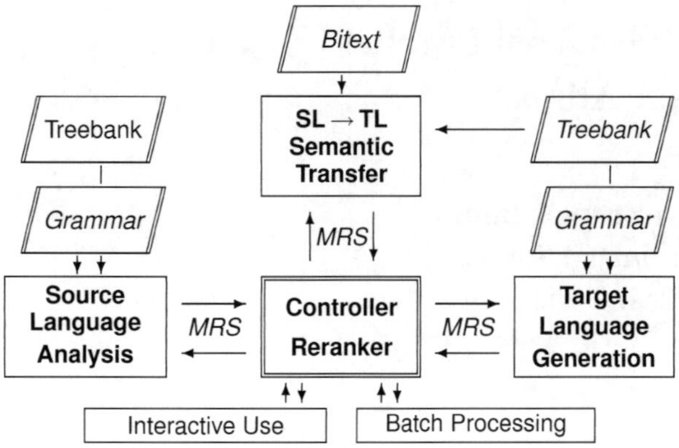

Figure 1: Architecture of the Jaen MT system.

is ranked by stochastic models. In the default configuration, only the 5 top ranked outputs at each step are kept, so the maximum number of translations is 125 (5x5x5). There is also a final reranking using a combined model (Oepen et al., 2007).

The architecture of the MT system is illustrated in Figure 1, where the contribution of the transfer rule extraction from parallel corpora is depicted by the arrow going from Bitext to Semantic Transfer.

Most of the rules in the transfer grammar are simple predicate changing rules, like the rule for mapping the predicate "_hon_n_rel" onto the predicate "_book_v_1_rel". Other rules are more complex, and transfers many Japanese relations into many English relations. In all, there are 61 types of transfer rules, the most frequent being the rules for nouns translated into nouns (44,572), noun noun compounds translated into noun noun compounds (38,197), and noun noun compounds translated into adjective plus noun (27,679). 31 transfer rule types have less than 10 instances. The most common rule types are given in Table 1.[1]

[1]Some of the rule types are extracted by only one extraction method. This holds for the types *n_adj+n_mtr*, *n+n+n_n+n_mtr*, *n+n_n_mtr*, *pp+np_np+pp_mtr*, and *arg1+pp_arg1+pp_mtr*, *adj_pp_mtr*, and *preposition_mtr*. The lemmatized extraction method extracts rules for triple compounds *n+n+n_n+n*. This is currently not done with the semantic extraction method, since a template for a triple compound would include 8 relations (each noun also has a quantifier and there are two compound relations in between), and the number of input relations are currently limited to 5 (but can be increased). The rest of the templates are new, and they have so far only been successfully integrated with the semantic extraction method.

The transfer grammar has a core set of 1,415 hand-written transfer rules, covering function words, proper nouns, pronouns, time expressions, spatial expressions, and the most common open class items. The rest of the transfer rules (190,356 unique rules) are automatically extracted from parallel corpora.

The full system is available from `http://moin.delph-in.net/LogonTop` (different components have different licenses, all are open source, mainly LGPL and MIT).

3 Two methods of rule extraction

The parallel corpus we use for rule extraction is a collection of four Japanese English parallel corpora and one bilingual dictionary. The corpora are the Tanaka Corpus (2,930,132 words: Tanaka, 2001), the Japanese Wordnet Corpus (3,355,984 words: Bond, Isahara, Uchimoto, Kuribayashi, and Kanzaki, 2010), the Japanese Wikipedia corpus (7,949,605 words),[2] and the Kyoto University Text Corpus with NICT translations (1,976,071 words: Uchimoto et al., 2004). The dictionary is Edict (3,822,642 words: Breen, 2004). The word totals include both English and Japanese words.

The corpora were divided into into development, test, and training data. The training data from the four corpora plus the bilingual dictionary was used for rule extraction. The combined corpus used for rule extraction consists of 9.6 million English words and 10.4 million Japanese words (20 million words in total).

3.1 Extraction from a lemmatized parallel corpus

In the first rule extraction procedure we extracted transfer rules directly from the surface lemmas of the parallel text. The four parallel corpora were tokenized and lemmatized, for Japanese with the MeCab morphological analyzer (Kudo et al., 2004), and for English with the Freeling analyzer (Padró et al., 2010), with MWE, quantities, dates and sentence segmentation turned off. (The bilingual dictionary was not tokenized and lemmatized, since the entries in the dictionary are lemmas).

[2]The Japanese-English Bilingual Corpus of Wikipedia's Kyoto Articles: `http://alaginrc.nict.go.jp/WikiCorpus/index_E.html`.

Rule type	Hand	Lemma	Pred	Intersect	Union	Total
noun_mtr	64	32,033	31,575	19,100	44,508	44,572
n+n_n+n_mtr	0	32,724	18,967	13,494	38,197	38,197
n+n_adj+n_mtr	0	22,777	15,406	10,504	27,679	27,679
arg12+np_arg12+np_mtr	0	9,788	1,774	618	10,944	10,944
arg1_v_mtr	22	8,325	1,031	391	8,965	8,987
pp_pp_mtr	2	146	8,584	19	8,711	8,713
adjective_mtr	27	4,914	4,034	2,183	6,765	6,792
arg12_v_mtr	50	4,720	1,846	646	5,920	5,970
n_adj+n_mtr	1	-	4,695	-	4,695	4,696
n+n_n_mtr	0	2,591	3,273	1,831	4,033	4,033
n+n+n_n+n_mtr	0	3,380	-	-	3,376	3,376
n+adj-adj-mtr	2	633	2,586	182	3,037	3,039
n_n+n_mtr	1	-	2,229	-	2,229	2,230
pp-adj_mtr	27	1,008	971	1	1,978	2,005
p+n+arg12_arg12_mtr	1	1,796	101	35	1,862	1,863
pp+np_np+pp_mtr	0	-	1,516	-	1,516	1,516
pp+arg12_arg12_mtr	0	852	62	26	888	888
arg1+pp_arg1+pp_mtr	1	-	296	-	296	297
monotonic_mtr	139	-	-	-	-	139
adj_pp_mtr	0	-	112	-	112	112
preposition_mtr	53	-	34	-	34	87
arg123_v_mtr	3	30	14	8	36	39

Table 1: Most common mtr rule types. The numbers in the Hand column show the number of hand-written rules for each type. The numbers in the Lemma column, show the number of rules extracted from the lemmatized parallel corpus. The numbers in the Pred column show the number of rules extracted from the semantic parallel corpus. The Intersect column, shows the number of intersecting rules of Lemma and Pred, and the Union column show the number of distinct rules of Lemma and Pred.

We then used MOSES (Koehn et al., 2007) and Anymalign (Lardilleux and Lepage, 2009) to align the lemmatized parallel corpus. We got two phrase tables with 10,812,423 and 5,765,262 entries, respectively. MOSES was run with the default settings, and Anymalign ran for approximately 16 hours.

We selected the entries that had (i) a translation probability, P(English|Japanese) of more than 0.1,[3] (ii) an absolute frequency of more than 1,[4] (iii) fewer than 5 lemmas on the Japanese side and fewer than 4 lemmas on the English side,[5] and (iv) lexical entries for all lemmas in Jacy for Japanese and the ERG for English. This gave us 2,183,700 Moses entries and 435,259 Anymalign entries, all phrase table entries with a relatively high probability, containing lexical items known both to the parser and the generator.

The alignments were a mix of one-to-one-or-many and many-to-one-or-many. For each lemma in each alignment, we listed the possible predicates according to the lexicons of the parsing grammar (Jacy) and the generating grammar (ERG). Since many lemmas are ambiguous, we often ended up with many semantic alignments for each surface alignment. If a surface alignment contained 3 lemmas with two readings each, we would get 8 (2x2x2) semantic alignments. However, some of the seman-

[3]This number is set based on a manual inspection of the transfer rules produced. The output for each transfer rule template is inspected, and for some of the templates, in particular the multi-word expression templates, the threshold is set higher.

[4]The absolute frequency number can, according to Adrien Lardilleux (p.c.), be thought of as a confidence score. The larger, the more accurate and reliable the translation probabilities. 1 is the lowest score.

[5]These numbers are based on the maximal number of lemmas needed for the template matching on either side.

tic relations associated with a lemma had very rare readings. In order to filter out semantic alignments with such rare readings, we parsed the training corpus and made a list of 1-grams of the semantic relations in the highest ranked output. Only the relations that could be linked to a lemma with a probability of more than 0.2 were considered in the semantic alignment. The semantic alignments were matched against 16 templates. Six of the templates are simple one-to-one mapping templates:

1.	noun	⇒	noun
2.	adjective	⇒	adjective
3.	adjective	⇒	intransitive verb
4.	intransitive verb	⇒	intransitive verb
5.	transitive verb	⇒	transitive verb
6.	ditransitive verb	⇒	ditransitive verb

The rest of the templates have more than one lemma on the Japanese side and one or more lemmas on the English side. In all, we extracted 126,964 rules with this method. Some of these are relatively simple, such as 7 which takes a noun compound and translates it into a single noun, or 8 which takes a VP and translates it into a VP (without checking for compositionality, if it is a common pattern we will make a rule for it).

7. n+n ⇒ n

(1) 小 テスト-が あっ-た。
minor test had
I had a quiz.

8. arg12+np ⇒ arg12+np_mtr

(2) その 仕事-を 終え-まし-た。
that job finished
I finished the job.

Other examples, such as 9 are more complex, here the rule takes a Japanese noun-adjective combination and translates it to an adjective, with the external argument in Japanese (the so-called second subject) linked to the subject of the English adjective. Even though we are applying the templates to learn rules to lemma n-grams, in the translation system these rules apply to the semantic representation, so they can apply to a wide variety of syntactic variations (we give an example of a relative clause below).

9. n+adj ⇒ adj

(3) 前-の 冬-は 雪-が 多かっ-た。
previous winter snow much-be
Previous winter was snowy.

(4) 雪-の 多い 冬 だっ-た。
snow much winter was
It was a snowy winter.

Given the ambiguity of the lemmas used for the extraction of transfer rules, we were forced to filter semantic relations that have a low probability in order to avoid translations that do not generalize. One consequence of this is that we were not building rules that should have been built in cases where an ambiguous lemma has one dominant reading, and one or more less frequent, but plausible, readings. Another consequence is that we were building rules where the dominant reading is used, but where a less frequent reading is correct. The method is not very precise since it is based on simple 1-gram counts, and we are not considering the context of the individual lemma. A way to improve the quality of the assignment of the relation to the lemma would be to use a tagger or a parser. However, instead of going down that path, we decided to parse the whole parallel training corpus with the parsing grammar and the generation grammar of the MT system and produce a parallel corpus of semantic relations instead of lemmas. In this way, we use the linguistic grammars as high-precision semantic taggers.

3.2 Extraction from a parallel corpus of predicates

The second rule extraction procedure is based on a parallel corpus of semantic representations, rather than lemmatized sentences. We parsed the training corpus (1,578,602 items) with the parsing grammar (Jacy) and the generation grammar (ERG) of the MT system, and got a parse with both grammars for 630,082 items. The grammars employ statistical models trained on treebanks in order to select the most probable analysis. For our semantic corpus, we used the semantic representation of the highest ranked analysis on either side.

The semantic representation produced by the ERG for the sentence *The white dog barks* is given in Figure 2. The relations in the MRSs are represented in the order they appear in the analysis.[6] In the semantic parallel corpus we kept the predicates, e.g. *_the_q_rel*, *_white_a_1_rel*, and so on, but we did not keep the information about linking. For verbs, we attached information about the valency. Verbs that were analyzed as intransitive, like *bark* in Figure 2, were represented with a suffix *1x*, where *1* indicates argument 1 and *x* indicates a referential index: *_bark_v_1_rel@1x*. If a verb was analyzed as being transitive or ditransitive, this would be reflected in the suffix: *_give_v_1_rel@1x2x3x*. The item corresponding to *The white dog barks* in the semantic corpus would be *_the_q_rel _white_a_1_rel _dog_n_1_rel _bark_v_1_rel@1x*.

The resulting parallel corpus of semantic representations consists of 4,712,301 relations for Japanese and 3,806,316 relations for English. This means that the size of the semantic parallel corpus is a little more than a third of the lemmatized parallel corpus. The grammars used for parsing are deep linguistic grammars, and they do not always perform very well on out of domain data, like for example the Japanese Wikipedia corpus. One way to increase the coverage of the grammars would be to include robustness rules. This would decrease the reliability of the assignment of semantic relations, but still be more reliable than simply using 1-grams to assign the relation.

The procedure for extracting semantic transfer rules from the semantic parallel corpus is similar to the procedure for extraction from the lemmatized corpus. The major difference is that the semantic corpus is disambiguated by the grammars.

As with the lemmatized corpus, the semantic parallel corpus was aligned with MOSES and Anymalign. They produced 4,830,000 and 4,095,744 alignments respectively. Alignments with more than 5 relations on either side and with a probability of less than 0.01 were filtered out.[7] This left us with 4,898,366 alignments, which were checked against 22 rule templates.[8] This produced 112,579 rules, which is slightly fewer than the number of rules extracted from the lemmatized corpus (126,964). 49,187 of the rules overlap with the rules extracted from the lemmatized corpus, which gives us a total number of unique rules of 190,356. The distribution of the rules is shown in Table 1.

Some of the more complex transfer rules types like *p+n+arg12_arg12_mtr* and *pp+arg12_arg12_mtr* were extracted in far greater numbers from the lemmatized corpus than from the corpus of semantic representations. This is partially due to the fact that the method involving the lemmatized corpus is more robust, which means that the alignments are done on 3 times as much data as the method involving the corpus of semantic predicates. Another reason is that the number of items that need to be aligned to match these kinds of multi-word templates is larger when the rules are extracted from the corpus of semantic representations. (For example, a noun relation always has a quantifier binding it, even if there is no particular word expressing the quantifier.) Since the number of items to be aligned is bigger, the chance of getting an alignment with a high probability that matches the template becomes smaller.

One of the transfer rule templates (*pp_pp_mtr*) generates many more rules with the method involving the semantic predicates than the method involving lemmas. This is because we restricted the rule to only one preposition pair (*_de_p_rel* ↔ *_by_p_means_rel*) with the lemmatized corpus method, while all preposition pairs are accepted with the semantic predicate method since the confidence in the output of this method is higher.

4 Experiment and Results

In order to compare the methods for rule extraction, we made three versions of the transfer grammar, one including only the rules extracted from the lemma-

[6]Each predicate has the character span of the corresponding word(s) attached.

[7]A manual inspection of the rules produced by the template matching showed that most of the rules produced for several of the templates were good, even with a probability as low as 0.01. For some of the templates, the threshold was set higher.

[8]The reason why the number of rule templates is higher with this extraction method, is that the confidence in the results is higher. This holds in particular for many-to-one rules, were the quality of the rules extracted with from the lemmatized corpus is quite low.

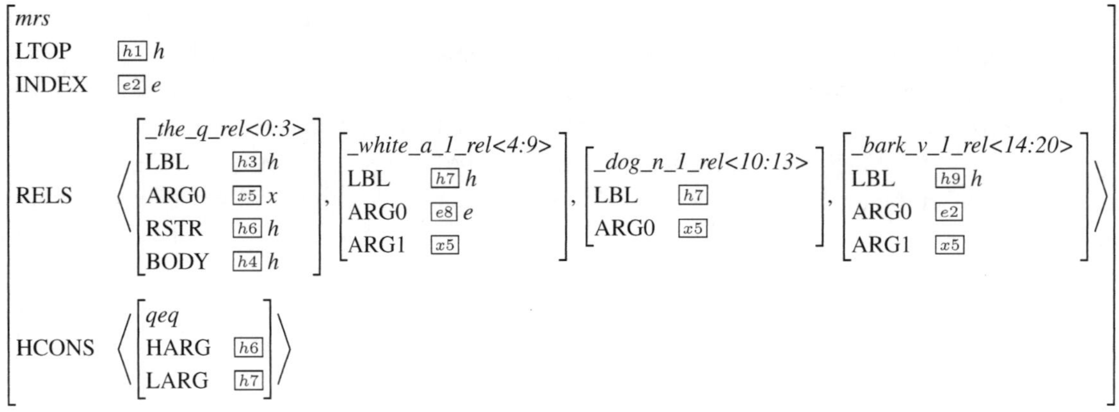

Figure 2: MRS of *The white dog barks*

tized corpus (Lemm), one including only the rules extracted from the corpus of semantic representations (Pred), and one including the union of the two (Combined). In the Combined grammar, the Lemm rules with a probability lower than 0.4 were filtered out if the input relation(s) are already translated by either handwritten rules or Pred rules since the confidence in the Lemm rules is lower.

Since the two methods for rule extraction involve different sets of templates, we also made two versions of the transfer grammar including only the 15 templates used in both Lemm and Pred. These were named LemmCore and PredCore.

The five versions of the transfer grammar were tested on sections 003, 004, and 005 of the Tanaka Corpus (4,500 test sentences), and the results are shown in Table 2. The table shows how the versions of Jaen performs with regard to parsing (constant), transfer, generation, and overall coverage. It also shows the NEVA[9] scores of the highest ranked translated sentences (NEVA), and the highest NEVA score of the 5 highest ranked translations (Oracle). The F1 is calculated based on the overall coverage and the NEVA.

The coverage of Lemm and Pred is the same; 20.8%, but Pred gets a higher NEVA score than Lemm (21.11 vs. 18.65), and the F1 score is one percent higher. When the Lemm and Pred rules are combined in Combined, the coverage is increased by almost 6%. This increase is due to the fact that the Lemm and Pred rule sets are relatively complimentary. Although the use of the Lemm and Pred transfer grammars gives the same coverage (20.8%), only 648 (14.4%) of the test sentences are translated by both systems. The NEVA score of Combined is between that of Lemm and Pred while the F1 score beats both Lemm and Pred.

When comparing the core versions of Lemm and Pred, LemmCore and PredCore, we see the same trend, namely that coverage is about the same and the NEVA score is higher when the Pred rules are used.

644 of the test sentences were translated by all versions of the transfer grammar (Lemm, Pred, and Combined). Table 3 shows how the different versions of Jaen perform on these sentences. The results show that the quality of the transfer rules extracted from the MRS parallel corpus is higher than the quality of the transfer rules based on the lemmatized parallel corpus. It also shows that there is a small decrease of quality when the rules from the lemmatized parallel corpus are added to the rules from the MRS corpus.

Version	NEVA
Lemmatized	20.44
MRS	**23.55**
Lemma + MRS	23.04

Table 3: NEVA scores of intersecting translations

The two best-performing versions of JaEn, Pred and Combined, were compared to MOSES (see Table 4 and Table 5). The BLEU scores were calculated with `multi-bleu.perl`, and the METEOR

[9]NEVA (N-gram EVAluation: Forsbom (2003)) is a modified version of BLEU.

	Parsing	Transfer	Generation	Overall	NEVA	Oracle	F1
LemmCore	3590/4500	1661/3590	930/1661	930/4500	18.65	22.99	19.61
	79.8%	46.3%	56.0%	20.7%			
Lemm	3590/4500	1674/3590	938/1674	938/4500	18.65	22.99	19.69
	79.8%	46.6%	56.0%	20.8%			
PredCore	3590/4500	1748/3590	925/1748	925/4500	20.40	24.81	20.48
	79.8%	48.7%	52.9%	20.6%			
Pred	3590/4500	1782/3589	937/1782	937/4500	**21.11**	**25.75**	20.96
	79.8%	49.7%	52.6%	20.8%			
Combined	3590/4500	2184/3589	1194/2184	1194/4500	19.77	24.00	**22.66**
	79.8%	60.9%	54.7%	**26.5%**			

Table 2: Evaluation of the Tanaka Corpus Test Data

scores were calculated with `meteor-1.3.jar` using default settings.[10] The human score is a direct comparison, an evaluator[11] was given the Japanese source, a reference translation and the output from the two systems, randomly presented as A or B. They then indicated which they preferred, or if the quality was the same (in which case each system gets 0.5). All the translations, including the reference translations, were tokenized and lower-cased. In both comparisons, MOSES gets better BLEU and METEOR scores, while the Jaen translation is preferred by the human evaluator in 58 out of 100 cases.

	BLEU	METEOR	HUMAN
JaEn First	16.77	28.02	**58**
MOSES	**30.19**	**31.98**	42

Table 4: BLEU Comparison of Jaen loaded with the Combined rules, and MOSES (1194 items)

	BLEU	METEOR	HUMAN
JaEn	18.34	29.02	**58**
MOSES	**31.37**	**32.14**	42

Table 5: BLEU Comparison of Jaen loaded with the Pred rules, and MOSES (936 items)

The two systems make different kinds of mistakes. The output of Jaen is mostly grammatical, but it may not always make sense. An example of a nonsense translation from Jaen is given in (5).[12]

(5) S: 我々は魚を生で食べる。
R: We eat fish raw.
M: We eat fish raw.
J: We eat fish in the camcorder.

Jaen sometimes gets the arguments wrong:

(6) S: 彼は大統領に選ばれた。
R: He was elected president.
M: He was elected president.
J: The president chose him.

The output of Moses on the other hand is more likely to lack words in the translation, and it is also more likely to be ungrammatical. A translation with a missing word is shown in (7).

(7) S: カーテンがゆっくり引かれた。
R: The curtains were drawn slowly.
M: The curtain was slowly.
J: The curtain was drawn slowly.

Missing words become extra problematic when a negation is not transferred:

(8) S: 偏見は持つべきではない。
R: We shouldn't have any prejudice.
M: You should have a bias.
J: I shouldn't have prejudice.

Sometimes the Moses output is lacking so many words that it is impossible to follow the meaning:

[10] The METEOR evaluation metric differs from BLEU in that it does not only give a score for exact match, but it also gives partial scores for stem, synonym, and paraphrase matches.

[11] A Japanese lecturer at NTU, trilingual in English, Japanese and Korean, not involved in the development of this system, but with experience in Japanese/Korean MT research.

[12] The examples below are taken from the development data of the Tanaka Corpus. 'S' stands for 'Source', 'R' stands for 'Reference translation', 'M' stands for 'Moses translation,' and 'J' stands for 'Jaen translation.'

(9) S: 脳が私達の活動を支配している。
R: Our brains control our activities.
M: The brain to us.
J: The brain is controlling our activities.

Also the output of Moses is more likely to be ungrammatical, as illustrated in (10) and (11).

(10) S: 私は日本を深く愛している。
R: I have a deep love for Japan.
M: I is devoted to Japan.
J: I am deeply loving Japan.

(11) S: 彼女はタオルを固く絞った。
R: She wrung the towel dry.
M: She squeezed pressed the towel.
J: She wrung the towel hard.

5 Discussion

In order to get a system with full coverage, Jaen could be used with Moses as a fallback. This would combine the precision of the rule-based system with the robustness of Moses. The coverage and the quality of Jaen itself can be extended by using more training data. Our experience is that this holds even if the training data is from a different domain. By adding training data, we are incrementally adding rules to the system. We still build the rules we built before, plus some more rules extracted from the new data. Learning rules that are not applicable for the translation task does not harm or slow down the system. Jaen has a rule pre-selection program which, before each translation task selects the applicable rules. When the system does a batch translation of 1,500 sentences, the program selects about 15,000 of the 190,000 automatically extracted rules, and only these will be loaded. Rules that have been learned but are not applicable are not used.[13]

We can also extend the system by adding more transfer templates. So far, we are using 23 templates, and by adding new templates for multi-word expressions, we can increase the precision.

The predicate alignments produced from the parallel corpus of predicates are relatively precise since the predicates are assigned by the grammars. This allows us to extract transfer rules from alignments that are given a low probability (down to 0.01) by the aligner.

We would also like to get more from the data we have, by making the parser more robust. Two approaches that have been shown to work with other grammars is making more use of morphological information (Adolphs et al., 2008) or adding robustness rules (Cramer and Zhang, 2010).

6 Conclusion

We have shown how semantic transfer rules can be learned from parallel corpora that have been aligned in SMT phrase tables. We employed two strategies. The first strategy was to lemmatize the parallel corpus and use SMT aligners to create phrase tables of lemmas. We then looked up the relations associated with the lemmas using the lexicons of the parser and generator. This gave us a phrase table of aligned relations. We were able to extract 127,000 rules by matching the aligned relations with 16 semantic transfer rule templates.

The second strategy was to parse the parallel corpus with the parsing grammar and the generating grammar of the MT system. This gave us a parallel corpus of predicates, which, because of lack of coverage of the grammars, was about a third the size of the full corpus. The parallel corpus of predicates was aligned with SMT aligners, and we got a second phrase table of aligned relations. We extracted 113,000 rules by matching the alignments against 22 rule templates. These transfer rules produced the same number of translation as the rules produced with the first strategy (20.8%), but they proved to be more precise.

The two rule extraction methods complement each other. About 30% of the sentences translated with one rule set are not translated by the other. By merging the two rule sets into one, we increased the coverage of the system to 26.6%. A human evaluator preferred Jaen's translation to that of Moses for 58 out of a random sample of 100 translations.

References

Peter Adolphs, Stephan Oepen, Ulrich Callmeier, Berthold Crysmann, Dan Flickinger, and Bernd Kiefer. 2008. Some fine points of hybrid natural language parsing. In European Language Re-

[13]The pre-selection program speeds up the system by a factor of three.

sources Association (ELRA), editor, *Proceedings of the Sixth International Language Resources and Evaluation (LREC'08)*, pages 1380–1387. Marrakech, Morocco.

Francis Bond, Hitoshi Isahara, Kiyotaka Uchimoto, Takayuki Kuribayashi, and Kyoko Kanzaki. 2010. Japanese WordNet 1.0. In *16th Annual Meeting of the Association for Natural Language Processing*, pages A5–3. Tokyo.

Francis Bond, Stephan Oepen, Eric Nichols, Dan Flickinger, Erik Velldal, and Petter Haugereid. 2011. Deep open source machine translation. *Machine Translation*, 25(2):87–105. URL `http://dx.doi.org/10.1007/s10590-011-9099-4`, (Special Issue on Open source Machine Translation).

James W. Breen. 2004. JMDict: a Japanese-multilingual dictionary. In *Coling 2004 Workshop on Multilingual Linguistic Resources*, pages 71–78. Geneva.

Ann Copestake, Dan Flickinger, Carl Pollard, and Ivan A. Sag. 2005. Minimal Recursion Semantics. An introduction. *Research on Language and Computation*, 3(4):281–332.

Bart Cramer and Yi Zhang. 2010. Constraining robust constructions for broad-coverage parsing with precision grammars. In *Proceedings of COLING-2010*, pages 223–231. Beijing.

Dan Flickinger. 2000. On building a more efficient grammar by exploiting types. *Natural Language Engineering*, 6(1):15–28. (Special Issue on Efficient Processing with HPSG).

Eva Forsbom. 2003. Training a super model look-alike: Featuring edit distance, n-gram occurrence, and one reference translation. In *In Proceedings of the Workshop on Machine Translation Evaluation. Towards Systemizing MT Evaluation*.

Philipp Koehn, Wade Shen, Marcello Federico, Nicola Bertoldi, Chris Callison-Burch, Brooke Cowan, Chris Dyer, Hieu Hoang, Ondrej Bojar, Richard Zens, Alexandra Constantin, Evan Herbst, Christine Moran, and Alexandra Birch. 2007. Moses: Open source toolkit for statistical machine translation. In *Proceedings of the ACL 2007 Interactive Presentation Sessions*. Prague. URL `http://www.statmt.org/moses/`.

Taku Kudo, Kaoru Yamamoto, and Yuji Matsumoto. 2004. Applying Conditional Random Fields to Japanese Morphological Analysis. In Dekang Lin and Dekai Wu, editors, *Proceedings of EMNLP 2004*, pages 230–237. Association for Computational Linguistics, Barcelona, Spain.

Adrien Lardilleux and Yves Lepage. 2009. Sampling-based multilingual alignment. In *Proceedings of Recent Advances in Natural Language Processing (RANLP 2009)*, pages 214–218. Borovets, Bulgaria.

Stephan Oepen, Erik Velldal, Jan Tore Lønning, Paul Meurer, and Victoria Rosen. 2007. Towards hybrid quality-oriented machine translation. on linguistics and probabilities in MT. In *11th International Conference on Theoretical and Methodological Issues in Machine Translation: TMI-2007*, pages 144–153.

Lluís Padró, Miquel Collado, Samuel Reese, Marina Lloberes, and Irene Castellón. 2010. Freeling 2.1: Five years of open-source language processing tools. In *Proceedings of 7th Language Resources and Evaluation Conference (LREC 2010)*. La Valletta. (`http://nlp.lsi.upc.edu/freeling`.

Melanie Siegel and Emily M. Bender. 2002. Efficient deep processing of Japanese. In *Proceedings of the 3rd Workshop on Asian Language Resources and International Standardization at the 19th International Conference on Computational Linguistics*, pages 1–8. Taipei.

Yasuhito Tanaka. 2001. Compilation of a multilingual parallel corpus. In *Proceedings of PACLING 2001*, pages 265–268. Kyushu. (`http://www.colips.org/afnlp/archives/pacling2001/pdf/tanaka.pdf`).

Kiyotaka Uchimoto, Yujie Zhang, Kiyoshi Sudo, Masaki Murata, Satoshi Sekine, and Hitoshi Isahara. 2004. Multilingual aligned parallel treebank corpus reflecting contextual information and its applications. In Gilles Sérasset, editor, *COLING 2004 Multilingual Linguistic Resources*, pages 57–64. COLING, Geneva, Switzerland. URL `http://acl.ldc.upenn.edu/W/W04/W04-2208.bib`.

Towards Probabilistic Acceptors and Transducers for Feature Structures

Daniel Quernheim
Institute for Natural Language Processing
Universität Stuttgart, Germany
Pfaffenwaldring 5b, 70569 Stuttgart
daniel@ims.uni-stuttgart.de

Kevin Knight
University of Southern California
Information Sciences Institute
Marina del Rey, California 90292
knight@isi.edu

Abstract

Weighted finite-state acceptors and transducers (Pereira and Riley, 1997) are a critical technology for NLP and speech systems. They flexibly capture many kinds of stateful left-to-right substitution, simple transducers can be composed into more complex ones, and they are EM- trainable. They are unable to handle long-range syntactic movement, but tree acceptors and transducers address this weakness (Knight and Graehl, 2005). Tree automata have been profitably used in syntax-based MT systems. Still, strings and trees are both weak at representing linguistic structure involving semantics and reference ("who did what to whom"). Feature structures provide an attractive, well-studied, standard format (Shieber, 1986; Rounds and Kasper, 1986), which we can view computationally as directed acyclic graphs. In this paper, we develop probabilistic acceptors and transducers for feature structures, demonstrate them on linguistic problems, and lay down a foundation for semantics-based MT.

1 Introduction

Weighted finite-state acceptors and transducers (Pereira and Riley, 1997) provide a clean and practical knowledge representation for string-based speech and language problems. Complex problems can be broken down into cascades of simple transducers, and generic algorithms (best path, composition, EM, etc) can be re-used across problems.

String automata only have limited memory and cannot handle complex transformations needed in machine translation (MT). Weighted *tree* acceptors and transducers (Gécseg and Steinby, 1984; Knight and Graehl, 2005) have proven valuable in these scenarios. For example, systems that transduce source strings into target syntactic trees performed well in recent MT evaluations (NIST, 2009).

To build the next generation of language systems, we would like to represent and transform deeper linguistic structures, e.g., ones that explicitly capture semantic "who does what to whom" relationships, with syntactic sugar stripped away. *Feature structures* are a well-studied formalism for capturing natural language semantics; Shieber (1986) and Knight (1989) provide overviews. A feature structure is defined as a collection of unordered features, each of which has a value. The value may be an atomic symbol, or it may itself be another feature structure. Furthermore, structures may be re-entrant, which means that two feature paths may point to the same value.

Figure 1 shows a feature structure that captures the meaning of a sample sentence. This semantic structure provides much more information than a typical parse, including semantic roles on both nouns and verbs. Note how "Pascale" plays four different semantic roles, even though it appears only once overtly in the string. The feature structure also makes clear which roles are unfilled (such as the agent of the charging), by omitting them. For computational purposes, feature structures are often represented as rooted, directed acyclic *graphs* with edge and leaf labels.

While feature structures are widely used in hand-built grammars, there has been no compelling proposal for weighted acceptors and transducers for

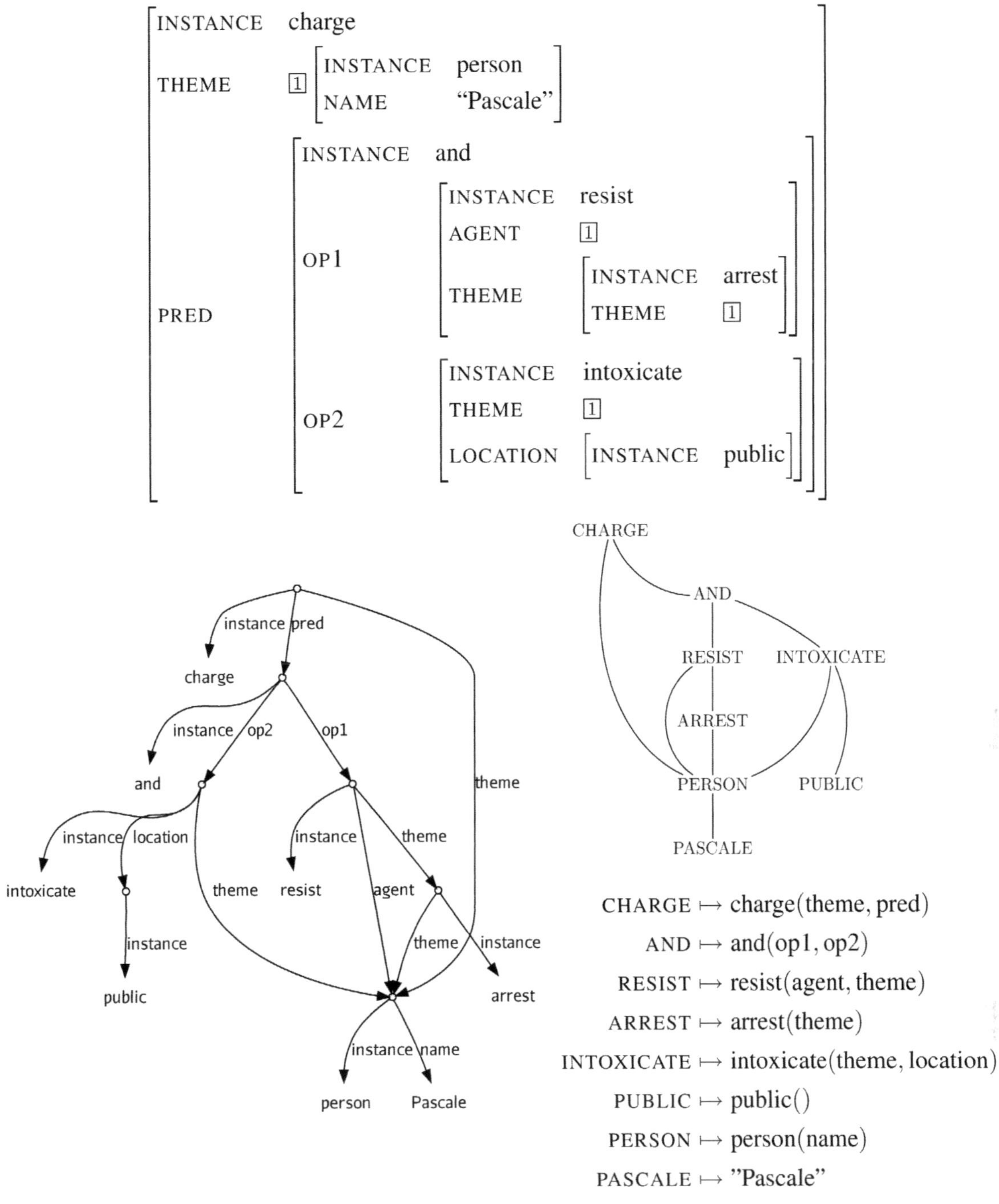

Figure 1: A feature structure representing the semantics of "Pascale was charged with resisting arrest and public intoxication," the corresponding dag, and the simplified dag with argument mapping. Dag edges always point downward.

$$\underset{\text{FSA}}{\text{fstring}} \longrightarrow \overset{\text{nl-XTOPs}^{-1}}{\boxed{\text{translate}}} \longrightarrow \underset{\text{RTG}}{\text{etree}} \longrightarrow \overset{\text{FSA}}{\boxed{\text{rank}}} \longrightarrow \underset{\text{FSA}}{\text{estring}}$$

$$\text{fstring} \longrightarrow \boxed{\text{parse + understand}} \longrightarrow \text{esem} \longrightarrow \boxed{\text{rank}} \longrightarrow \text{esem} \longrightarrow \boxed{\text{generate}} \longrightarrow \text{etree} \longrightarrow \boxed{\text{rank}} \longrightarrow \text{estring}$$

Figure 2: Pipelines for syntax-based and for semantics-based MT. Devices: FSA = finite string automaton; ln-XTOPs = linear non-deleting extended top-down tree-to-string transducer; RTG = regular tree grammar.

	string automata	tree automata	graph automata
k-best	...paths through a WFSA (Viterbi, 1967; Eppstein, 1998)	...trees in a weighted forest (Jiménez and Marzal, 2000; Huang and Chiang, 2005)	?
EM training	Forward-backward EM (Baum et al., 1970; Eisner, 2003)	Tree transducer EM training (Graehl et al., 2008)	?
Determinization	...of weighted string acceptors (Mohri, 1997)	...of weighted tree acceptors (Borchardt and Vogler, 2003; May and Knight, 2006a)	?
Transducer composition	WFST composition (Pereira and Riley, 1997)	Many transducers not closed under composition (Maletti et al., 2009)	?
General tools	AT&T FSM (Mohri et al., 2000), Carmel (Graehl, 1997), OpenFST (Riley et al., 2009)	Tiburon (May and Knight, 2006b)	?

Table 1: General-purpose algorithms for strings, trees and feature structures.

them. Such automata would be of great use. For example, a weighted graph acceptor could form the basis of a semantic language model, and a weighted graph-to-tree transducer could form the basis of a natural language understanding (NLU) or generation (NLG) system, depending on which direction it is employed. Putting NLU and NLG together, we can also envision semantics-based MT systems (Figure 2). A similar approach has been taken by Graham et al. (2009) who incorporate LFG f-structures, which are deep syntax feature structures, into their (automatically acquired) transfer rules. Feature structure graph acceptors and transducers could themselves be learned from semantically-annotated data, and their weights trained by EM.

However, there is some distance to be traveled. Table 1 gives a snapshot of some efficient, generic algorithms for string automata (mainly developed in the last century), plus algorithms for tree automata (mainly developed in the last ten years). These algorithms have been packaged in general-purpose software toolkits like AT&T FSM (Mohri et al., 2000), OpenFST (Riley et al., 2009), and Tiburon (May and Knight, 2006b). A research program for graphs should hold similar value.

Formal graph manipulation has, fortunately, received prior attention. A unification grammar can specify semantic mappings for strings (Moore, 1989), effectively capturing an infinite set of string/graph pairs. But unification grammars seem too powerful to admit the efficient algorithms we desire in Table 1, and weighted versions are not popular. Hyperedge replacement grammars (Drewes et al., 1997; Courcelle and Engelfriet, 1995) are another natural candidate for graph acceptors, and a synchronous hyperedge replacement grammar might serve as a graph transducer. Finally, Kamimura and Slutzki (1981, 1982) propose graph acceptor and graph-to-tree transducer formalisms for rooted directed acyclic graphs. Their model has been extended to multi-rooted dags (Bossut et al., 1988; Bossut and Warin, 1992; Bossut et al., 1995) and arbitrary hypergraphs (Bozapalidis and Kalampakas, 2006; Bozapalidis and Kalampakas, 2008); however, these extensions seem too powerful for NLP. Hence, we use the model of Kamimura and Slutzki (1981, 1982) as a starting point for our definition, then we give a natural language example, followed by an initial set of generic algorithms for graph automata.

2 Preliminaries

In this section, we will define directed acyclic graphs which are our model for semantic structures.

Let us just define some basic notions: We will write $\mathbb{R}$ for the real numbers. An alphabet is just a finite set of symbols.

Intuitively, a rooted ordered directed acyclic graph, or *dag* for short, can be seen as a tree that allows sharing of subtrees. However, it is not necessarily a *maximally* shared tree that has no isomorphic subtrees (consider the examples in Figure 3).

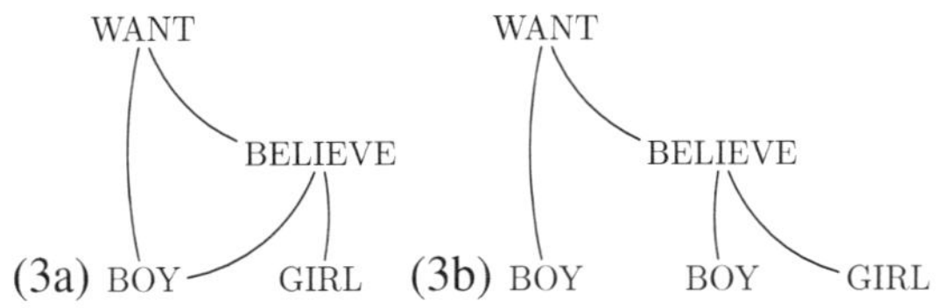

Figure 3: Maximally shared tree (a) and not maximally shared tree (b; note the two BOY nodes) can be distinct dags. The dag in (a) means "The boy wants to believe the girl," while the dag in (b) means "The boy wants some other boy to believe the girl."

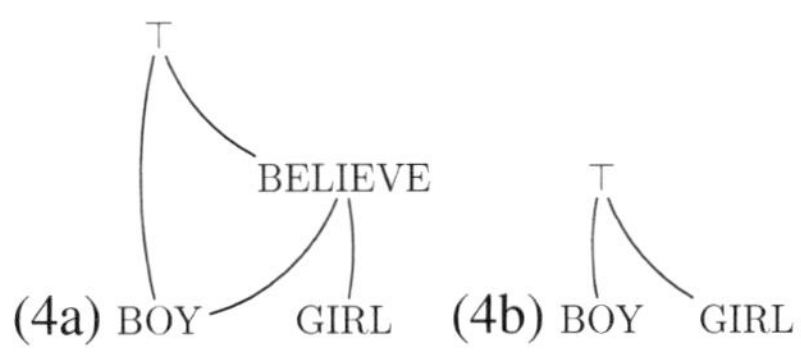

Figure 4: Subdag of dag (3a) and subdag of dag (3b) in Figure 3.

More formally, we define a directed graph over an alphabet Σ as a triple $G = (V, E, \ell)$ of a finite set of nodes V, a finite set of edges $E \subset V \times V$ connecting two nodes each and a labeling function $\ell : V \rightarrow \Sigma$. We say that (v, w) is an outgoing edge of v and an incoming edge of w, and we say that w is a child of v and v is a parent of w. A directed graph is a dag if it is

- acyclic: V is totally ordered such that there is no $(v, w) \in E$ with $v > w$;
- ordered: for each V, there is a total order both on the incoming edges and the outgoing edges;
- and rooted: $\min(V)$ is transitively connected by to all other nodes.

This is a simplified account of the dags presented in Section 1. Instead of edge-labels, we will assume that this information is encoded explicitely in the node-labels for the INSTANCE feature and implicitly in the node-labels and the order of the outgoing edges for the remaining features. Figure 1 shows a feature structure and its corresponding dag. Nodes with differently-labeled outgoing edges can thus be differentiated. Since the number of ingoing edges is not fixed, a node can have arbitrary many parents. For instance, the PERSON node in Figure 1 has four parents. We call the number of incoming edges of a given node its *head rank*, and the number of outgoing edges its *tail rank*.

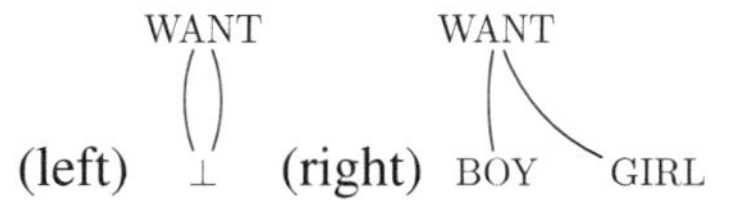

Figure 5: (left) Remainder of (3a) after removing (4a). (right) Dag resulting from replacing (4a) by (4b) in (3a).

We also need incomplete dags in order to compose larger dags from smaller ones. An incomplete dag is a dag in which some edges does not necessarily have to be connected to two nodes; they can be "dangling" from one node. We represent this by adding special nodes $\top$ and $\bot$ to the dag. If an incomplete dag has m edges $(\top, v)$ and n edges $(v, \bot)$, we call it an (m, n)-dag. An (m, n)-dag G can be composed with an (n, o)-dag G' by identifying the n downward-dangling edges of G with the n upward-dangling edges of G' in the right order; the result $G \circ G'$ is a (m, o)-dag. Furthermore, two dags H and H' of type (m, n) and (m', n') can be composed horizontally by putting their upward-dangling edges next to each other and their downward-dangling edges next to each other, resulting in a new $(m + m', n + n')$ dag $H \oplus H'$. If $G_1, \ldots, G_\ell$ can be composed (vertically and horizontally) in such a way that we obtain G, then G_i are called *subdags* of G.

An (m, n)-subdag H of a dag G can be replaced by an (m, n)-subdag H', resulting in the dag G', written $G[H \rightarrow H'] = G'$. An example is depicted in Figure 5, showing how a dag is split into two subdags, of which one is replaced by another incomplete dag. Our account of dag replacement is a simplified version of general hypergraph replacement that has been formulated by Engelfriet and Vereijken (1997) and axiomatized by Bozapalidis and Kalampakas (2004).

Trees are dags where every node has at most one incoming edge. Tree substitution is then just a special case of dag composition. We will write the set of dags over an alphabet Σ as D_Σ and the set of trees over Σ as T_Σ, and $T_\Sigma(V)$ is the set of trees with leaves labeled with variables from the set V.

3 Dag acceptors and transducers

The purpose of dag acceptors and dag transducers is to compactly represent (i) a possibly-infinite set of dags, (ii) a possibly-infinite set of (dag, tree) pairs, and (iii) a possibly-infinite set of (graph, tree, weight) triples.

Dag acceptors and dag transducers are a generalization of tree acceptors and transducers (Comon et al., 2007). Our model is a variant of the dag acceptors defined by Kamimura and Slutzki (1981) and the dag-to-tree transducers by Kamimura and Slutzki (1982). The original definition imposed stricter constraints on the class of dags. Their devices operated on graphs called *derivation dags* (short: d-dags) which are always planar. In particular, the authors required all the parents and children of a given node to be adjacent, which was due to the fact that they were interested in derivation graphs of unrestricted phrase-structure grammar. (While the derivation structures of context-free grammar are trees, the derivation structures of type-0 grammars are d-dags.) We dropped this constraint since it would render the class of dags unsuitable for linguistic purposes. Also, we do not require planarity.

Kamimura and Slutzki (1981, 1982) defined three devices: (i) the bottom-up dag acceptor, (ii) the top-down dag acceptor (both accepting d-dags) and (iii) the bottom-up dag-to-tree transducer (transforming d-dags into trees). We demonstrate the application of a slightly extended version of (ii) to unrestricted dags (semantic dags) and describe a top-down dag-to-tree transducer model, which they did not investigate. Furthermore, we add weights to the models.

A (weighted) *finite dag acceptor* is a structure $M = (Q, q_0, \Sigma, R, w)$ where Q is a finite set of states and q_0 the start state, Σ is an alphabet of node labels, and R is a set of rules of the form $r : \alpha \rightarrow \beta$, where r is the (unique) rule identifier and (i) $\alpha \in Q^m(\sigma)$ and $\beta \in r(Q^n)$ for $m, n \in \mathbb{N}$ and some $\sigma \in \Sigma$ (an explicit rule of type (m, n)) or (ii) $\alpha \in Q^m$ and $\beta \in r(Q)$ (an implicit rule of type $(m, 1)$). The function $w : R \rightarrow \mathbb{R}$ assigns a weight to each rule.

Intuitively, explicit rules consume input, while implicit rules are used for state changes and joining edges only. The devices introduced by Kamimura and Slutzki (1981) only had explicit rules.

We define the derivation relation of M by rewriting of configurations. A *configuration* of M is a dag over $\Sigma \cup R \cup Q$ with the restriction that every state-labeled node has head and tail rank 1. Let c be a configuration of M and $r : \alpha \rightarrow \beta$ an explicit rule of type (m, n). Then $c \Longrightarrow_r c'$ if α matches a subdag of c, and $c' = c[\alpha \rightarrow \beta]$.

$$(q)\text{WANT} \rightarrow 1(r, q)\ \langle 0.3 \rangle \quad (1)$$
$$(q)\text{BELIEVE} \rightarrow 2(r, q)\ \langle 0.2 \rangle \quad (2)$$
$$(r)\text{BOY} \rightarrow 3\ \langle 0.3 \rangle \quad (3)$$
$$(r)\text{GIRL} \rightarrow 4\ \langle 0.3 \rangle \quad (4)$$
$$(r)\emptyset \rightarrow 5\ \langle 0.1 \rangle \quad (5)$$
$$(q)\emptyset \rightarrow 6\ \langle 0.1 \rangle \quad (6)$$
$$(q) \rightarrow 7(r)\ \langle 0.4 \rangle \quad (7)$$

Figure 7: Ruleset of the dag acceptor in Example 1.

Now let c be a configuration of M and $r : \alpha \rightarrow \beta$ an implicit rule of type $(m, 1)$. If a configuration c' can be obtained by replacing m nodes labeled α such that all tails lead to the same node and are in the right order, by the single state-node β, then we say $c \Longrightarrow_r c'$. Example derivation steps are shown in Figure 6 (see Example 1). We denote the transitive and reflexive closure of $\Longrightarrow$ by $\Longrightarrow^*$.

A dag G is accepted by M if there is a derivation $q_0(G) \Longrightarrow^* G'$, where G' is a dag over $\sigma(R)$. Note that the derivation steps of a given derivation are partially ordered; many derivations can share the same partial order. In order to avoid spurious derivations, recall that the nodes of G are ordered, and assume that nodes are rewritten according to this order: the resulting derivation is called a *canonical derivation*. The set of all canonical derivations for a given graph G is $D(G)$. The set of all dags accepted by M is the dag language $L(M)$. The weight $w(d)$ of a derivation dag (represented by its canonical derivation) $d = G \Longrightarrow_{r_1} G_1 \Longrightarrow_{r_2} \ldots \Longrightarrow_{r_n} G_n$ is $\prod_{i=1}^{n} w(r_n)$, and the weight of a dag G is $\sum_{d \in D(G)} w(d)$. The weighted language $L(N)$ is a function that maps every dag to its weight in N.

Example 1. *Let*

$$\Sigma = \{\text{GIRL}, \text{BOY}, \text{BELIEVE}, \text{WANT}, \emptyset\}$$

and consider the top-down dag acceptor $M = (\{q, r\}, q, \Sigma, R, w)$ *which has a ruleset containing the explicit and implicit* $(1, 1)$ *rules given in Figure 7. The weights defined by* w *have been written directly after the rules in angle brackets. This ac-*

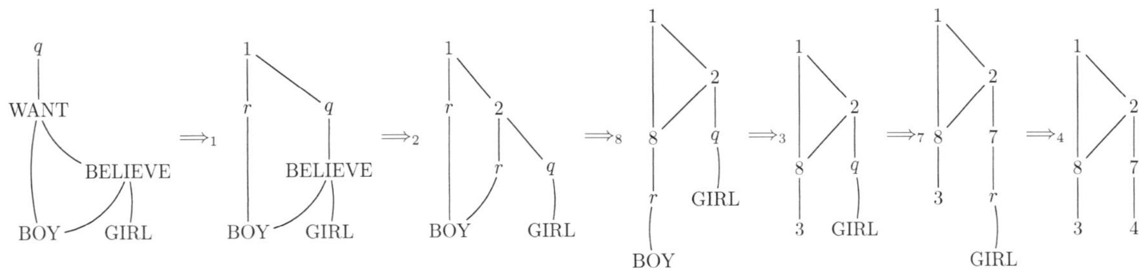

Figure 6: Derivation of a dag using the dag acceptor of Example 1. The weight of the derivation is $w(1) \cdot w(2) \cdot w(8) \cdot w(3) \cdot w(7) \cdot w(4) = 0.3 \cdot 0.2 \cdot 0.2 \cdot 0.3 \cdot 0.4 \cdot 0.3 = 0.000432$.

ceptor can accept dags that involve boys and girls believing and wanting. One of them is given in Figure 3b. To obtain dags that are not trees, let us add the following implicit $(2, 1)$ *and* $(3, 1)$ *rules:*

$$(r, r) \rightarrow 8(r) \langle 0.2 \rangle \tag{8}$$

$$(r, r, r) \rightarrow 9(r) \langle 0.1 \rangle \tag{9}$$

A non-treelike dag is given in Figure 3a, while its derivation is given in Figure 6. Note that the effect of rule (8) could be simulated by rule (9).

Let us now define dag-to-tree transducers. Contrarily to Kamimura and Slutzki (1982), who defined only the bottom-up case and were skeptical of an elegant top-down formulation, we only consider top-down devices.

A (weighted) *top-down dag-to-tree transducer* is a machine $T = (Q, q_0, \Sigma, \Delta, R, w)$ which is defined in the same way as a finite dag acceptor, except for the additional output alphabet Δ and the rules' right-hand side. A dag-to-tree transducer explicit rule has the form $r : \alpha \rightarrow \beta$ where $\alpha \in Q^m(\Sigma)$ and $\beta \in (T_\Delta(Q(X_n)))^m$ for $m, n \in \mathbb{N}$. Intuitively, this means that the left-hand side still consists of a symbol and m "incoming states", while the right-hand side now are m trees over Δ with states and n variables used to process the n child subdags. Implicit $(m, 1)$ rules are defined in the same way, having m output trees over one variable. The dag-to-tree transducer T defines a relation $L(T) \subseteq D_\Sigma \times T_\Delta \times \mathbb{R}$.

A derivation step of T is defined analogously to the acceptor case by replacement of α by β. However, copying rules (those that use a variable more than once in a right-hand side) and deleting rules (those that do not use a rule at all) are problematic in the dag case. In the tree world, every tree can be broken up into a root symbol and independent subtrees. This is not true in the dag world, where there is sharing between subdags. Therefore, if an edge reaching a given symbol σ is not followed at all (deleting rule), the transducer is going to choke if not every edge entering σ is ignored. In the case of copying rules, the part of the input dag that has not yet been processed must be copied, and the configuration is split into two sub-configurations which must both be derived in parallel. We will therefore restrict ourselves to linear (non-copying) non-deleting rules in this paper.

4 NLP example

Recall the example dag acceptor from Example 1. This acceptor generates an sentences about boys and girls wanting and believing. Figure 3 shows some sample graphs from this language.

Next, we build a transducer that relates these graphs to corresponding English. This is quite challenging, as BOY may be referred to in many ways ("the boy", "he", "him", "himself", "his", or zero), and of course, there are many syntactic devices for representing semantic role clusters. Because of ambiguity, the mapping between graphs and English is many-to-many. Figure 8 is a fragment of our transducer, and Figure 9 shows a sample derivation.

Passives are useful for realizing graphs with empty roles ("the girl is wanted" or "the girl wants to be believed"). Note that we can remove syntactic 0 (zero) elements with a standard tree-to-tree transducer, should we desire.

$$(q_s)\text{WANT}(x, y) \rightarrow \text{S}(q_{nomg}(x), \text{is wanted}, q_{zero}(y))$$

$$(q_{infg})\text{BELIEVE}(x, y) \rightarrow \text{INF}(q_{zero}(y), \text{ to be believed}, q_{zerog}(y))$$

$$(q_{zero})\emptyset \rightarrow 0$$

$$(q_s)\text{WANT}(x,y) \rightarrow \text{S}(q_{nomb}(x), \text{wants}, q_{infb}(y)) \quad (10)$$
$$(q_{infb})\text{BELIEVE}(x,y) \rightarrow \text{INF}(q_{accg}(x), \text{to believe}, q_{accb}(y)) \quad (11)$$
$$(q_{accg})\text{GIRL} \rightarrow \text{NP(the girl)} \quad (12)$$
$$(q_{nomb}, q_{accb})\text{BOY} \rightarrow \text{NP(the boy), NP(him)} \quad (13)$$

Figure 8: Transducer rules mapping semantic graphs to syntactic trees.

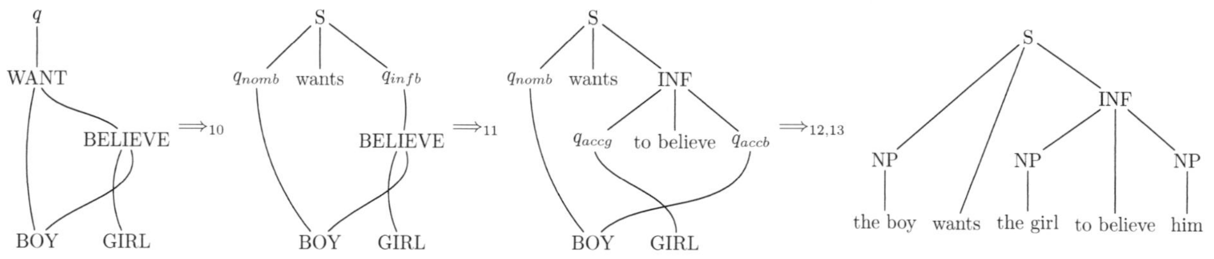

Figure 9: Derivation from graph to tree "the boy wants the girl to believe him".

Events can be realized with nouns as well as verbs ("his desire for her, to believe, him"):

$$(q_{np})\text{WANT}(x,y) \rightarrow \text{NP}(q_{possb}(x), \text{'s desire}, q_{infb}(y))$$

We note that transducer rules can be applied in either direction, semantics-to-English or English-to-semantics. Though this microworld is small, it certainly presents interesting challenges for any graph transduction framework. For example, given "the boy's desire is to be believed by the girl," the transducer's graph must make BOY the theme of BELIEVE.

5 Generic dag acceptor and transducer algorithms

In this section we give algorithms for standard tasks.

5.1 Membership checking

Membership checking is the task of determining, for a given finite dag acceptor M and an input dag G, whether $G \in L(M)$, or in the weighted case, compute the weight of G. Recall that the set of nodes of G is ordered. We can therefore walk through G according to this order and process each node on its own. A very simple algorithm can be given in the framework of "parsing as deduction" (Shieber et al., 1995):

Items: configurations, i.e. dags over $\Sigma \cup Q \cup R$

Axiom: G, a dag over Σ

Goal: dag over R

Inference rule: if an item has only ancestors from Q, apply a matching rule from R to obtain a new item

This algorithm is correct and complete and can be implemented in time $O(2^{|G|})$ since there are exponentially many configurations. Moreover, the set of derivation dags is the result of this parser, and a finite dag acceptor representing the derivation dags can be constructed on the fly. It can be easily extended to check membership of (dag, tree) pairs in a dag-to-tree transducer and to generate all the trees that are obtained from a given dag ("forward application"). In order to compute weights, the techniques by Goodman (1999) can be used.

5.2 1-best and k-best generation

The k-best algorithm finds the highest-weighted k derivations (not dags) in a given (weighted) dag acceptor. If no weights are available, other measures can be used (e.g. the number of derivation steps or symbol frequencies). We can implement the k-best algorithm (of which 1-best is a special case) by generating graphs and putting incomplete graphs on a priority queue sorted by weight. If rule weights are probabilities between 0 and 1, monotonicity ensures that the k-best graphs are found, as the weights of incomplete hypotheses never increase.

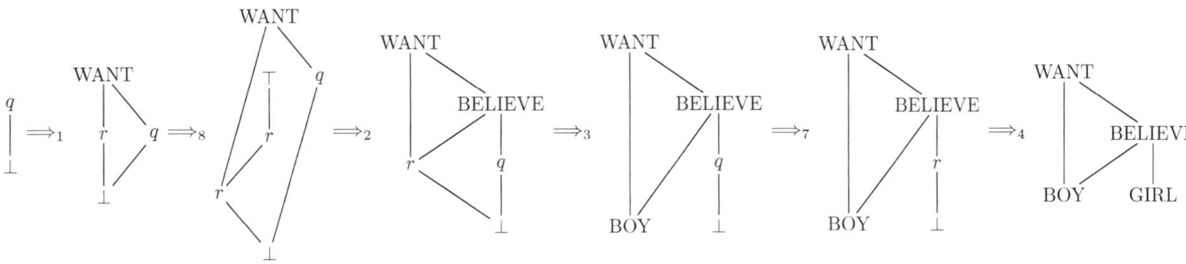

Figure 10: Example derivation in "generation mode".

Dags are generated by taking the basic incomplete dags (rule dags) defined by each rule and concatenating them using the dangling edges. Every dangling edge of the rule dag can be identified with a dangling edge of the current hypothesis (if the orientation matches) or be left unconnected for later connection. In that way, all children and parents for a given node are eventually created. Strictly speaking, the resulting structures are not dags anymore as they can contain multiple $\top$ and $\bot$ symbols. A sample generation is shown in Figure 10. Note how the order of rules applied is different from the example in Figure 6.

Using the dag acceptor as a generating device in this way is unproblematic, but poses two challenges. First, we have to avoid cyclicity, which is easily confirmed by keeping nodes topologically sorted.

Second, to avoid spurious ambiguity (where derivations describe the same derivation dag, but only differ by the order of rule application), special care is needed. A simple solution is to sort the edges in each incomplete dag to obtain a canonical ("leftmost") derivation. We start with the start state (which has head rank 0). This is the first incomplete dag that is pushed on the dag queue. Then we repeatedly pop an incomplete dag G from the dag queue. The first unused edge e of G is then attached to a new node v by identifying e with one of v's edges if the states are compatible. Remaining edges of the new node (incoming or outgoing) can be identified with other unused edges of G or left for later attachment. The resulting dags are pushed onto the queue.

Whenever a dag has no unused edges, it is complete and the corresponding derivation can be returned. The generation process stops when k complete derivations have been produced. This k-best algorithm can also be used to generate tree output for a dag-to-tree transducer, and by restricting the shape of the output tree, for "backward application" (given a tree, which dags map to it?).

6 Future work

The work presented in this paper is being implemented in a toolkit that will be made publicly available. Of course, there is a lot of room for improvement, both from the theoretical and the practical viewpoint. This is a brief list of items for future research:

- Complexity analysis of the algorithms.
- Closure properties of dag acceptors and dag-to-tree transducers as well as composition with tree transducers.
- Investigate a reasonable probabilistic model and training procedures.
- Extended left-hand sides to condition on a larger semantic context, just like extended top-down tree transducers (Maletti et al., 2009).
- Handling flat, unordered, sparse sets of relations that are typical of feature structures. Currently, rules are very specific to the number of children and parents. A first step in this direction is given by implicit rules that can handle a potentially arbitrary number of parents.
- Hand-annotated resources such as (dag, tree) pairs, similar to treebanks for syntactic representations.

Acknowledgements

This research was supported in part by ARO grant W911NF-10-1-0533. The first author was supported by the German Research Foundation (DFG) grant MA 4959/1–1.

References

L. E. Baum, T. Petrie, G. Soules, and N. Weiss. 1970. A maximization technique occurring in the statistical analysis of probabilistic functions of Markov chains. *Ann. Math. Statist.*, 41(1):164171.

Björn Borchardt and Heiko Vogler. 2003. Determinization of finite state weighted tree automata. *J. Autom. Lang. Comb.*, 8(3):417–463.

Francis Bossut and Bruno Warin. 1992. Automata and pattern matching in planar directed acyclic graphs. In Imre Simon, editor, *Proc. LATIN*, volume 583 of *LNCS*, pages 76–86. Springer.

Francis Bossut, Max Dauchet, and Bruno Warin. 1988. Automata and rational expressions on planar graphs. In Michal Chytil, Ladislav Janiga, and Václav Koubek, editors, *Proc. MFCS*, volume 324 of *LNCS*, pages 190–200. Springer.

Francis Bossut, Max Dauchet, and Bruno Warin. 1995. A kleene theorem for a class of planar acyclic graphs. *Inf. Comput.*, 117(2):251–265.

Symeon Bozapalidis and Antonios Kalampakas. 2004. An axiomatization of graphs. *Acta Inf.*, 41(1):19–61.

Symeon Bozapalidis and Antonios Kalampakas. 2006. Recognizability of graph and pattern languages. *Acta Inf.*, 42(8-9):553–581.

Symeon Bozapalidis and Antonios Kalampakas. 2008. Graph automata. *Theor. Comput. Sci.*, 393(1-3):147–165.

H. Comon, M. Dauchet, R. Gilleron, C. Löding, F. Jacquemard, D. Lugiez, S. Tison, and M. Tommasi. 2007. Tree automata techniques and applications. Available on: `http://www.grappa.univ-lille3.fr/tata`. release October, 12th 2007.

Bruno Courcelle and Joost Engelfriet. 1995. A logical characterization of the sets of hypergraphs defined by hyperedge replacement grammars. *Math. Syst. Theory*, 28(6):515–552.

Frank Drewes, Hans-Jörg Kreowski, and Annegret Habel. 1997. Hyperedge replacement, graph grammars. In Grzegorz Rozenberg, editor, *Handbook of Graph Grammars*, pages 95–162. World Scientific.

Jason Eisner. 2003. Learning non-isomorphic tree mappings for machine translation. In *Proc. ACL*, pages 205–208. ACL.

Joost Engelfriet and Jan Joris Vereijken. 1997. Context-free graph grammars and concatenation of graphs. *Acta Inf.*, 34(10):773–803.

David Eppstein. 1998. Finding the k shortest paths. *SIAM J. Comput.*, 28(2):652–673.

Ferenc Gécseg and Magnus Steinby. 1984. *Tree Automata*. Akadémiai Kiadó, Budapest, Hungary.

Joshua Goodman. 1999. Semiring parsing. *Comput. Linguist.*, 25:573–605.

Jonathan Graehl, Kevin Knight, and Jonathan May. 2008. Training tree transducers. *Comput. Linguist.*, 34(3):391–427.

Jonathan Graehl. 1997. Carmel finite-state toolkit. `http://www.isi.edu/licensed-sw/carmel`.

Yvette Graham, Josef van Genabith, and Anton Bryl. 2009. F-structure transfer-based statistical machine translation. In *Proc. LFG*.

Liang Huang and David Chiang. 2005. Better k-best parsing. In *Proc. IWPT*.

Víctor M. Jiménez and Andrés Marzal. 2000. Computation of the n best parse trees for weighted and stochastic context-free grammars. In *Proc. SSPR/SPR*, volume 1876 of *LNCS*, pages 183–192. Springer.

Tsutomu Kamimura and Giora Slutzki. 1981. Parallel and two-way automata on directed ordered acyclic graphs. *Inf. Control*, 49(1):10–51.

Tsutomu Kamimura and Giora Slutzki. 1982. Transductions of dags and trees. *Math. Syst. Theory*, 15(3):225–249.

Kevin Knight and Jonathan Graehl. 2005. An overview of probabilistic tree transducers for natural language processing. In *Proc. CICLing*, volume 3406 of *LNCS*, pages 1–24. Springer.

Kevin Knight. 1989. Unification: A multidisciplinary survey. *ACM Comput. Surv.*, 21(1):93–124.

Andreas Maletti, Jonathan Graehl, Mark Hopkins, and Kevin Knight. 2009. The power of extended top-down tree transducers. *SIAM J. Comput.*, 39(2):410–430.

Jonathan May and Kevin Knight. 2006a. A better n-best list: Practical determinization of weighted finite tree automata. In *Proc. HLT-NAACL*. ACL.

Jonathan May and Kevin Knight. 2006b. Tiburon: A weighted tree automata toolkit. In Oscar H. Ibarra and Hsu-Chun Yen, editors, *Proc. CIAA*, volume 4094 of *LNCS*, pages 102–113. Springer.

Mehryar Mohri, Fernando C. N. Pereira, and Michael Riley. 2000. The design principles of a weighted finite-state transducer library. *Theor. Comput. Sci.*, 231(1):17–32.

Mehryar Mohri. 1997. Finite-state transducers in language and speech processing. *Computational Linguistics*, 23(2):269–311.

Robert C. Moore. 1989. Unification-based semantic interpretation. In *Proc. ACL*, pages 33–41. ACL.

NIST. 2009. NIST Open Machine Translation 2009 Evaluation (MT09). `http://www.itl.nist.gov/iad/mig/tests/mt/2009/`.

Fernando Pereira and Michael Riley. 1997. Speech recognition by composition of weighted finite automata. In *Finite-State Language Processing*, pages 431–453. MIT Press.

Michael Riley, Cyril Allauzen, and Martin Jansche. 2009. OpenFST: An open-source, weighted finite-state transducer library and its applications to speech and language. In Ciprian Chelba, Paul B. Kantor, and Brian Roark, editors, *Proc. HLT-NAACL (Tutorial Abstracts)*, pages 9–10. ACL.

William C. Rounds and Robert T. Kasper. 1986. A complete logical calculus for record structures representing linguistic information. In *Proc. LICS*, pages 38–43. IEEE Computer Society.

Stuart M. Shieber, Yves Schabes, and Fernando C. N. Pereira. 1995. Principles and implementation of deductive parsing. *J. Log. Program.*, 24(1&2):3–36.

Stuart M. Shieber. 1986. *An Introduction to Unification-Based Approaches to Grammar*, volume 4 of *CSLI Lecture Notes*. CSLI Publications, Stanford, CA.

Andrew Viterbi. 1967. Error bounds for convolutional codes and an asymptotically optimum decoding algorithm. *IEEE Transactions on Information Theory*, 13(2):260–269.

Using Domain-specific and Collaborative Resources for Term Translation

Mihael Arcan, Paul Buitelaar
Unit for Natural Language Processing
Digital Enterprise Research Institute
Galway, Ireland
firstname.lastname@deri.org

Christian Federmann
Language Technology Lab
German Research Center for AI
Saarbrücken, Germany
cfedermann@dfki.de

Abstract

In this article we investigate the translation of terms from English into German and vice versa in the isolation of an ontology vocabulary. For this study we built new domain-specific resources from the translation search engine Linguee and from the online encyclopedia Wikipedia. We learned that a domain-specific resource produces better results than a bigger, but more general one. The first finding of our research is that the vocabulary and the structure of the parallel corpus are important. By integrating the multilingual knowledge base Wikipedia, we further improved the translation wrt. the domain-specific resources, whereby some translation evaluation metrics outperformed the results of Google Translate. This finding leads us to the conclusion that a hybrid translation system, a combination of bilingual terminological resources and statistical machine translation can help to improve translation of domain-specific terms.

1 Introduction

Our research on translation of ontology vocabularies is motivated by the challenge of translating domain-specific terms with restricted or no additional textual context that in other cases can be used for translation improvement. For our experiment we started by translating financial terms with baseline systems trained on the EuroParl (Koehn, 2005) corpus and the JRC-Acquis (Steinberger et al., 2006) corpus. Although both resources contain a large amount of parallel data, the translations were not satisfying. To improve the translations of the financial ontology vocabulary we built a new parallel resource, which was generated using Linguee[1], an online translation query service. With this data, we could train a small system, which produced better translations than the baseline model using only general resources.

Since the manual development of terminological resources is a time intensive and expensive task, we used Wikipedia as a background knowledge base and examined articles, tagged with domain-specific categories. With this extracted domain-specific data we built a specialised English-German lexicon to store translations of domain-specific terms. These terms were then used in a pre-processing method in the decoding approach. This approach incorporates the work by Aggarwal et al. (2011), which suggests a sub-term analysis. We split the financial terms into n-grams and search for financial sub-terms in Wikipedia.

The remainder of the paper is organised like this. In Section 2 we describe related work while in Section 3 the ontology data, the training data that we used in training the language model, and the translation decoder are discussed. Section 4 presents the new resources which were used for improving the term translation. In Section 5 we discuss the results of exploiting the different resources. We conclude with a summary and give an outlook on future work in Section 6.

2 Related Work

Kerremans (2010) presents the issue of terminological variation in the context of specialised translation on a parallel corpus of biodiversity texts. He shows that a term often cannot be aligned to any term in

[1] See www.linguee.com

the target language. As a result, he proposes that specialised translation dictionaries should store different translation possibilities or term variants.

Weller et al. (2011) describe methods for terminology extraction and bilingual term alignment from comparable corpora. In their compound translation task, they are using a dictionary to avoid out-of-domain translation.

Zesch et al. (2008) address issues in accessing the largest collaborative resources: Wikipedia and Wiktionary. They describe several modules and APIs for converting a Wikipedia XML Dump into a more suitable format. Instead of parsing the large Wikipedia XML Dump, they suggest to store the Dump into a database, which significantly increases the performance in retrieval time of queries.

Wikipedia has not only a dense link structure between articles, it has also inter-language links between articles in different languages, which was the main reason to use this invaluable collaborative resource. Erdmann et al. (2008) regarded the titles of Wikipedia articles as terminology. They assumed that two articles connected by an Interlanguage link are likely to have the same content and thus an equivalent title.

Vivaldi and Rodriguez (2010) proposed a methodology for term extraction in the biomedical domain with the help of Wikipedia. As a starting point, they manually select a set of seed words for a domain, which is used to find corresponding nodes in this resource. For cleaning their collected data, they use thresholds to avoid storing undesirable categories.

Müller and Gurevych (2008) use Wikipedia and Wiktionary as knowledge bases to integrate semantic knowledge into Information retrieval. Their models, text semantic relatedness (for Wikipedia) and word semantic relatedness (for Wiktionary), are compared to a statistical model implemented in Lucene. In their approach to Bilingual Retrieval, they use the cross-language links in Wikipedia, which improved the retrieval performance in their experiment, especially when the machine translation system generated incorrect translations.

3 Experiments

Our experiment started with an analysis of the terms in the ontology to be translated, which was stored in RDF[2] data model. These terms were used to automatically extract any corresponding Wikipedia Categories, which helped us to define more exactly the domain(s) of the ontology to be translated. The collected Categories were further used to build a domain-specific lexicon to be used for improving term translation. At the same time a new parallel corpus was built, which was also generated with the help of the ontology terms. This new data was then used to pre-process the input data for the decoder and to build a specialised training model which yielded to a translation improvement.

In this section, several types of data will be presented and furthermore the translation decoder, which has to access this data to build the training models. Section 3.1 gives an overview of the data that was used in translation. In Sections 3.2 and 3.3 we describe the data that is used to train the translation and language model. We used different parallel corpora, JRC-Acquis, EuroParl and a domain-specific corpus built from Linguee. In Section 3.4, we discuss a domain-specific lexicon, extracted from Wikipedia. In the last Section 3.5 we describe the phrase-based machine translation decoder Moses that we used for our experiments.

3.1 xEBR Dataset

For the translation dataset a financial ontology developed by the XBRL European Business Registers[3] (xEBR) Working Group was used. This financial ontology is a framework for describing financial accounting and profile information of business entities across Europe, see also Declerck et al. (2010). The ontology holds 263 concepts and is partially translated into German, Dutch, Spanish, French and Italian. The terms in each language are aligned via the SKOS[4] Exact Match mechanism to the xEBR core taxonomy. In this partially translated taxonomy, we identified 63 English financial terms and their German equivalents, which were used as reference translations in evaluating the different experiment steps.

The xEBR financial terms are not really terms from a linguistic point of view, but they are used in financial or accounting reports as unique finan-

[2]RDF: Resource Description Framework
[3]XBRL: eXtensible Business Reporting Language
[4]SKOS: Simple Knowledge Organization System

Length	Count	Examples
11	1	Taxes Remuneration And Social Security Payable After More Than One Year
10	2	Amounts Owed To Credit Institutions After More Than One Year, Variation In Stocks Of Finished Goods And Work In Progress
		...
2	57	Net Turnover, Liquid Assets, ...
1	10	Assets, Capital, Equity, ...

Table 1: Examples of xEBR terms

cial expressions or tags to organize and retrieve automatically reported information. Therefore it is important to translate these financial terms exactly.

Table 1 illustrates the structure of xEBR terms. It is obvious that they are not comparable to general language, but instead are more like headlines in newspapers, which are often short, very informative and written in a telegraphic style. xEBR terms are often only noun phrases without determiners. The length of the financial terms varies, e.g. the longest financial term considered for translation has a length of 11 tokens, while others may consist of 1 or 2.

3.2 General Resources: EuroParl and JRC-Acquis

As a baseline, the largest available parallel corpora were used: EuroParl and the JRC-Acquis parallel corpus. The EuroParl parallel corpus holds the proceedings of the European Parliament in 11 European languages. The JRC-Acquis corpus is available in almost all EU official languages (except Irish) and is a collection of legislative texts written between 1950 and today.

Although research work proved, that a training model built by using a general resource cannot be used to translate domain-specific terms (Wu et al., 2008), we decided to train a baseline model on these resources to illustrate any improvement steps from a general resource to specialised domain resources.

3.3 Domain Resource: Linguee

Linguee is a combination of a dictionary and a search engine, which indexes around 100 Million bilingual texts on words and expressions. Linguee search results show example sentences that depict how the searched expression has been translated in context.

In contrast to translation engines like Google Translate and Bing Translator, which give you the most probable translation of a source text, every entry in the Linguee database has been translated by humans. The bilingual dataset was gathered from the web, particularly from multilingual websites of companies, organisations or universities. Other sources include EU documents and patent specifications.

The language pairs available for querying are English↔German, English↔Spanish, English↔French and English↔Portuguese.

Since Linguee includes EU documents, they also use parallel sentences from EuroParl and JRC-Acquis. We investigated the proportion of sentences returned by Linguee which are contained in EuroParl or JRC-Acquis. The outcome is that the number of sentences is very low, where 131 sentences (0.54%) are gathered from JRC-Acquis corpus and 466 (1.92%) from EuroParl.

3.4 Collaborative Resource: Wikipedia

Wikipedia is a multilingual, freely available encyclopedia that was built by a collaborative effort of voluntary contributors. All combined Wikipedias hold approximately 20 million articles or more than 8 billion words in more than 280 languages. With these facts it is the largest collection of freely available knowledge[5].

With the heavily interlinked information base, Wikipedia forms a rich lexical and semantic resource. Besides a large amount of articles, it also holds a hierarchy of Categories that Wikipedia Articles are tagged with. It includes knowledge about named entities, domain-specific terms and word senses. Furthermore, the redirect system of Wikipedia articles can be used as a dictionary for synonyms, spelling variations and abbreviations.

3.5 Translation System: Moses

For generating translations from English into German and vice versa, the statistical translation toolkit Moses (Koehn et al., 2007) was used to build the training model and for decoding. For this approach, a phrase-based approach was taken instead of a tree based model. Further, we aimed at improving the translations only on the surface level, and therefore no part-of-speech information was taken into account. Word and phrase alignments were built with

[5] http://en.wikipedia.org/wiki/Wikipedia:Size_comparison

the GIZA++ toolkit (Och and Ney, 2003), whereby the 5-gram language model was built by SRILM (Stolcke, 2002).

4 Domain-specific Resource Generation

In this section, two different types of data and the approach of building them will be presented. Section 4.1 gives an overview of generating a parallel resource from Linguee, which was used in generating a new domain-specific training model. In Section 4.2 a detailed description is given how we extracted terms from Wikipedia for generating a domain-specific lexicon.

4.1 Domain-specific parallel corpus generation

To build a new training model that is specialised on our xEBR ontology, we used the Linguee search engine. This resource can be queried on single words and on word expressions with or without quotation marks. We stored the HTML output of the Linguee queries on our financial terms and parsed these files to extract plain parallel text. From this, we built a financial parallel corpus with 13,289 translation pairs, including single words, multi-word expressions and sentences. The English part of the parallel resource contained 410,649 tokens, the German part 347,246.

4.2 Domain-specific lexicon generation

To improve translation based on the domain-specific parallel corpus, we built a cross-lingual terminological lexicon extracted from Wikipedia. From the Wikipedia Articles we used different information units, i.e. the Title of a Wikipedia Article, the Category (or Categories) of the Title and the internal Interwiki
Interlanguage links of the Title. The concept of Interwiki links can be used to make links to other Wikipedia Articles in the same language or to another Wikipedia language i.e. Interlanguage links.

In our first approach, we used Wikipedia to determine the domain (or several domains) of the ontology. This approach (a) is to understand as the identification of the domain through the vocabulary of the ontology. For this approach, the financial terms, which were extracted from the ontology, were used to query the Wikipedia knowledge base[6]. The

Collected Wikipedia Categories	
Frequency	Name
8	Generally Accepted Accounting Principles
4	Debt
4	Accounting terminology
	...
1	Political science terms
1	Physical punishments

Table 2: Collected Wikipedia Categories based on the extracted financial terms

Wikipedia Article was considered for further examination, if its Title is equivalent to our financial terms. In this first step, 7 terms of our ontology were identified in the Wikipedia knowledge base. With this step, we collected the Categories of these Titles, which was the main goal of this approach. In a second round, we split all financial terms into all possible n-grams and repeated the query again to find additional Categories based on the split n-grams. Table 2 shows the collected Categories of the first approach and how often they appeared in respect to the extracted financial terms.

After storing all Categories, only such Categories were considered, which frequency had a value more than the calculated arithmetic mean of all frequencies (> 3.15). For the calculation of the arithmetic mean only Categories were considered, which had a frequency more than 1, since 2,262 of 3,615 collected Categories (62.6%) had a frequency equals 1. With this threshold we avoided extraction of a vocabulary that is not related to the ontology. Without this threshold, out-of-domain Categories would be stored, which would extend the lexicon with vocabulary that would not benefit the ontology translation, e.g. *Physical punishments*, which was access by the financial term *Stocks*.

In the next step, we further extended the list of Categories collected previously by use of full and split terms. This was done by storing new Categories based on the Wikipedia Interwiki links of each Article which was tagged with a Category from Table 2. For example, we collected all Categories wherewith the Article *Balance sheet*[7] is tagged and the Categories of the 106 Interwiki links of the Article *Balance sheet*. The frequencies of these Categories were summed up for all Interwiki links. Finally a

[6]For the Wikipedia Query we used the Wikipedia XML dump; `enwiki-20120104-pages-articles.xml`

[7]Financial statements, Accounting terminology

Final Category List	
Frequency	Name
95	Economics terminology
62	Generally Accepted Accounting Principles
61	Macroeconomics
55	Accounting terminology
47	Finance
44	Economic theories
	...

Table 3: Most frequent Categories based on the xEBR terms and their Interwiki links

new Category was added to the final Category list, if the new Category frequency exceeds the arithmetic mean threshold (> 18.40).

The final Category list contained 33 financial Wikipedia Categories (Table 3), which was in the next step used for financial term extraction.

With the final list of Categories, we started an investigation of all Wikipedia articles tagged with these financial Categories. Each Wikipedia Title was considered as a useful domain-specific term and was stored in our lexicon if a German title in the Wikipedia knowledge base also existed. As an example, we examined the Category Accounting terminology and stored the English Wikipedia Title *Balance sheet* with the German equivalent Wikipedia Title *Bilanz*.

At the end of the lexicon generation we examined 5228 Wikipedia Articles, which were tagged with one or more financial Categories. From this set of Articles we were able to generate a terminological lexicon with 3228 English-German entities.

5 Evaluation

Tables 4 to 5 illustrate the final results for our experiments on translating xEBR ontology terms, using the NIST (Doddington, 2002), BLEU (Papineni et al., 2002), and Meteor (Lavie and Agarwal, 2005) algorithms. To further study any translation improvements of our experiment, we also used Google Translate[8] in translating 63 financial xEBR terms (cf. Section 3.1) from English into German and from German into English.

5.1 Interpretation of Evaluation Metrics

In our experiments translation models built from a general resource performed worst. These results show that building resources from general language does not improve the translation of terms. The Linguee financial corpus, which is built from 13,289 sentences and holds 304K English and German 250K words, however demonstrates the benefit of domain-specific resources. Its size is less than two percent of that of the JRC-Acquis corpus (1,131,922 sentences, 21M English words, 19M German words), but evaluation scores are more than double than those for JRC-Acquis. This is clear evidence that such a resource benefits the translation of terms in a specific domain.

[8]Translations were generated on February 2012.

		Scoring Metric		
Source	# correct	BLEU	NIST	Meteor
Google Translate	18	0.264	4.382	0.369
JRC-Acquis	12	0.167	3.598	0.323
EuroParl	4	0.113	2.630	0.326
Linguee	25	0.347	4.567	0.408
Lexical substitution	4	0.006	0.223	0.233
Linguee+Wiki	25	0.324	4.744	0.432

Table 4: Evaluation scores for German term translations

		Scoring Metric		
Source	# correct	BLEU	NIST	Meteor
Google Translate	21	0.452	4.830	0.641
JRC-Acquis	9	0.127	2.458	0.480
EuroParl	5	0.021	1.307	0.412
Linguee	15	0.364	3.938	0.631
Lexical substitution	4	0.006	0.243	0.260
Linguee+Wiki	22	0.348	3.993	0.644

Table 5: Evaluation scores for English term translations

The models produced by the Linguee search engine are generating better translations than those produced by general resources. This approach outperforms Google Translate translations from German into English for all used evaluation metrics.

The table further shows results for our approach in using extracted Wikipedia terms as an example-based approach. For this we used the terms extracted from Wikipedia and exchanged English terms with German translations and vice versa. The evaluation metrics are very low in this case; only for Correct Translation we generate four positive findings.

Finally, the table gives results for our approach in using a combination of domain-specific parallel financial corpus with the lexicon extracted from Wikipedia. The domain-specific lexicon contains 3228 English-German translations, which were extracted from 18 different financial Categories. This combination of highly specialised resources gives the best results in our experiment. Translating financial terms into German, we get more Correct Translations as well as the Meteor metric shows better results compared to Google Translate. For translations into English, all used evaluation metrics show better results than those of Google Translate. As a final observation, we learned that translations made by domain-specific resources are on the same quality level, either if we translate from English into German or vice versa. In comparison, we see that Google Translate has a larger discrepancy when translating into German or English respectively. Our research showed that translations from English into German built by specialised resources were slightly better, which goes along with Google Translate that also produces better translations into German.

5.2 Manual Evaluation of Translation Quality

In addition to the automatic evaluation with BLEU, NIST, and Meteor scores, we have also undertaken a manual evaluation campaign to assess the translation quality of the different systems. In this section, we will a) describe the annotation setup and task presented to the human annotators, b) report on the translation quality achieved by the different systems, and c) present inter-annotator agreement scores that allow to judge the reliability of the human rankings.

5.2.1 Annotation Setup

In order to manually assess the translation quality of the different systems under investigation, we designed a simple classification scheme consisting of three distinct classes:

1. *Acceptable (A)*: terms classified as acceptable are either fully identical to the reference term or semantically equivalent;
2. *Can easily be fixed (C)*: terms in this class require some minor correction (such as fixing of typos, removal of punctuation, etc.) but are nearly acceptable. The general semantics of the reference term are correctly conveyed to the reader.
3. *None of both (N)*: the translation of the term does not match the intended semantics or it is plain wrong. Items in this class are considered severe errors which cannot easily be fixed and hence should be avoided wherever possible.

	Classes		
System	A	C	N
Linguee+Wiki	58%	27%	15%
Google Translate	55%	31%	14%
Linguee	51%	37%	12%
JRC-Acquis	32%	28%	40%
EuroParl	5%	25%	70%

Table 6: Results from the manual evaluation into German

	Classes		
System	A	C	N
Linguee+Wiki	56%	32%	12%
Linguee	56%	31%	13%
Google Translate	39%	40%	21%
JRC-Acquis	39%	31%	30%
EuroParl	15%	30%	55%

Table 7: Results from the manual evaluation into English

5.2.2 Annotation Data

We setup ten evaluation tasks, five for translations into English, five for translations into German. Each of these sets was comprised of 63 term translations and the corresponding reference. Every set was given to at least three human annotators who then classified the observed translation output according to the classification scheme described above. The human annotators included both domain experts and lay users without knowledge of the terms domain.

In total, we collected 2,520 classification items from six annotators. Tables 6, 7 show the results from the manual evaluation for term translations into German and English, respectively. We report the distribution of classes per evaluation task which are displayed in *best-to-worst* order.

In order to better be able to interpret these rankings, we computed the inter-annotator agreement between human annotators. We report scores generated with the following agreement metrics:

- S (Bennet et al., 1954);
- π *(averaged across annotators)* (Scott, 1955);
- κ (Fleiss and others, 1971);
- α (Krippendorff, 1980).

Tables 8, 9 present the aforementioned metrics scores for German and English term translations.

Overall, we achieve an average κ score of 0.463, which can be interpreted as *moderate agreement* following (Landis and Koch, 1977). Notably, we also reach *substantial* agreement for one of the annotation tasks with a κ score of 0.657. Given the

	Agreement Metric			
System	S	π	κ	α
Linguee+Wiki	0.599	0.528	0.533	0.530
Google Translate	0.698	0.655	0.657	0.657
Linguee	0.484	0.416	0.437	0.419
JRC-Acquis	0.412	0.406	0.413	0.408
EuroParl	0.515	0.270	0.269	0.273

Table 8: Annotator agreement scores for German

	Agreement Metric			
System	S	π	κ	α
Linguee+Wiki	0.532	0.452	0.457	0.454
Linguee	0.599	0.537	0.540	0.539
Google Translate	0.480	0.460	0.465	0.463
JRC-Acquis	0.363	0.359	0.366	0.360
EuroParl	0.552	0.493	0.499	0.495

Table 9: Annotator agreement scores for English

observed inter-annotator agreement, we expect the reported ranking results to be meaningful. Our Linguee+Wiki system performs best for both translation directions while out-of-domain systems such as JRC-Acquis and EuroParl perform badly.

5.3 Manual error analysis

Table 10 provides a manual analysis of the provided translations from Google Translate and the combined Linguee and Wikipedia Lexicon approach. Example Ex. 1 shows the results for [*Other intangible*] *fixed assets*. Since both translating systems translate it the same, namely *Vermögenswerte*, they could be considered as term variants.

A similar example is [*Receivables and other*] *assets* in Ex. 4. Google Translate translates the segment *asset* into *Vermögensgegenstände*, whereby the domain-specific approach translates it into *Vermögenswerte*. These examples prove the research by Kerremans (2010) that one term does not necessarily have only one translation on the target side. As term variants can further be considered *Aufwendungen* and *Kosten*, which were translated from *Costs* [*of old age pensions*] (Ex. 5).

In contrast, the German term in [*sonstige betriebliche*] *Aufwendungen* (Ex. 8) is according to the xEBR translated into [*Other operating*] *expenses*, which was translated correctly by both systems.

A deeper terminological analysis has to be done in the translation of the English term [*Cost of*] *old age pensions* (Ex. 5). In general it can be translated into *Altersversorgung* (provided by Google Translate and xEBR) or *Altersrente* (generated by the domain-specific model). Doing a compound analysis, the translation of [*Alters*]*versorgung* is *supply* or *maintenance*. On the other side, the translation of [*Alters*]*rente* is pension, which has a stronger connection to the financial term in this domain.

Ex. 6 shows an improvement of domain specific translation model in comparison to a general resource. Both general resources translated *Securities* as *Sicherheiten*, which is correct but not in the financial domain. The domain-specific trained model translates the ambiguous term correctly, namely *Wertpapiere*. Google Translate generates the same term as on the source site, *Securities*. Further, the term *Equity* (Ex. 7) is translated by Google Translate as *Gerechtigkeit*, the domain-specific model translates it as *Eigenkapital*, which is the correct translation. Finally, Ex. 2 and Ex. 3 open the issue of accurateness of the references for translation evaluation. The translations of these terms are correct if we consider the source language. On the other hand, if we compare them with the proposed references, they are not the same. In Ex. 2 they are truncated or extended in Ex. 3, which opens up problems in translation evaluation.

5.4 Discussion

Our approach shows the differences between improving translations with different resources. It was shown to be necessary to use additional language resources, i.e. specialised parallel corpora and if available, specialised lexica with appropriate translations. Nevertheless, to move further in this direction, translation of specific terms, more research is required in several areas that we identified in our experiment. One is the quality of the translation model. Because the translation model can only translate terms that are in the training model, it is necessary to use a domain-specific resource. Although we got better results with a smaller resource (if we translate into English), comparing those results with Google Translate, we learned that more effort has to be done in the direction of extending the size and quality of domain-specific resources.

Apart from that, with the aid of Wikipedia, which can be easily adapted for other language pairs, we further improved the translations into English to a

	Term		Translations	
#	Source	Reference	Google	Domain-specific
1	Other intangible fixed assets	sonstige immaterielle Vermögensgegenstände	Sonstige immaterielle Vermögenswerte	Sonstige immaterielle Vermögenswerte
2	Long-term financial assets	Finanzanlagen	Langfristige finanzielle Vermögenswerte	Langfristige finanzielle Vermögenswerte
3	Financial result	Finanz- und Beteiligungsergebnis	Finanzergebnis	Finanzergebnis
4	Receivables and other assets	Forderungen und sonstige Vermögensgegenstände	Forderungen und sonstige Vermögensgegenstände	Forderungen und sonstige Vermögenswerte
5	Cost of old age pensions	Aufwendungen für Altersversorgung	Aufwendungen für Altersversorgung	Kosten der Altersrenten
6	Securities	Wertpapiere	Securities	Wertpapiere
7	Equity	Eigenkapital	Gerechtigkeit	Eigenkapital
8	sonstige betriebliche Aufwendungen	Other operating expenses (TC)	other operating expenses	other operating expenses

Table 10: Translations provided by Google Translate and by the domain-specific resource

point where we outperform translations provided by Google Translate. Nevertheless, our experiment showed that the translations into German were better in regard of Google translate only for the Meteor evaluation system, for BLEU and NIST we did not achieve significant improvements. Also here more work has to be done in domain adaptation in a more sophisticated way to avoid building out-of-domain vocabulary.

6 Conclusion

The approach of building new resources showed a large impact on the translation quality. Therefore, generating specialised resources for different domains will be the focus of our future work. On the one hand, building appropriate training models is important, but our experiment also highlighted the importance of additional collaborative resources, like Wikipedia, Wiktionary, and DBpedia. Besides extracting Wikipedia Articles with their multilingual equivalents, as shown in Section 4.2, Wikipedia holds much more information in the articles itself. Therefore exploiting non-parallel resources, shown by Fišer et al. (2011), would clearly help the translation system to improve performance. Future work needs to better include the redirect system, which would allow a better understanding of synonymy and spelling variety of terms.

Focusing on translating ontologies, we will try to better exploit the structure of the ontology itself. Therefore, more work has to be done in the combination of linguistic and semantic information (structure of an ontology) as demonstrated by Aggarwal et al. (2011), which showed first experiments in combining semantic, terminological and linguistic information. They suggest that a deeper semantic analysis of terms, i.e. understanding the relations between terms and analysing sub-terms needs to be considered. Another source of useful information may be found in using existing translations for improving the translation of other related terms in the ontology.

Acknowledgments

This work has been funded under the Seventh Framework Programme for Research and Technological Development of the European Commission through the T4ME contract (grant agreement no.: 249119) and in part by the European Union under Grant No. 248458 for the Monnet project as well as by the Science Foundation Ireland under Grant No. SFI/08/CE/I1380 (Lion-2). The authors would like to thank Susan-Marie Thomas, Tobias Wunner, Nitish Aggarwal and Derek De Brandt for their help with the manual evaluation. We are grateful to the anonymous reviewers for their valuable feedback.

References

Nitish Aggarwal, Tobias Wunner, Mihael Arcan, Paul Buitelaar, and Seán O'Riain. 2011. A similarity measure based on semantic, terminological and linguistic information. In *The Sixth International Workshop on Ontology Matching collocated with the 10th International Semantic Web Conference (ISWC'11)*.

E. M. Bennet, R. Alpert, and A. C. Goldstein. 1954. Communications through limited response questioning. *Public Opinion Quarterly*, 18:303–308.

Thierry Declerck, Hans-Ulrich Krieger, Susan M. Thomas, Paul Buitelaar, Sean O'Riain, Tobias Wunner, Gilles Maguet, John McCrae, Dennis Spohr, and Elena Montiel-Ponsoda. 2010. Ontology-based multilingual access to financial reports for sharing business knowledge across europe. In *Internal Financial Control Assessment Applying Multilingual Ontology Framework*.

George Doddington. 2002. Automatic evaluation of machine translation quality using n-gram co-occurrence statistics. In *Proceedings of the second international conference on Human Language Technology Research*, HLT '02, pages 138–145.

M. Erdmann, K. Nakayama, T. Hara, and S. Nishio. 2008. An approach for extracting bilingual terminology from wikipedia. *Lecture Notes in Computer Science*, (4947):380–392. Springer.

Darja Fišer, Špela Vintar, Nikola Ljubešić, and Senja Pollak. 2011. Building and using comparable corpora for domain-specific bilingual lexicon extraction. In *Proceedings of the 4th Workshop on Building and Using Comparable Corpora: Comparable Corpora and the Web*, BUCC '11, pages 19–26.

J.L. Fleiss et al. 1971. Measuring nominal scale agreement among many raters. *Psychological Bulletin*, 76(5):378–382.

Koen Kerremans. 2010. A comparative study of terminological variation in specialised translation. In *Reconceptualizing LSP Online proceedings of the XVII European LSP Symposium 2009*, pages 1–14.

Philipp Koehn, Hieu Hoang, Alexandra Birch, Chris Callison-Burch, Marcello Federico, Nicola Bertoldi, Brooke Cowan, Wade Shen, Christine Moran, Richard Zens, Chris Dyer, Ondřej Bojar, Alexandra Constantin, and Evan Herbst. 2007. Moses: Open Source Toolkit for Statistical Machine Translation. In *Proceedings of the 45th Annual Meeting of the ACL*, ACL '07, pages 177–180.

Philipp Koehn. 2005. Europarl: A Parallel Corpus for Statistical Machine Translation. In *Conference Proceedings: the tenth Machine Translation Summit*, pages 79–86. AAMT.

Klaus Krippendorff. 1980. *Content Analysis: An Introduction to Methodology*. Sage Publications, Inc.

J. R. Landis and G. G. Koch. 1977. The measurement of observer agreement for categorical data. *Biometrics*, 33(1):159–174.

Alon Lavie and Abhaya Agarwal. 2005. Meteor: An automatic metric for mt evaluation with improved correlation with human judgments. In *Proceedings of the EMNLP 2011 Workshop on Statistical Machine Translation*, pages 65–72.

Christof Müller and Iryna Gurevych. 2008. Using wikipedia and wiktionary in domain-specific information retrieval. In *Working Notes for the CLEF 2008 Workshop*.

Franz Josef Och and Hermann Ney. 2003. A systematic comparison of various statistical alignment models. *Computational Linguistics*, 29.

Kishore Papineni, Salim Roukos, Todd Ward, and Wei-Jing Zhu. 2002. Bleu: a method for automatic evaluation of machine translation. In *Proceedings of the 40th Annual Meeting on Association for Computational Linguistics*, ACL '02, pages 311–318.

W. A. Scott. 1955. Reliability of Content Analysis: The Case of Nominal Scale Coding. *Public Opinion Quarterly*, 19:321–325.

Ralf Steinberger, Bruno Pouliquen, Anna Widiger, Camelia Ignat, Tomaz Erjavec, Dan Tufis, and Dniel Varga. 2006. The jrc-acquis: A multilingual aligned parallel corpus with 20+ languages. In *Proceedings of the 5th International Conference on Language Resources and Evaluation (LREC'2006)*.

Andreas Stolcke. 2002. Srilm-an extensible language modeling toolkit. In *Proceedings International Conference on Spoken Language Processing*, pages 257–286.

Jorge Vivaldi and Horacio Rodriguez. 2010. Using wikipedia for term extraction in the biomedical domain: first experiences. *Procesamiento del Lenguaje Natural*, 45:251–254.

Marion Weller, Anita Gojun, Ulrich Heid, Béatrice Daille, and Rima Harastani. 2011. Simple methods for dealing with term variation and term alignment. In *Proceedings of the 9th International Conference on Terminology and Artificial Intelligence*, pages 87–93.

Hua Wu, Haifeng Wang, and Chengqing Zong. 2008. Domain adaptation for statistical machine translation with domain dictionary and monolingual corpora. In *Proceedings of the 22nd International Conference on Computational Linguistics - Volume 1*, COLING '08, pages 993–1000.

Torsten Zesch, Christof Müller, and Iryna Gurevych. 2008. Extracting lexical semantic knowledge from wikipedia and wiktionary. In *Proceedings of the Sixth International Conference on Language Resources and Evaluation (LREC'08)*.

Improving Statistical Machine Translation through co-joining parts of verbal constructs in English-Hindi translation

Karunesh Kumar Arora
CDAC, Anusandhan Bhawan
C 56/1, Sector 62,
Noida, India
karunesharora@cdac.in

R Mahesh K Sinha
JSS Academy of Technical Education,
C 20/1, Sector 62,
Noida, India
sinharmk@gmail.com

Abstract

Verb plays a crucial role of specifying the action or function performed in a sentence. In translating English to morphologically richer language like Hindi, the organization and the order of verbal constructs contributes to the fluency of the language. Mere statistical methods of machine translation are not sufficient enough to consider this aspect. Identification of verb parts in a sentence is essential for its understanding and they constitute as if they are a single entity. Considering them as a single entity improves the translation of the verbal construct and thus the overall quality of the translation. The paper describes a strategy for pre-processing and for identification of verb parts in source and target language corpora. The steps taken towards reducing sparsity further helped in improving the translation results.

1 Introduction

With the availability of parallel content, increased memory and processing speed, there has been growing trend moving towards Statistical Machine Translation. Most of the phrase based machine translation systems are based on the noisy-channel based IBM models (Koehn, Och & Marcu, 2003, Zens et al., 2004). Phrases refer to a number of consecutive words that may not be a valid syntactic phrase but are learnt through the statistical alignment between two languages. English and Hindi have differing syntactical structure and pose great challenge in aligning phrases of the two languages. The former follows SVO pattern while the later adheres to the SOV pattern. Hindi being morphologically richer offers several verbal constructs governed through Tense, Aspect and Modality (TAM). The non-monotonocity between the two languages causes inferior alignment of phrases especially verbal constructs.

There have been efforts towards single tokenization of MWE parts. Ueffing and Ney, 2003 reported use of POS information for SMT to morphologically richer language. They tried to transform the source language while the approach proposed here attempts transformations on both source and target laguage sides. Recent related works use statistical measures like Mutual Information and Log Likelihood Ratio (Seretan and Wehrli, 2007) to know the degree of cohesion between constituents of a MWE. These require defining threshold value above which the extracted phrase is qualified as a MWE.

Minkov et al. (2007) utilized the rich syntactic and morphological analyzers to generate the inflections. Hindi lacks availability of robust parsers and complex morphological analyzers. The paper describes the process of identifying verbal constructs of both languages and grouping them in single units to reduce the search space. For identification of the verbal constructs, the POS information is utilized with simple combining rules to make verb phrases. This yields better alignment of verbal phrases and results in more grammatical, fluent and acceptable translations. Besides that, the data sparseness generated from chunking is handled through extending the phrase table with verbal parts entries.

The paper is organized in sections, describing the phrase based SMT in brief, Hindi language and its verbal properties followed by sections describing identification of verbal constructs in English and Hindi. Further to it, corpus and pre-processing activities are detailed alongwith the experimental setup, process adopted to reduce sparcity, the translation process, observations and conclusion.

2 Overview of SMT

Candide SMT system [Brown et al., 1990], presented by the IBM researchers paved the path for statistical approach to machine translation.
In statistical machine translation, we are given a source language sentence $S = s^I_1 = s_1 \ldots s_i \ldots s_I$, which is to be translated into a target language ('English') sentence $T = t^J_1 = t_1 \ldots t_j \ldots t_J$. Statistical machine translation is based on a noisy channel model. It considers T to be the target of a communication channel, and its translation S to be the source of the channel. System may generate multiple translation sentences options and the problem of translation becomes identifying sentence T which fits as the best translation of the source sentence S. Hence the machine translation task becomes to recover the source from the target. So, we need to maximize P(T|S). According to the Bayes rule,

$$t^* = \arg\max_t P(t \mid s) = \arg\max_t \frac{P(s \mid t) * P(t)}{P(s)}$$

As, P(S) is constant,

$$t^* = \arg\max_t P(s \mid t) * P(t)$$

Here, P(s|t) represents Translation model and P(t) represents language model. Translation model plays the role of ensuring translation faithfulness and Language model to ensure the fluency of translated output.

3 Hindi language and its verbal properties

Indian languages are classified in four major families: Indo-Aryan (a branch of the Indo-European family), Dravidian, Austro-Asiatic (Austric), and Sino-Tibetan, with the overwhelming majority of the population speaking languages belonging to the first two families. There are 22 languages listed in eighth schedule of constitution of India. The four major families are different in their form and construction, but they share many orthographic similarities, because their scripts originate from Brahmi (Ishida, 2002).

Hindi language belongs to the Indo-Aryan language family. It is spoken in vast areas of northern India and is written in Devanagari script. In Hindi, words belonging to various grammatical categories appear in lemma and inflectional forms. Hindi Verbal constructs system is based on the TAM of the action. The Verbal costructs are formed by placement of auxiliary verbs after the main verb. The main verb that carries the lexical meaning may appear in the root or inflected form. Auxiliary verbs of the main verb denote the TAM property of the verbal construct.

Tense is a grammatization of the relations between time of some event and the refrence time. Aspect markers are semantically very sensitive and often convey subtle meanings and nuances that are not generally expressed through simple lexical words. Here we look at the two example sentences,

1. वह दिन भर बैठा रहता है

vaha din bhar baithaa rahataa hai

('He remains seated whole day').

2. वह बार-बार बैठता रहता है

vaha baar-baar baithtaa rahataa hai

('He sits frequetly')

Here, aspect marker या रह 'yaa raha' in first sentence, denotes the resultant state of the action and रह 'raha' gives perception of a longer period of time. While in a slightly modified second sentence, the aspect marker ता रह 'taa raha' gives the sense of repetition or infinity of the action and रह 'raha' gives the perception of a time spread.

The mood reflects speaker's attitude towards the action and is manifested in many ways in a language. In Hindi the moods can be of Imperative,

Subjunctive, Indefinite and definite potential, conditional and future etc. Here we look at the following three sentences.

1. तू पढ़ tu padh ('You read')
2. तुम पढ़ो tu padh ('You read')
3. आप पढ़िए tu padh ('You read')

All the above three sentences are imperative in nature but there is subtle difference in speaker's attitude. The first sentence is the impolite form of expression, the second one is common form and the third sentence is the polite form of expressing the same thing.

All constituents of the verbal constructs are obligatory. Semantically TAM markers are so closely interlinked that it would be appropriate to treat them as a single entity rather than treating them sperately. Besides that, the main verb appears frequently in compound and conjunct forms in the verbal constrcuts (Singh, 2010). Compound verbs follow the pattern of verb-verb (V-V) combination while conjunct verbs are formed with either noun-verb (N-V) or adjective-verb (A-V) combinations. In V-V expressions the first verb word carries verbal stem while successive verb words play the role of auxiliary or light verbs (LV). The LVs loose their independent meaning and are used to reflect the shade of main verb. The compound and conjunct verb expressions are also referred as complex predicates (CP). The CPs are multi-word expressions (MWEs) which may be compositional or non-compositional in nature (Sinha, 2011). These should be treated as a single verbal unit to infer the intended meaning or semantics. The CP adds to the expressiveness of the expression but pose difficulty for automatic identification.

4 Identification and treatment verbal constructs

The elements of verbal constructs, if treated as individual words leave too many entries in the sentences to get aligned through statistical alignment. This makes the probability distribution unfocussed. Co-joining parts of verbal constructs reduces the sentence length and thus helps in better alignment.

4.1 English verbal constructs

The Stanford POS tagger (Kristina Toutanova et al., 2003) is used for tagging words in a sentence with their POS categories. The POS tags are based on Penn Treebank POS tagset (Mitchell et al., 1993). The verbal parts to be chunked together are identified with the help of a set of rules. Some of these rules are listed in the Table 1. As an example, the rule 'get NP VBN' specifies, that if Noun Phrase appears in between the word 'get' and VBN, this is considered as a verbal construct.

POS based Verb Chunking Rules
VBP/VBD/VBZ VBG
MD not VB
get NP VBN

Table 1: Sample rules for identiying English Verbal constructs

These rules are impletemented in the form of a Finite State Machine (FSM). The NP-phrase appearing in between the verb construct parts is identified and FSM implementation helps in achieving this. Similarly, the model auxiliaries like 'can be' are also co-joined with successive verbs. These simple rules help in identifying the constituents of verbal constructs. The negation markers or noun phrases that appear in between verbal constructs are moved out to reduce sparsity. Table 2 shows some English verbal constructs and how these are co-joined.

Verbal Constructs	Co-joined Verbal Constructs
is going	is_going
can not be done	not can_be_done
get the work done	get_done the work

Table 2: Sample English Verbal constructs

4.2 Identification of Hindi verbal constructs

For identifying the Hindi verbal constructs, a combination of POS tagging and presence of the TAM markers appearing as verb ending sequences are used. The POS tags are based on modified Penn Treebank POS tagset. The POS tagging identifies possible verbal parts to be chunked, while the TAM rules help in confirmation of them. Table 3 lists some of the TAM rules. Here $ indicates the presence of main verb stem.

Verbal constructs	TAM Rules
जा सकता है jaa saktaa hai	$_सकता_है $_saktaa_hai
जाने मत दो jaane mat do	मत $ने _दो mat $ne_do
खाया जा रहा होगा khaaya jaa rahaa hogaa	$या_जा_रहा_होगा $yaa_jaa_rahaa_hogaa
जा नहीं रहा है jaa nahi rahaa hai	नहीं $_रहा_है nahi $_rahaa_hai
जाता तो था jaataa to thaa	तो $ता_था to $taa_thaa

Table 3: Sample rules for identiying Hindi Verbal constructs

Table 4 shows some of the verbal constrcts and their co-joined forms after processing. The negation markers, such as, नहीं nahi ('not') and particles, such as, तो (emphatic marker) occurring in between are moved out of the verbal expressions to reduce the sparsity.

Verbal Constructs	Co-joined Verbal Constructs
जा सकता है jaa saktaa hai	जा_सकता_है jaa_saktaa_hai
जाने मत दो jaane mat do	मत जाने _दो mat jaane_do
खाया जा रहा होगा khaayaa jaa rahaa hogaa	खाया_जा_रहा_होगा khaaya_jaa_rahaa_hogaa
जा नहीं रहा है jaa nahi rahaa hai	नहीं जा_रहा_है nahi jaa_rahaa_hai
जाता तो था jaataa to thaa	तो जाता_था to jaataa_thaa

Table 4: Sample Hindi Verbal constructs

Complex Predicates are identified using the approach of Sinha (2009). Here, we make use of parallel corpus, English-Hindi dictionary of Light Verbs and TAM rules. Table below shows some sample Complex predicates in Compound and Conjuct forms and their treatment.

Compound Verbs	
Verbal Constructs	Co-joined Verbal Constructs
बैठ जा baith jaa	बैठ_जा baith_jaa
पढ़ लिया होगा padh liyaa hogaa	पढ़_लिया_होगा padh_liyaa_hogaa
कर दिया kar diyaa	कर_दिया kar_diyaa
Conjunct Verbs	
Verbal Constructs	Co-joined Verbal Constructs
परीक्षा दे parikshaa de	परीक्षा_दे parikshaa_de
बात कर रहा है baat kar rahaa hai	बात _कर_रहा_है baat_kar_rahaa_hai
बंद हो गया band ho gayaa	बंद_हो_गया band_ho_gayaa

Table 5: Sample Hindi complex predicates

5 Corpus and pre-processing

Basic Travel Expressions Corpus (BTEC) containing travel conversations is used for performing the experiments (Kikui, 2006). This contains travel expressions which are generally used when a person travels to another country and covers the utterances of potential subjects in travel situations. The expressions contained more than one sentence in single expression. These have been separated by sentence end markers (dot). Such sentences have been treated as separate sentence entities. This increased the number of independent sentences in parallel corpus. The Tables 6 and 7 list corpus statistics.

Corpus	Training	Development	Test
English:			
# sentences	19972	2343	2371
# words	153066	17806	18257
# avg words / sentence	7.7	7.6	7.7
Hindi:			
# sentences	19972	2043	2071
# words	171347	17774	17811
# avg words / sentence	8.6	8.7	8.6

Table 6: Corpus Statistics before pre-processing

Corpus	Training	Development	Test
English:			
# sentences	24056	2581	2575
# avg words / sentence	6.3	6.4	6.3
Hindi:			
# sentences	24056	2581	2575
# avg words / sentence	7.2	7.1	7.2

Table 7: Corpus Statistics after pre-processing

The average sentence length in the English corpus before pre-processing was 7.7 words per sentence and after pre-processing it came down to 6.3 words per sentence. Hindi corpus had 8.7 words per sentence and it became 7.2 words per sentence after pre-processing.

The pre-processing activity also included expanding of common abbreviated expressions e.g. I'll to 'I will' etc. This has been performed with a set of simple expansion rules. Besides that, dots appearing after titles are also replaced with hash (#), to avoid being treated them as sentence end-markers.

6 Experimental setup

For the training of the statistical models, standard word alignment GIZA++ (Och & Ney, 2003) and language modelling toolkit SRILM (Stolcke, 2002) tools were used. For translation, MOSES phrase-based SMT decoder (Koehn, 2007) has been used. For evaluation, the automatic evaluation metrics, BLEU (Papineni, 2002) was applied to the translation output.

7 Translation process

The overall process can be classified as Training and Testing processes. The training process describes the steps involved in building models. These steps include – pre-processing of training corpus, POS tagging source and target language training corpus, chunking words forming the verbal constructs, building translation and language models.

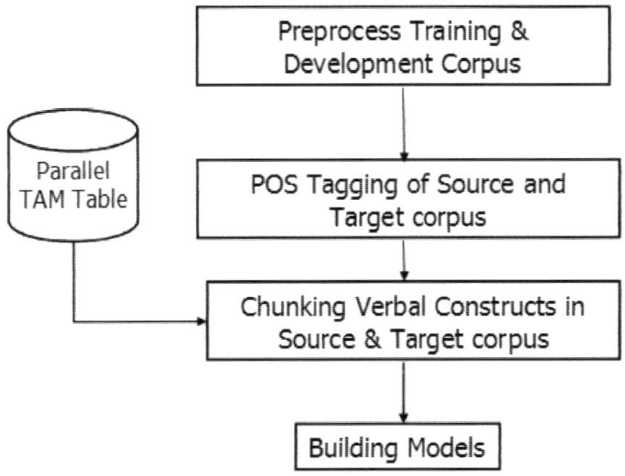

Figure 1: Training process

Testing process describes steps while translating. It involves - pre-processing of test corpus, POS tagging of test corpus, chunking the words forming the verbal constructs and searching words in the vocabulary of training models. If some words are unseen but are lexical words of verbal constructs, they are handled as described in section 8 below.

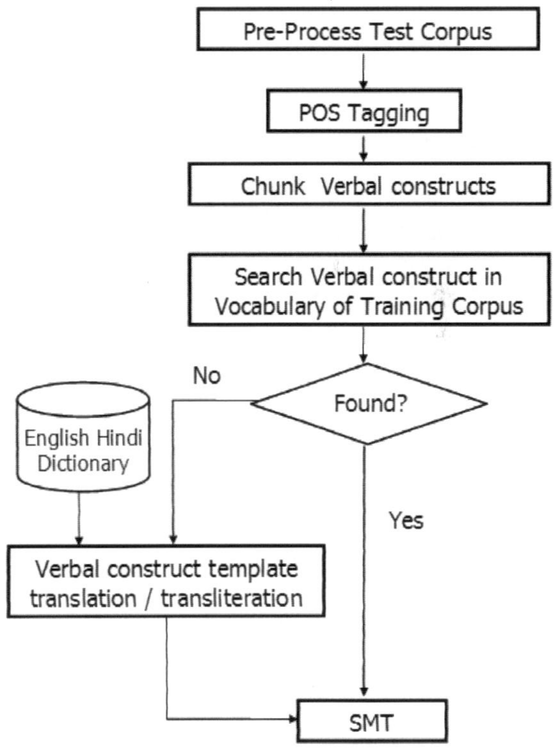

Figure 2: Testing process

8 Handling sparsity

Due to limited size of parallel corpus used for training the models, it is quite probable that some verbal constructs may appear which is unseen by the training model and is out of vocabulary (OOV). The probability of such occurrence increases due to the co-joining of words forming verbal constructs. To meet this situation, templates of different verbal constructs with their translations are used. The Table 8 shows some sample templates with their translations.

If verbal construct is OOV, it is changed to its translation template form. After that, its equivalent translation is picked up and is replaced in the sentence to be translated. As an example, if the verbal construct 'would_have_been_cleaning' is OOV. It is changed to its template form would_have_been_VBG and its respective translation VB_रहा_होगा is picked up from the translation template table. Now, with the help of English-Hindi dictionary, translation of verbal construct 'would_have_been_cleaning' in the sentence is replaced with the translated as 'साफ़_कर_रहा_होगा and is sent for final translation.

Verbal construct template	Translation template
can_VB	VB_सकता_है VB_saktaa_hai
would_have_been_VBG	VB_रहा_होगा VB_rahaa_hogaa
has_not_VBN	नहीं_VBया_है nahi_VByaa_hai

Table 8: Verbal Construct template translation

If the verb is not present in the English-Hindi dictionary too, it is translierated and 'कर' is added to it. Now, the verbal construct in the source sentence is replaced with its transliterated form before sending for translation. As an example, if word 'clean' is not found in English-Hindi dictionary, its translterated form 'क्लीन' is generated and 'कर' is added to it. The verbal construct 'would_have_been_cleaning' in the source sentence is replaced with transliterated verbal construct 'क्लीन_कर_रहा_होगा' before sending for SMT. For trnasliteration in-house statistical transliteration system is used.

9 Experiments

The experiments were carried on original, pre-processed and chunked verbal constructs based models. Table 9 below show that there is improvement in BLUE score when we pre-process the raw corpus. Better alignment is achieved due to reduced sentence length and data being in normalized form. The chunked verbal constructs corpus further improves the BLUE score. Though the BLUE score gain is marginal but on human inspection, better order and organization of Verbal constructs is observed. The table below shows the BLEU score for experiments.

Corpus	BLEU Score	Gain in BLEU score
BPP *	0.1596	
APP *	0.1672	0.0076
APP + VCC *	0.1694	0.0022

Table 9: BLEU scores for different experiments

* BPP - Before Pre-processing the corpus
* APP - After Pre-processing the corpus
* APP + VCC - After Pre-Processing corpus + Verbal Constructs Chunking

10 Conclusion and Future Work

Results show, moderate gain in BLUE score is obtained with pre-processing of the corpus. This can be attributed to better alignment due to reduced length of sentences. Marginal gain is observed with chunking of Verbal constructs, yet manual inspection show fluent translation of verbal parts.

Hindi verb forms are sensitive to gender, number and person information, which is not considered in current implementation. Work on interrogatives, prepositional phrases and other multi-word expressions, is in progress. There is scope to improve the statistical alignment using linguitic knowledge. The investigations on these are currently in progress.

Acknowledgments

We would like to thank Centre for Development of Advanced Computing (CDAC) for providing conducive environment for this work. We also would like to thank NICT, Japan for providing the English version of BTEC corpus for performing experiments. Thanks are also due to Mr Mukund Kumar Roy and Mr Pramod Kumar Gupta for setting up the software and programming efforts. Thanks are also extended to Mr VN Shukla for extending support.

References

Philipp Koehn, Franz Josef Och, and Daniel Marcu. 2003. Statistical Phrase-Based Translation, Proc. of the Human Language Technology Conference (HLT/NAACL)

Richard Zens and Hermann Ney. 2004. Improvements in Phrase-Based Statistical Machine Translation, Proc. of the Human Language Technology Conference (HLT-NAACL) , Boston, MA, pp. 257-264.

Nicola Ueffing and Hermann Ney. 2003. Using pos information for statistical machine translation into morphologically rich languages. In Proc. of the 10th Conference of the European Chapter of the ACL (EACL), Budapest, Hungary

Seretan V. and Wehrli E. 2007. Collocation translation based onalignment and parsing. Proceedings of TALN. Toulouse, France.

Einat Minkov, Krishna Toutanova and Hisami Suzuki. 2007. Generating Complex Morphology for Machine Translation, in Proc. 45th Annual Meeting of the Association for Computational Linguistics, pp 128-135.

Brown, P., Cocke, J., Pietra, S. A. D., Pietra, V. J. D., Jelinek, F., La_erty, J. D., Mercer, R. L., and Rossin, P. 1990. A statistical approach to machine translation. Computational Linguistics, 16(2):76{85.

R. Ishida. 2002. An introduction to Indic scripts, in Proc. of the 22nd International Unicode Conference.

Singh, Suraj Bhan. 2010. A Syntactic Grammar of Hindi (first ed.), Ocean Books.

R. Mahesh K. Sinha. 2011. Stepwise Mining of Multi-Word Expressions in Hindi, ACL-HLT, Workshop on Multiword expressions, Portland, USA

Kristina Toutanova, Dan Klein, Christopher Manning, and Yoram Singer. 2003. Feature-Rich Part-of-Speech Tagging with a Cyclic Dependency Network. In Proceedings of HLT-NAACL, pp. 252-259.

Mitchell P. Marcus, Beatrice Santorini, and Mary Ann Marcinkiewicz. 1993. Building a Large Annotated Corpus of English: The Penn Treebank, in Computational Linguistics, Volume 19, Number 2, pp. 313--330

R. Mahesh K. Sinha. 2009. Mining Complex Predicates In Hindi Using Parallel Hindi-English Corpus, ACL-IJCNLP, Workshop on Multi Word Expression, Singapore.

G. Kikui et al. 2006. Comparative study on corpora for speech translation, IEEE Transactions on Audio, Speech and Language, vol. 14(5), pp. 1674–1682.

F. Och and H. Ney. 2003. A Systematic Comparison of Various Statistical Alignment Models, Computational Linguistics, vol. 29(1), pp. 19–51.

A. Stolcke. 2002. SRILM -an extensible language modelling toolkit, in Proc. of ICSLP, Denver, pp. 901–904.

P. Koehn et al. 2007. Moses: Open Source Toolkit for SMT," in Proc. of the 45th ACL, Demonstration Session, Prague, Czech Republic, , pp. 177–180.

K. Papineni et al. 2002. BLEU: a Method for Automatic Evaluation of Machine Translation, in Proc. of the 40th ACL, Philadelphia, USA, , pp. 311–318.

Application of Clause Alignment for Statistical Machine Translation

Svetla Koeva, Borislav Rizov, Ivelina Stoyanova, Svetlozara Leseva, Rositsa Dekova, Angel Genov, Ekaterina Tarpomanova, Tsvetana Dimitrova and **Hristina Kukova**

Department of Computational Linguistics
Institute for Bulgarian Language, Bulgarian Academy of Sciences
Sofia 1113, Bulgaria

{svetla,boby,iva,zarka,rosdek,angel,katja,cvetana,hristina}@dcl.bas.bg

Abstract

The paper presents a new resource light flexible method for clause alignment which combines the Gale-Church algorithm with internally collected textual information. The method does not resort to any pre-developed linguistic resources which makes it very appropriate for resource light clause alignment. We experiment with a combination of the method with the original Gale-Church algorithm (1993) applied for clause alignment. The performance of this flexible method, as it will be referred to hereafter, is measured over a specially designed test corpus.

The clause alignment is explored as means to provide improved training data for the purposes of Statistical Machine Translation (SMT). A series of experiments with Moses demonstrate ways to modify the parallel resource and effects on translation quality: (1) baseline training with a Bulgarian-English parallel corpus aligned at sentence level; (2) training based on parallel clause pairs; (3) training with clause reordering, where clauses in each source language (SL) sentence are reordered according to order of the clauses in the target language (TL) sentence. Evaluation is based on BLEU score and shows small improvement when using the clause aligned corpus.

1 Motivation

Evaluation on the performance of MT systems has shown that a pervasive shortcoming shared by both the phrase-based and the syntax-based SMT systems is translating long and (syntactically) complex sentences (Koehn et al., 2003; Li et al., 2007; Sudoh et al., 2010).

The power of phrase-based SMT lies in local lexical choice and short-distance reordering (Li et al., 2007). Syntax-based SMT is better suited to cope with long-distance dependencies, however there also are problems, some of them originated from the linguistic motivation itself – incorrect parse-trees, or reordering that might involve blocks that are not constituents (Li et al., 2007).

An efficient way to overcome the problem of sentence length and complexity is to process the clauses in a similar way as sentences. This has incited growing interest towards the alignment and processing of clauses – a group of syntactically and semantically related words expressing predicative relation and positioned between sentence borders or clause connectors. (It is known that some predicative relations can be considered complex being saturated with another predicative relation – but with the above given definition this case is simplified).

The differences in word order and phrase structure across languages can be better captured at a clause rather than at a sentence level, therefore, monolingual and parallel text processing in the scope of the clauses may significantly improve syntactic parsing, automatic translation, etc. The sentences can be very long and complex in structure, may consist of a considerable number of clauses which in turn may vary with respect to their relative position to each other in parallel texts both due to linguistic reasons per se and translators' choices.

The flexible order, length and number of clauses

in sentences, along with the different word order and ways of lexicalisation across languages contribute to the complexity of clause alignment as compared to sentence alignment and call for more sophisticated approaches. These findings have inspired growing research into clause-to-clause machine translation involving clause splitting, alignment and word order restructuring within the clauses (Cowan et al., 2006; Ramanathan et al., 2011; Sudoh et al., 2010; Goh et al., 2011).

A fixed clause order in a language (i.e. relative clauses in Bulgarian, English, French and many other languages follow the head noun, while in Chinese, Japanese, Turkish, etc. they precede it) may correspond to a free order in another (i.e. Bulgarian and English adverbial clauses). The hypothesis is that a SMT model can be improved by inducing a straightforward clause alignment through reordering the clauses of the source language text so as to correspond to the order of the clauses in the target language text.

2 State-of-the-art

The task of clause alignment is closely related to that of sentence alignment (Brown et al., 1990; Gale and Church, 1993; Kay and Roscheisen, 1993) and phrase alignment (DeNero and Klein, 2008; Koehn et al., 2003). There are two main approaches – statistical and lexical, often employed together to produce hybrid methods. Machine learning techniques are applied to extract models from the data and reduce the need of predefined linguistic resources.

Boutsis, Piperidis and others (Boutsis and Piperidis, 1998; Boutsis and Piperidis, 1998; Piperidis et al., 2000) employ a method combining statistical techniques and shallow linguistic processing applied on a bilingual parallel corpus of software documentation which is sentence-aligned, POS-tagged and shallow parsed. The combined task of clause borders identification uses linguistic information (POS tagging and shallow parsing) and clause alignment based on pure statistical analysis. The reported precision is 85.7%. Kit et al. (2004) propose a method for aligning clauses in Hong Kong legal texts to English which relies on linguistic information derived from a glossary of bilingual legal terms and a large-scale bilingual dictionary. The algorithm selects a minimal optimal set of scores in the similarity matrix that covers all clauses in both languages. The authors report 94.60% alignment accuracy of the clauses, corresponding to 88.64% of the words.

The quality of the parallel resources is of crucial importance to the performance of SMT systems and substantial research is focused on developing good parallel corpora of high standard. Most clause alignment methods are applied on domain specific corpora, in particular administrative corpora and are not extensively tested and evaluated on general corpora or on texts of other domains. Although clause segmentation is often performed together with clause alignment (Papageorgiou, 1997) the former tends to be more language-specific and therefore clause alignment is performed and evaluated independently. The majority of the available comparative analyses discuss modifications of one method rather than the performance of different methods. Moreover, the performance of resource-free against resource-rich methods has been poorly explored. To the best of our knowledge, there is no purely resource-free method for clause alignment offered so far.

In recent years, handling machine translation at the clause level has been found to overcome some of the limitations of phrase-based SMT. Clause aligned corpora have been successfully employed in the training of models for clause-to-clause translation, reordering and subsequent sentence reconstruction in SMT – Cowan et al. (2006) for syntax-based German-to-English SMT, Sudoh et al. (2010) for English-to-Japanese phrase-based SMT, among others.

Cowan et al. (2006) discuss an approach for tree-to-tree SMT using Tree Adjoining Grammars. Clause alignment is performed on a corpus (Europarl) which is then used in the training of a model for mapping parse trees in the source language to parse trees in the target language. The performance of this syntax-based method is similar to the phrase-based model of Koehn et al. (2003).

Sudoh et al. (2010) propose a method for clause-to-clause translation by means of a standard SMT method. The clauses may contain non-terminals as placeholders for embedded clauses. After translation is performed, the non-terminals are replaced by their clause translations. The model for clause translation is trained using a clause-aligned bilingual corpus of research paper abstract. The proposed improvement by using Moses is 1.4% in BLEU (33.19% to 34.60%), and 1.3% in TER (57.83% to 56.50%) and 2.2% in BLEU (32.39% to 34.55%) and 3.5% in TER (58.36% to 54.87%) using a hierarchical phrase-based SMT system.

The potential of clause alignment along with other sub-sentence levels of alignment in extracting matching translation equivalents from translation archives has been recognised within the EBMT framework, as well (Piperidis et al., 2000).

3 Bootstrapping clause alignment

The clause alignment is modelled as a bipartite graph. Each node in the graph corresponds to a clause in either the source or the target language. A pair of clauses that are fully or partially translational equivalents is connected by an edge in the graph. The connected components of the graph are beads (the smallest group of aligned clauses). In these terms, the task of clause alignment is the task of the identification of the edges in a bipartite graph, where the nodes are the clauses (Brown et al., 1990).

A bootstrapping method for clause alignment that does not exploit any pre-developed linguistic resources is elaborated. The method uses length-balance based alignment algorithm – i.e. Gale-Church (Gale and Church, 1993), for the data collecting. The bootstrapping algorithm attains high precision and relatively good recall. In order to improve the recall while preserving the precision the method is combined with the Gale-Church algorithm applied to clause alignment.

The proposed method consists of the following stages:

1. Initial clause alignment that serves as training data.
2. Identifying similarities between clauses in different languages.
3. Building the clause alignment.

3.1 The Gale and Church algorithm

Gale and Church (1993) describe a method for aligning sentences based on a simple statistical model of sentence lengths measured in number of characters. It relies on the fact that longer sentences in one language tend to be translated into longer sentences in the other language, and vice versa. A probabilistic score is assigned to each proposed correspondence of sentences, based on the scaled difference and the variance of the lengths of the two sentences. The method is reported to give less than 4% error in terms of alignment and is probably the most widely used sentence alignment method.

The extended version of the Gale-Church aligner from the Natural Language Toolkit[1] is applied for clause alignment. The original Gale-Church method applies the 1:1, 0:1, 1:0, 1:2, 2:1 and 2:2 bead models; in the extended version – the 1:3, 3:1, 2:3, 3:2, 3:3 models are added.

3.2 Clause alignment training data

The clause beads are identified by applying the Gale-Church algorithm. The aim is to select a set of aligned beads which are to serve as a training set for the subsequent stages. Only beads showing high probability of correctness are used. For any probability p we could find δ so that for the Gale-Church measure within $[-\delta, \delta]$ the corresponding bead is correct with probability p.

3.3 Clause similarity

Clause similarity is measured by means of: a) partial word alignment, b) length similarity, and c) weighted punctuation similarity.

3.3.1 Word alignment

To align words in the scope of parallel clauses, word-to-word connections (weighted links between two words based on word similarity) are calculated using several methods given below:

- Vector space model

  A given word is assigned a vector

  $$< x_1,\ x_2,\ \cdots,\ x_n >$$

  in an n-dimensional vector space, where each dimension represents a bead in the preliminary clause alignment and x_i is the number of the occurrences of the word in the bead. The set of these vectors is a matrix.

[1] http://nltk.googlecode.com

The vector space word similarity is the cosine of the angle between the vectors of the words (Ruge, 1992; Schütze, 1992). Two words are similar if the cosine is above a specified threshold. The observations over the training and test data show that the translation equivalents are identified best when the cosine is higher than 0.7. However, the word-to-word alignment reduces some of the errors which increase in number when lowering the threshold. Therefore, the threshold is set at 0.4 acquiring a good balance between the number of the connections obtained and the error rate.

A second vector space matrix is built using the first two words in each clause on the assumption that clause-introducing words may express stronger word-to-word connections.

Some experiments with word similarity association measures e.g. the chi-square measure (Evert, 2005) failed to show any improvements.

Word forms are treated as instances of one and the same word if either their actual or normalised forms are equal (Kay and Roscheisen, 1993). The normalised forms cover correspondences between grammatically and semantically related words in languages with rich inflectional and derivational morphology. The morphology algorithm proposed by Kay and Roscheisen (1993) is applied for splitting potential suffixes and prefixes and for obtaining the normalised word forms. The vector space word-to-word connections are calculated for both actual and normalised forms and the obtained similarity measures are summed up.

- Levenshtein measure (Levenshtein, 1966)

  Church (1993) employs a method that induces sentence alignment by employing cognates (words that are spelled similarly across languages). Instead the standard Levenshtein distance (the number of edits required to transform a string A into another string B) is applied. The non-Latin characters are transliterated into Latin ones. The distance is calculated within a tolerance different for a different word length. The distance is then transformed into similarity by means of the tolerance.

$$\sqrt{1 - \frac{\text{levenshtein}}{\text{tolerance} + 1}}.$$

- Punctuation

  Similarity is calculated also if two words contain identical prefixes or suffixes which are punctuation marks or special characters. Punctuation and special characters are not all equal. Some of them are more robust, e.g. marks for currency and measurement, or mathematical symbols ($, , , %, +, <, >, =) or the different types of brackets. Others (e.g. comma, hyphen, colon, semi-colon) may be governed by language specific rules and may lead to improvement only for those pairs of languages that employ similar rules.

The word-to-word similarity measure is the weighted sum of the above measures where the Levenshtein similarity is multiplied by 3, the punctuation similarity by 0.4 and the vector space similarity measure by 1, which is defined as a base.

The similarity connections are sorted descendingly and sequentially processed. At each iteration only connections between dangling words are stored. Thus there is only one connection left for each word resulting in partial word alignment. The weights of all obtained word-to-word connections are summed up to produce the weight of the clause association that is propagated to the clause similarity calculation stage.

3.3.2 Length similarity

Zero-weighted similarity connections between clauses are collected using Gale-Church's distance measure. Thus connections are added without increasing the weight of the existing ones.

3.3.3 Weighted punctuation similarity

This similarity is calculated by the following formula

$$\sum_{Z \in PU} \min(\text{count}(Z \in cl_1),\ \text{count}(Z \in cl_2)),$$

where PU is the set of the punctuation marks and special symbols being prefixes and suffixes of words in the clauses processed.

3.4 Clause alignment with the bootstrapping method

The bipartite graph is built by filtering the set of the calculated clause similarity connections. The connected components of this graph form the clause beads. A conservative fallback strategy is applied to add the dangling clauses to the most appropriate bead. The filtering process starts by defining a threshold for grouping (1,2) and every clause similarity connection with weight above it is considered strong. In a way similar to word alignment, the remaining (weak) connections are sorted descendingly and processed one by one. If the processed connection relates clauses that are not attached to any bead, it passes the filter. In other words these two clauses form a 1:1 bead.

The bootstrapping method evaluated on the test corpus has precision above 94% and recall of 77%. To overcome this low recall we combine the Gale-Church algorithm with the core method.

3.5 Combined clause alignment

The combined method also distinguishes strong and weak clause connections by means of a threshold constant. At the beginning the Gale-Church results in clause alignment are compared with the strong connections. If they comply with the Gale-Church's beads, the weak connections are processed. The weak connections are added to the final graph if they do not contradict Gale-Church's output, i.e. when they do not connect clauses from two different beads.

In case of a strong connection the Gale-Church's alignment is discarded, assuming that the semantic and the syntactic similarities between clauses are more significant than the length.

4 Clause alignment evaluation

4.1 Test corpus

A test corpus was constructed for the purposes of method evaluation. It consists of 363,402 tokens altogether (174,790 for Bulgarian and 188,612 for English) distributed over five thematic domains: Fiction (21.4%), News (37.1%), Administrative (20.5%), Science (11.2%) and Subtitles (9.8%). The purpose of using a general testing corpus with texts from a variety of domains is to investigate method performance in a wider range of contexts.

Both Bulgarian and English parts of the corpus are first automatically segmented and then aligned at sentence level. The task of sentence detection in Bulgarian is carried out using a Bulgarian sentence splitter (Koeva and Genov, 2011). For sentence splitting of the English texts a pre-trained OpenNLP[2] model is used. Sentence alignment is produced using HunAlign[3] (Varga et al., 2005), with the alignment manually verified by human experts.

Clause splitting is considered a highly language dependent task and separate linguistic models need to be developed for each language. For the purposes of the present study, Bulgarian sentences are manually or semiautomatically split into clauses and for the English texts a pre-trained OpenNLP parser is used to determine clause boundaries followed by manual expert verification and post-editing (the task of automatic clause splitting falls outside the scope of the present study).

Subsequently, manual clause alignment is performed. Tables 1 and 2 present the number of sentences and clauses, respectively, in Bulgarian and English with their average length in tokens ($L_S(t)$) and in characters ($L_S(ch)$).

Language	**Sentences**		
	number	$L_S(t)$	$L_S(ch)$
Bulgarian	13,213	13.23	73.04
English	13,896	13.57	69.21
Total	**27,109**	–	–

Table 1: Number of sentences and their length.

Different models of clause alignment reflect interlingual symmetry or assymetry, such as: 1:1 for equivalent clauses in both languages; 0:1 or 1:0 if a clause in one of the languages is missing in the other; $1:N$ and $N:1$ ($N>1$) in the cases of different clause segmentation, when clauses contain the same information; $N:M$ ($N,M>1$) in relatively rare cases when the information is crossed among

[2]http://opennlp.apache.org/index.html

[3]http://mokk.bme.hu/resources/hunalign/

Language	Clauses		
	number	$L_S(t)$	$L_S(ch)$
Bulgarian	24,409	7.20	39.54
English	28,949	6.57	33.22
Total	**53,358**	–	–

Table 2: Number of clauses and their length.

clauses. The distribution of the models is given in Table 3.

Model	Frequency	% of all
0:1	553	2.53
1:0	412	1.88
1:1	17,708	80.88
1:2	2,055	9.39
1:3	309	1.41
1:4	98	0.45
2:1	588	2.69
2:2	81	0.37
2:3	15	0.07
3:1	31	0.14
3:2	7	0.03

Table 3: Distribution of bead models in the manually aligned corpus.

4.2 Evaluation

The precision is calculated as the number of true connections (between clauses in the two languages) divided by the number of the proposed connections, while the recall is the proportion of true connections to all connections in the corpus. The connections in a bead are the Cartesian product of the clauses in the first and the second language. The $K : 0$ and $0 : K$ bead models are considered as $K : 1$ and $1 : K$ by adding a fake clause.

The evaluation is performed both over the corpus as a whole and on each of the domain specific subcorpora included in it.

The evaluation of the clause alignment implementation of the Gale-Church algorithm on the same corpus shows overall precision of 0.902, recall – 0.891 and F_1 measure – 0.897. Although the original Gale-Church method performs very well in terms of both precision and recall, sentence alignment poses a greater challenge. The explanation for this fact lies

Domain	Precision	Recall	F_1
Total	**0.910**	**0.911**	**0.911**
Administrative	0.865	0.857	0.861
Fiction	0.899	0.902	0.901
News	0.933	0.946	0.940
Science	0.874	0.852	0.862
Subtitles	0.934	0.934	0.934

Table 4: Performance of the flexible method.

in the broader scope of variations of clause correspondences as compared to sentences.

The bootstrapping method performs better in the translations with clause reordering. An example is the administrative subcorpus where Gale-Church gives precision/recall – 81.5%/79.7% compared to 86.6%/85.8% shown by the bootstrapping method. In the texts with less clause order asymmetries the results are close.

5 Application of clause alignment in SMT

Typical Moses[4] (Koehn et al., 2007) models are built on a large amount of parallel data aligned at the sentence level. For the purposes of the present study a specially designed parallel corpus is used. The aim is to demonstrate the effect of using syntactically enhanced parallel data (clause segmentation and alignment, reordering of clauses, etc.).

A series of experiments with Moses is designed to demonstrate the effect of training data modification on the performance of the SMT system. The different training datasets comprise the same sentences but differ in their syntactic representation. The baseline model is constructed on the basis of aligned sentence pairs. The first experiment is based on aligned clauses rather than sentences. The second experiment demonstrates the effect of reordering of the clauses within the source language sentences. The main purpose of the experiments is to demonstrate possible applications of the clause alignment method for training an SMT system, enhanced with linguistic information.

5.1 Training corpus

For the demonstration purposes of the present study we apply a small corpus of 27,408 aligned sen-

[4]http://www.statmt.org/moses/

tence pairs (comprising 382,950 tokens in Bulgarian and 409,757 tokens in English) which is semi-automatically split into clauses and automatically aligned at clause level. The current purposes of the research do not include the development of a full SMT model but focus on the demonstration of the effect of syntactical information on the performance of the SMT system. Thus, the size of the training corpus is considered sufficient for demonstration purposes. The parallel texts are extracted from several domains – Administrative, Fiction, News, Science, Subtitles.

5.2 Test corpus

The test corpus compiled for the purposes of evaluation of the SMT performance is independently derived from the Bulgarian-English parallel corpus and does not overlap with the training corpus. It however, resembles its structure and contains texts from the same domains as the training data. Table 5 gives the number of tokens in the Bulgarian and in the English part of the test corpus, with percent of tokens in the Bulgarian texts.

Domain	BG	ENl	% (BG)
Administrative	36,042	35,185	21.10
Fiction	34,518	38,723	20.21
News	64,169	62,848	37.57
Science	18,912	19,856	11.07
Subtitles	17,147	18,951	10.04
Total	**170,788**	**175,563**	

Table 5: Number of tokens in the test corpus.

5.3 Baseline model

The baseline model corresponds to the traditional Moses trained models and is constructed from aligned sentences in Bulgarian and English. The BLEU score for translation from Bulgarian into English is 16.99 while for the reverse it is substantially lower – 15.23. In the subsequent tests we observe the results for the Bulgarian-to-English translation only.

5.4 Clause level trained model

The first experiment aims to demonstrate that training of the model based on aligned clauses rather than sentences yields improvement. The assumption is that alignment at a sub-sentential level would improve word and phrase alignment precision by limiting the scope of occurrence of translational equivalents. On the other hand, however, lower level alignment reduces the number of aligned phrases. For this purpose clauses are the optimal scope for alignment as phrases rarely cross clause boundaries.

The results of the clause level training show small improvement of 0.11 in the BLEU score from 16.99 (baseline) to 17.10 for the Bulgarian-to-English translation.

5.5 Reordering of clauses

The second experiment relies on reordering of clauses within aligned sentences. The experiment aims at showing that reordering improves performance of SMT system.

A simple clause reordering task was carried out within the sentences on the parallel training corpus. Clause reordering involves linear reordering of clauses in the source language sentences to match the linear order of corresponding clauses in the target language sentences.

Reordering applies to cases where asymmetries are present in the alignment i.e. crossed connections between clauses, which is expected to vary across languages and domains. This suggests that the proportion of the corpus affected by reordering also depends on the language and on the domain. Based on an experiment with a smaller corpus, approximately 7% of the Bulgarian sentences are affected by reordering when adjusted to the English sentences.

The result is BLEU score of 17.12 compared to 16.99 (baseline) which yields an improvement of 0.13.

5.6 Analysis

The results obtained from the above two experiments show a small yet consistent improvement in the BLEU score. It shows a possibility to improve the results by applying parallel data enhanced by syntactic information, namely, aligned pairs at clause level, or sentences with reordered clauses.

The data, however, are not sufficient to draw a definite conclusion both on whether the improvement is stable and on which of the two methods –

using clause aligned pairs or reordered sentences – performs better.

6 Conclusions

The research done in the scope of this paper has shown that, on the one hand, the Gale-Church algorithm is applicable for clause alignment. The results achieved by the bootstrapping method, on the other hand, show that clause alignment may be appropriately improved by means of similarity measurement especially for the domain dependent tasks – particularly for the domains for which non-linear order of the translated clauses is typical. Experiments showed that especially for texts exhibiting alignment asymmetries our method for clause alignment outperforms Gale-Church considerably.

We applied automatic clause alignment for building a Moses training dataset enhanced with syntactic information. Two experiments were performed – first, involving aligned clause pairs, and the second using clause reordering in the source language assuming that the order of clauses in the target language defines relations specific for the particular language. The experiments suggest that the clause reordering might improve translation models.

The series of experiments conducted with Moses showed possible applications of the clause alignment method for training an SMT system, enhanced with linguistic information.

References

Sotiris Boutsis and Stelios Piperidis. 1998. OK with alignment of sentences. What about clauses? *Proceedings of the Panhellenic Conference on New Information Technology (NIT98)*. pp. 288–297.

Sotiris Boutsis and Stelios Piperidis. 1998. Aligning clauses in parallel texts. *Proceedings of the 3rd Conference on Empirical Methods in Natural Language Processing (EMNLP 1998)*. pp. 17–26.

Peter F. Brown, John Cocke, Stephen A. Della Pietra, Vincent J. Della Pietra, Frederick Jelinek, Robert L. Mercer and Paul S. Roossin. 1990. A statistical approach to language translation. *Computational Linguistics*, 16(2): 79–85.

Kenneth Church. 1993. Charalign: A program for aligning parallel texts at the character level. *Proceedings of the 31st Annual Meeting of the Association for Computational Linguistics (ACL 1993)*. pp. 1–8.

Brooke Cowan, Ivona Kucerová and Michael Collins. 2006. A Discriminative Model for Tree-to-Tree Translation. *Proceedings of the Conference on Empirical Methods in Natural Language Processing (EMNLP 2006)*. pp. 232–241.

John DeNero and Dan Klein. 2008. The Complexity of Phrase Alignment Models. *Proceedings of the 46th Annual Meeting of the Association for Computational Linguistics (ACL 2008)*, Short Paper Track.

Stefan Evert. 2005. *The Statistics of Word Cooccurrences: Word Pairs and Collocations. Ph.D. thesis*. Institut fur maschinelle Sprachverarbeitung, University of Stuttgart.

William A. Gale and Kenneth. W. Church. 1993. A Program for Aligning Sentences in Bilingual Corpora. *Computational Linguistics*, 19(1): 75–102. URL: `http://acl.ldc.upenn.edu/J/J93/J93-1004.pdf`.

Chooi-Ling Goh, Takashi Onishi and Eiichiro Sumita. 2011. Rule-based Reordering Constraints for Phrase-based SMT. Mikel L. Forcada, Heidi Depraetere, Vincent Vandeghinste (eds.) *Proceedings of the 15th Conference of the European Association for Machine Translation (EAMT 2011)*. pp. 113–120.

Mridul Gupta, Sanjika Hewavitharana and Stephan Vogel. 2011. Extending a probabilistic phrase alignment approach for SMT. *Proceedings of the International Workshop on Spoken Language Translation (IWSLT 2011)*. pp. 175-182.

Martin Kay and Martin Roscheisen. 1993. Text translation alignment. *Computational Linguistics*, 19(1): 121–142.

Chunyu Kit, Jonathan J. Webster, King Kui Sin, Haihua Pan, Heng Li. 2004. Clause Alignment for Hong Kong Legal Texts: A Lexical-based Approach. *International Journal of Corpus Linguistics*, 9(1): 29–51.

Philipp Koehn, Franz J. Och and Daniel Marcu. 2003. Statistical phrase-based translation. *Proceedings of the North American Chapter of the Association for Computational Linguistics (NAACL 2003)*. pp. 48–54.

Philipp Koehn, Hieu Hoang, Alexandra Birch, Chris Callison-Burch, Marcello Federico, Nicola Bertoldi, Brooke Cowan, Wade Shen, Christine Moran, Richard Zens, Chris Dyer, Ondrej Bojar, Alexandra Constantin, Evan Herbst. 2007. Moses: Open Source Toolkit for Statistical Machine Translation. *Annual Meeting of the Association for Computational Linguistics (ACL), demonstration session*. Prague, Czech Republic, June 2007.

Svetla Koeva, Diana Blagoeva and Siya Kolkovska. 2010. Bulgarian National Corpus Project. Nicoletta Calzolari, Khalid Choukri, Bente Maegaard, Joseph Mariani, Jan Odijk, Stelios Piperidis, Mike Rosner,

Daniel Tapias (eds.) *Proceedings of the 7th conference on International Language Resources and Evaluation (LREC 2010)*. pp. 3678–3684.

Svetla Koeva and Angel Genov. 2011. Bulgarian language processing chain. *Proceedings of Integration of multilingual resources and tools in Web applications. Workshop in conjunction with GSCL 2011, 26 September 2011, University of Hamburg*. (to appear)

Vladimir Levenshtein 1966. Binary codes capable of correcting deletions, insertions, and reversals. *Soviet Physics Doklady*, 10. pp. 707–710.

Chi-Ho Li, Minghui Li, Dongdong Zhang, Mu Li, Ming Zhou and Yi Guan. 2007. A probabilistic approach to syntax-based reordering for statistical machine translation. *Proceedings of the 45rd Annual Meeting of the Association for Computational Linguistics (ACL 2007)*. pp. 720–727.

Harris Papageorgiou 1997. Clause recognition in the framework of alignment. Ruslan Mitkov and Nicolas Nicolov, N. (eds.) *Current Issues in Linguistic Theory*, 136: 417–425. John Benjamins B.V.

Stelios Piperidis, Harris Papageorgiou and Sotiris Boutsis. 2000. From sentences to words and clauses. Chapter 6. Jean Veronis and Nancy Ide (eds.) *Parallel Text Processing: Alignment and Use of Translation Corpora. Text, Speech and Language Technology series*, 13: 117–137.

Ananthakrishnan Ramanathan, Pushpak Bhattacharyya, Karthik Visweswariah, Kushal Ladha and Ankur Gandhe. 2011. Clause-Based Reordering Constraints to Improve Statistical Machine Translation. *Proceedings of the 5th International Joint Conference on Natural Language Processing (IJCNLP 2011)*. pp. 1351–1355.

Gerda Ruge. 1992. Experiments on linguistically based term associations. *Information Processing & Management*. 28(3):317-332.

Hinrich Schütze. 1992. Context Space. *Working Notes of the AAAI Fall Symposium on Probabilistic Approaches to Natural Language*. pp. 113-120

Katsuhito Sudoh, Kevin Duh, Hajime Tsukada, Tsutomu Hirao, Masaaki Nagata. 2010. Divide and Translate: Improving Long Distance Reordering in Statistical Machine Translation. *Proceedings of the Joint 5th Workshop on Statistical Machine Translation and MetricsMATR*. pp. 418–427.

Daniel Varga, Laszlo Nemeth, Peter Halacsy, Andras Kornai, Viktor Tron, Viktor Nagy. 2005. Parallel corpora for medium density languages. *Proceedings of the RANLP 2005*. pp. 590–596.

Zero Pronoun Resolution can Improve the Quality of J-E Translation

Hirotoshi Taira, Katsuhito Sudoh, Masaaki Nagata
NTT Communication Science Laboratories
2-4, Hikaridai, Seika-cho, Keihanna Science City
Kyoto 619-0237, Japan
{taira.hirotoshi,sudoh.katsuhito,nagata.masaaki}@lab.ntt.co.jp

Abstract

In Japanese, particularly, spoken Japanese, subjective, objective and possessive cases are very often omitted. Such Japanese sentences are often translated by Japanese-English statistical machine translation to the English sentence whose subjective, objective and possessive cases are omitted, and it causes to decrease the quality of translation. We performed experiments of J-E phrase based translation using Japanese sentence, whose omitted pronouns are complemented by human. We introduced 'antecedent F-measure' as a score for measuring quality of the translated English. As a result, we found that it improves the scores of antecedent F-measure while the BLEU scores were almost unchanged. Every effectiveness of the zero pronoun resolution differs depending on the type and case of each zero pronoun.

1 Introduction

Today, statistical translation systems have been able to translate between languages at high accuracy using a lot of corpora . However, the quality of translation of Japanese to English is not high comparing with the other language pairs that have the similar syntactic structure such as the French-English pair. Particularly, the quality of translation from spoken Japanese to English is in low. There are many reasons for the low quality. One is the different syntactic structures, that is, Japanese sentence structure is SOV while English one is SVO. This problem has been partly solved by head finalization techniques (Isozaki et al., 2010). Another big problem is that subject, object and possessive cases are often eliminated in Japanese, particularly, spoken Japanese (Nariyama, 2003). In the case of Japanese to English translation, the source language has lesser information in surface than the target language, and the quality of the translation tends to be low. We show the example of the omissions in Fig 1. In this example, the Japanese subject *watashi wa* ('I') and the object *anata ni* ('to you') are eliminated in the sentence. These omissions are not problems for human speakers and hearers because people easily recognize who is the questioner or responder (that is, 'I' and 'you') from the context. However, generally speaking, the recognition is difficult for statistical translation systems.

Some European languages allow the elimination of subject. We show an example in Spanish in Fig 2. In this case, the subject is eliminated, and it leaves traces including the case and the sex, on the related verb. The Spanish word, *tengo* is the first person singular form of the verb, *tener* (it means 'have'). So it is easier to resolve elimination comparing with Japanese one for SMT.

Otherwise, Japanese verbs usually have no inflectional form depending on the case and sex. So, we need take another way for elimination resolution. For example, if the eliminated Japanese subject is always 'I' when the sentence is declarative, and the subject is always 'you' when the sentence is a question sentence, phrase based translation systems are probably able to translate subject-eliminated Japanese sentences to correct English sentences. However, the hypothesis is not always

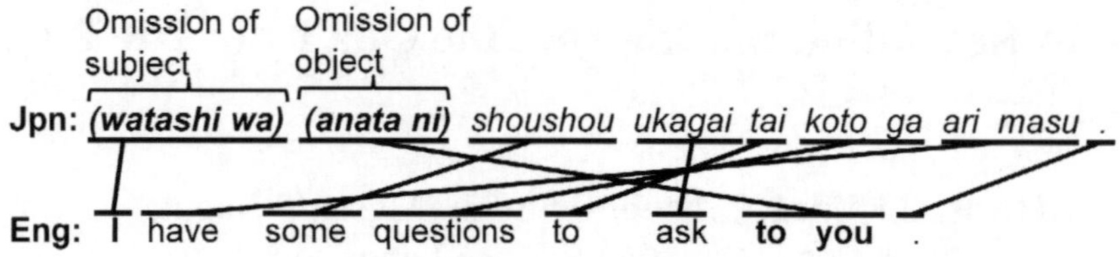

Figure 1: Example of Japanese Ellipsis (Zero Pronoun)

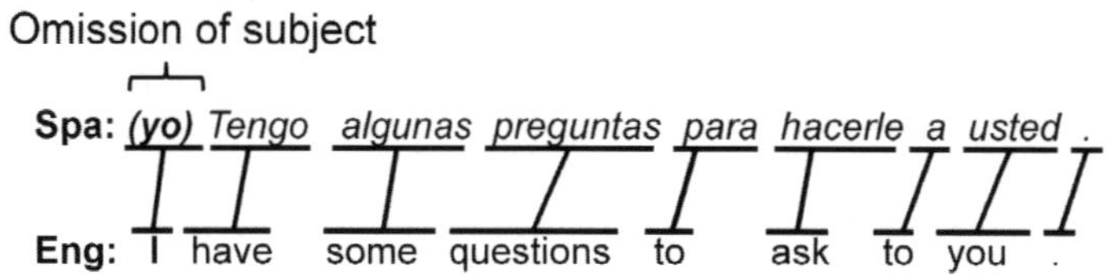

Figure 2: Spanish Ellipsis

true.

In this paper, we show that the quality of spoken Japanese to English translation can improve using a phrase-based translation system if we can use an ideal elimination resolution system. However, we also show that a simple elimination resolution system is not effective to the improvement and it is necessary to recognize correctly the modality of the sentence.

2 Previous Work

There are a few researches for adaptation of ellipsis resolution to statistical translation systems while there are a lot of researches for one to rule-based translation systems in Japanese (Yoshimoto, 1988; Dohsaka, 1990; Nakaiwa and Yamada, 1997; Yamamoto et al., 1997).

As a research of SMT using elimination resolution, we have (Furuichi et al., 2011). However, the target of the research is illustrative sentences in English to Japanese dictionary. Our research aims spoken language translation and it is different from the paper.

3 Setup of the Data of Subjects and Objects Ellipsis in Spoken Japanese

3.1 Ellipsis Resolved Data by Human

In this section, we describe the data used in our experiments. We used BTEC (Basic Travel Expression Corpus) corpus (Kikui et al., 2003) distributed in IWSLT07 (Fordyce, 2007). The corpus consists of tourism-related sentences similar to those that are usually found in phrasebooks for tourists going abroad. The characteristics of the dataset are shown in Table 1. We used 'train' for training, 'devset1-3' for tuning, and 'test' for evaluation. We did not use the 'devset4' and 'devset5' sets because of the different number of English references.

We annotated zero pronouns and the antecedents to the sentences by hand. Here, zero pronoun is defined as an obligatory case noun phrase that is not expressed in the utterance but can be understood through other utterances in the discourse, context, or out-of-context knowledge (Yoshimoto, 1988). We annotated the zero pronouns based on pronouns in the translated English sentences. The BTEC corpus has multi-references in English. We first chose the most syntactically and lexically similar translation in the references and annotated zero pronouns in it. Our target pronouns are *I, my, me, mine, myself, we, our, us, ours, ourselves, you, your, yourself, yourselves, he, his, him, himself, she, her, herself, it, its, itself, they, their, them, theirs and themselves* in English. We show the distribution of the annotation types in the test set in Table 2.

3.2 Baseline System

We also examined a simple baseline zero pronoun resolution system for the same data. We defined

Table 1: Data distribution

	train	devset1-3	devset4	devset5	test
# of References	1	16	7	7	16
# of Source Segments	39,953	1,512	489	500	489

Japanese predicate as verb, adjective, and copula (*da* form) in the experiments. If the inputted Japanese sentence contains predicates and it does not contain 'wa' (a binding particle and a topic marker), 'mo' (a binding particle, which means 'also' and can often replace 'wa' and 'ga'), and 'ga' (a case particle and subjective marker), the system regards the sentence as a candidate sentence to solve the zero pronouns. Then, if the candidate sentence is declarative, the system inserts '*watashi wa* (I)' when the predicate is a verb, and '*sore wa* (it)' when the predicate is a adjective or a copula. In the same way, if the candidate sentence is a question, the system inserts '*anata wa* (you)' when the predicate is a verb, and '*sore wa* (it)' when the predicate is a adjective or a copula. These inserted position is the beginning of the sentence. In the case that the sentence is imperative, the system does not solve the zero pronouns (Fig. 3).

4 Experiments

4.1 Experimental Setting

Fig. 4 shows the outline of the procedure of our experiment. We used Moses (Koehn et al., 2007) for the training of the translation and language models, tuning with MERT (Och, 2003) and the decoding. First, we prepared the data for learning which consists of parallel English and Japanese sentences. We used MeCab [1] as Japanese tokenizer and the tokenizer in Moses Tool kit as English tokenizer. We used default settings for the parameters of Moses. Next, Moses learns language model and translation model from the Japanese and English sentence pairs. Then, the learned model was tuned by completed sentences with MERT. and Moses decoded the completed Japanese sentences to English sentences.

4.2 Evaluation Method

We used BLEU (Papineni et al., 2002) and antecedent Precision, Recall and F-measure for the evaluation of the performances, comparing the system outputs with the English references of test data. Using only BLEU score is not adequate for evaluation of pronoun translation (Hardmeier et al., 2010).

We were inspired empty node recovery evaluation by (Johnson, 2002) and defined antecedent Precision (P), Recall (R) and F-measure (F) as follows,

$$P = \frac{|G \cap S|}{|S|}$$

$$R = \frac{|G \cap S|}{|G|}$$

$$F = \frac{2PR}{P + R}$$

Here, S is the set of each pronoun in English translated by decoder, G is the set of the gold standard zero pronoun.

We evaluated the effect of performance of every case among completed sentences by human, ones by the baseline system, and the original sentences.

4.3 Experimental Result

We show the BLEU scores in Table 3. and the antecedent precision, recall and F-measure in Table 4. The BLEU scores for experiments using our baseline system and human annotation, are slightly better than for one without ellipsis resolution, 45.4% and 45.6%, respectively. However, the scores of antecedent F-measure have major difference between 'original' and 'human'. Particularly, the recall is improved. Each 1st, 2nd and 3rd person score is better than original one.

5 Discussion and Conclusion

We performed experiments of J-E phrase based translation using Japanese sentences, whose omitted pronouns are complemented by human and a baseline system. Using 'antecedent F-measure' as a score for measuring the quality of the translated English, it improves the score of antecedent F-measure. Every effectiveness of the zero pronoun resolution

[1]http://mecab.sourceforge.net/

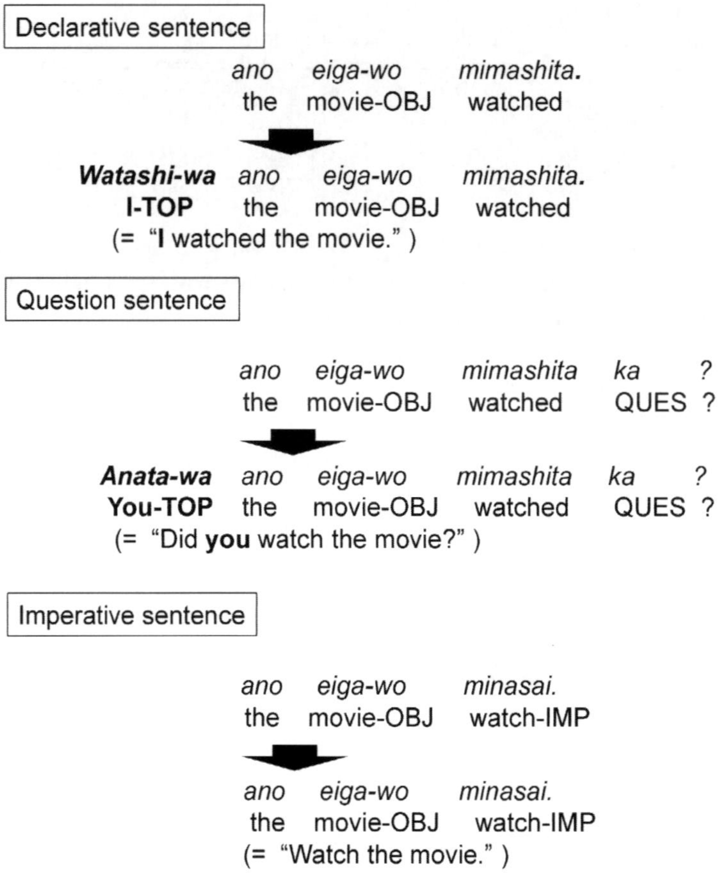

Figure 3: Our baseline system of zero pronoun resolution

differed, depending on the type and case of each zero pronoun. The F-measures for the first person pronoun were smaller than expected ones, Rather, the scores for and possessive pronouns second person were greater (Table. 3).

We show a better, a worse, and an unchanged cases of translation using the baseline system of the elimination resolution in Fig. 5. The left-hand is the result of the alignment between the original Japanese sentence and the decoded English sentence. The right-hand is the result of one using the Japanese the baseline system solved zero pronouns. In the 'better' case, the alignment of *todoke-te* (send) is better than one of the original sentence, and 'Can you' is compensated by the solved zero pronoun *anata-wa* (you-TOP). Otherwise, in the 'worse' case, our baseline system could not recognize that the sentence is imperative, and inserted *watashi-wa* (I-TOP) incorrectly into the sentence. It indicates that we need a highly accurate recognition of the modalities of sentences for more correct completion of the antecedent of zero pronouns. In the 'unchanged' case, the translation results are the same. However, the alignment of the right-hand is more correct than one of the left-hand.

References

Kohji Dohsaka. 1990. Identifying the referents of zero-pronouns in japanese based on pragmatic constraint interpretation. In *Proceedings of ECAI*, pages 240–245.

C.S. Fordyce. 2007. Overview of the iwslt 2007 evaluation campaign. In *Proceedings of the International Workshop on Spoken Language Translation*, pages 1–12.

M. Furuichi, J. Murakami, M. Tokuhisa, and M. Murata. 2011. The effect of complement subject in japanese to english statistical machine translation (in Japanese). In *Proceedings of the 17th Annual Meeting of The*

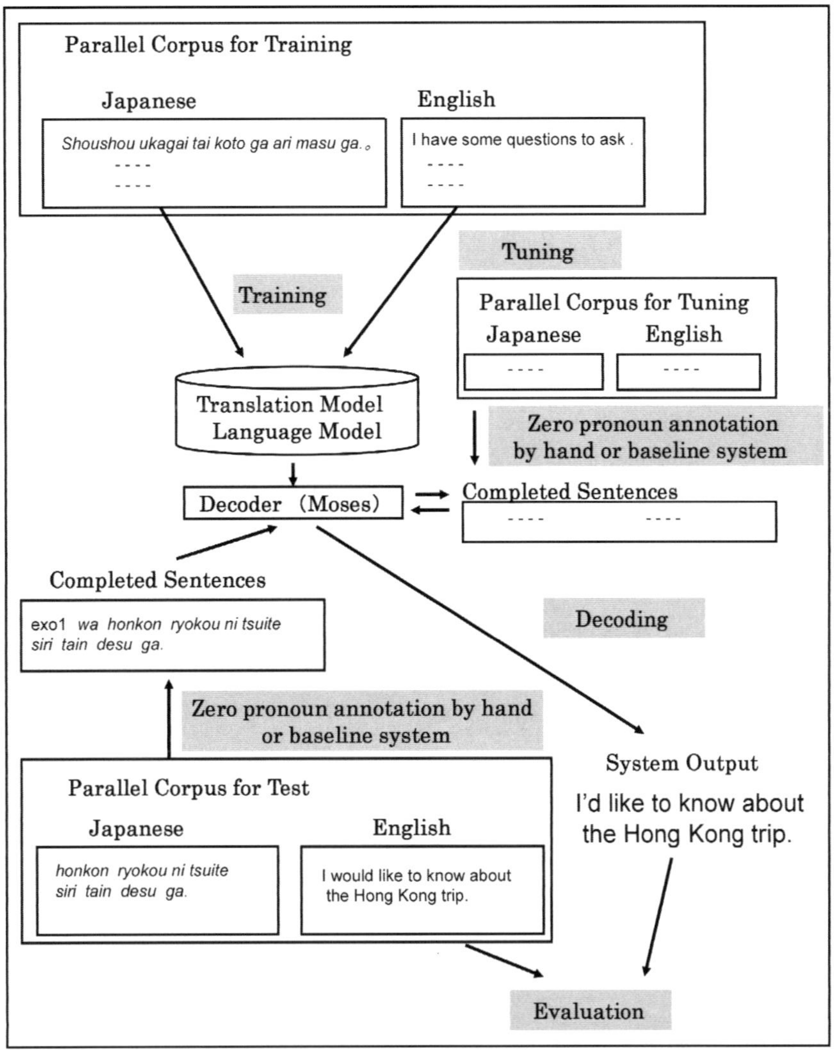

Figure 4: Outline of the experiment

Association for Natural Language Processing (NLP-2012).

C. Hardmeier, M. Federico, and F.B. Kessler. 2010. Modelling pronominal anaphora in statistical machine translation. In *Proceedings of the seventh International Workshop on Spoken Language Translation (IWSLT)*, pages 283–289.

H. Isozaki, K. Sudoh, H. Tsukada, and K. Duh. 2010. Head finalization: A simple reordering rule for sov languages. In *Proceedings of the Joint Fifth Workshop on Statistical Machine Translation and Metrics-MATR*, pages 244–251. Association for Computational Linguistics.

Mark Johnson. 2002. A simple pattern-matching algorithm for recovering empty nodes and their antecedents. In *Proceedings of 40th Annual Meeting of the Association for Computational Linguistics*, pages 136–143, Philadelphia, Pennsylvania, USA, July. Association for Computational Linguistics.

G. Kikui, E. Sumita, T. Takezawa, and S. Yamamoto. 2003. Creating corpora for speech-to-speech translation. In *Proceedings of EUROSPEECH*, pages 381–384.

Philipp Koehn, Hieu Hoang, Alexandra Birch, Chris Callison-Burch, Marcello Federico, Nicola Bertoldi, Brooke Cowan, Wade Shen, Christine Moran, Richard Zens, Chris Dyer, Ondrej Bojar, Alexandra Constantin, and Evan Herbst. 2007. Moses: open source toolkit for statistical machine translation. In *Proc. of the 45th Annual Conference of the Association for*

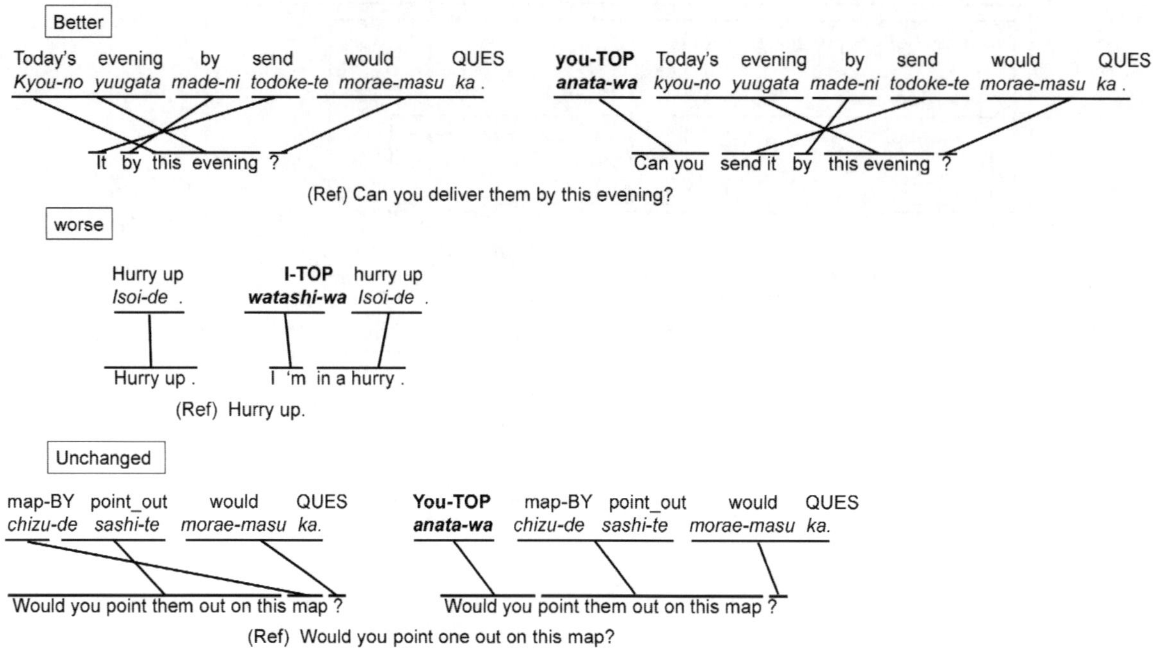

Figure 5: Effectiveness of zero pronoun resolution for decoding

Computational Linguistics (ACL-07), Demonstration Session, pages 177–180.

H. Nakaiwa and S. Yamada. 1997. Automatic identification of zero pronouns and their antecedents within aligned sentence pairs. In *Proc. of the 3rd Annual Meeting of the Association for Natural Language Processing*.

S. Nariyama. 2003. *Ellipsis and reference tracking in Japanese*, volume 66. John Benjamins Publishing Company.

Franz Josef Och. 2003. Minimum error rate training for statistical machine translation. In *Proc. of the ACL*.

Kishore Papineni, Salim Roukos, Todd Ward, and Wei-Jing Zhu. 2002. BLEU: A method for automatic evaluation of machine translation. In *Proc. of the 40th Annual Conference of the Association for Computational Linguistics (ACL-02)*.

K. Yamamoto, E. Sumita, O. Furuse, and H. Iida. 1997. Ellipsis resolution in dialogues via decision-tree learning. In *Proc. of NLPRS*, volume 97. Citeseer.

K. Yoshimoto. 1988. Identifying zero pronouns in japanese dialogue. In *Proceedings of the 12th conference on Computational linguistics-Volume 2*, pages 779–784. Association for Computational Linguistics.

Table 2: The Type Distributions of Zero Pronouns in Test Set

Type	Pronoun	#
First personal pronoun	i	121
	my	39
	me	32
	mine	1
	myself	0
	we	7
	our	2
	us	2
	ours	0
	ourselves	0
	total	204
Second personal pronoun	you	95
	your	23
	yours	0
	yourself	0
	yourselves	0
	total	118
Third personal pronoun	he	1
	his	0
	him	0
	himself	0
	she	0
	her	2
	hers	0
	herself	0
	it	51
	its	0
	itself	0
	they	2
	their	0
	them	5
	theirs	0
	themselves	0
	total	61
all	total	383

Table 3: BLEU score

	BLEU	F(Avg.)	P	R	F (1st person)	F (2nd person)	F (3rd person)
original	45.1	59.7	63.8	56.1	61.6	59.9	52.3
baseline	45.4	58.5	64.1	53.7	61.2	59.2	47.7
human	**45.6**	**71.8**	**67.5**	**76.7**	**70.6**	**77.6**	**63.7**

Table 4: Antecedent precision, recall and F-measure for every pronoun

		i (ref:121)			my (ref:39)			me (ref:32)		
	BLEU	P	R	F	P	R	F	P	R	F
original	45.1	**56.8**	51.2	53.9	55.5	51.2	53.3	58.0	56.2	57.1
baseline	45.4	51.8	46.2	48.9	**67.8**	48.7	56.7	**66.6**	50.0	57.1
human	**45.6**	50.9	**68.6**	**58.4**	65.2	**76.9**	**70.5**	61.2	**59.3**	**60.3**

	we (ref:7)			our (ref:2)			us (ref:2)		
	P	R	F	P	R	F	P	R	F
original	20.0	14.2	16.6	100.0	50.0	66.6	0.00	0.00	0.00
baseline	25.0	14.2	18.1	100.0	50.0	66.6	0.00	0.00	0.00
human	**40.0**	**28.5**	**33.3**	100.0	50.0	66.6	0.00	0.00	0.00

	you (ref:95)			your (ref:23)		
	P	R	F	P	R	F
original	55.3	54.7	55.0	**80.0**	52.1	63.1
baseline	57.1	54.7	55.9	58.8	43.4	50.0
human	**68.4**	**80.0**	**73.7**	73.0	**82.6**	**77.5**

	it (ref:51)			its (ref:0)		
	P	R	F	P	R	F
original	56.1	45.1	50.0	0.00	0.00	0.00
baseline	51.2	41.1	45.6	0.00	0.00	0.00
human	**58.3**	**54.9**	**56.5**	0.00	0.00	0.00

	they (ref:2)			their (ref:0)			them (ref:5)		
	P	R	F	P	R	F	P	R	F
original	**100.0**	50.0	**66.6**	0.00	0.00	0.00	0.00	0.00	0.00
baseline	**100.0**	50.0	**66.6**	0.00	0.00	0.00	0.00	0.00	0.00
human	58.3	**54.9**	56.5	0.00	0.00	0.00	0.00	0.00	0.00

Author Index

Association for Computational Linguistics
209 N. Eighth Street
Stroudsburg, Pennsylvania 18360

CURRAN ASSOCIATES INC
proceedings
.com

Workshop on Biomedical Natural Language Processing

(BioNLP 2013)

Sofia, Bulgaria
8 August 2013

ISBN: 978-1-62748-980-5